Matplotlib for Python Developers

Build remarkable publication quality plots the easy way

Sandro Tosi

BIRMINGHAM - MUMBAI

Matplotlib for Python Developers

First published: November 2009

Production Reference: 2221009

Published by Packt Publishing Ltd.
32 Lincoln Road
Olton
Birmingham, B27 6PA, UK.

ISBN 978-1-847197-90-0

www.packtpub.com

Cover Image by Raghuram Ashok (raghuram.ashok@gmail.com)

Credits

Author
Sandro Tosi

Reviewers
Michael Droettboom
Reinier Heeres

Acquisition Editor
Usha Iyer

Development Editor
Rakesh Shejwal

Technical Editor
Namita Sahni

Copy Editor
Leonard D'Silva

Indexers
Monica Ajmera
Hemangini Bari

Editorial Team Leader
Akshara Aware

Project Team Leader
Priya Mukherji

Project Coordinator
Zainab Bagasrawala

Proofreader
Lesley Harrison

Graphics
Nilesh Mohite

Production Coordinator
Adline Swetha Jesuthas

Cover Work
Adline Swetha Jesuthas

About the Author

Sandro Tosi was born in Firenze (Italy) in the early 80s, and graduated with a B.Sc. in Computer Science from the University of Firenze.

His personal passions for Linux, Python (and programming), and computer technology are luckily a part of his daily job, where he has gained a lot of experience in systems and applications management, database administration, as well as project management and development.

After having worked for five years as an EAI and an Application architect in an energy multinational, he's now working as a system administrator for an important European Internet company.

I'd like to thank Laura, who has assisted and supported me while writing this book.

About the Reviewers

Michael Droettboom holds a Master's Degree in Computer Music Research from The Johns Hopkins University. His research in optical music recognition lead to the development of the Gamera document image analysis framework, which has been used to recognize features in documents as diverse as medieval manuscript, Navajo texts, historical Scottish census data, and early American sheet music. His focus on computer graphics has lead to specializations in consumer electronics, computer-assisted engineering, and most recently, the science software for the Space Telescope Science Institute. He is currently one of the most active developers on the Matplotlib project.

I wish to thank my son, Kai, for asking all the hard questions.

Reinier Heeres has an MSc degree in Applied Physics from the Delft University of Technology, The Netherlands. He is currently pursuing a PhD there in the Quantum Transport group of the nanoscience department.

He has previously worked on Sugar, the child-friendly user interface mainly in use by One Laptop Per Child's $100 laptop. For this project, he designed the Calculator application.

Recently, he revived and extended the 3D plotting functionalities for Matplotlib to make it an excellent 2D graphing library, and a simple 3D plotting tool again.

Table of Contents

Preface

This book is about Matplotlib, a Python package for 2D plotting that generates production quality graphs. Its variety of output formats, several chart types, and capability to run either interactively (from Python or IPython consoles) and non-interactively (useful, for example, when included into web applications), makes Matplotlib suitable for use in many different situations.

Matplotlib is a big package with several dependencies and having them all installed and running properly is the first step that needs to be taken. We provide some ways to have a system ready to explore Matplotlib. Then we start describing the basic functions required for plotting lines, exploring any useful or advanced commands for our plots until we come to the core of Matplotlib: the object-oriented interface. This is the root for the next big section of the book—embedding Matplotlib into GUI libraries applications. We cannot limit it only to desktop programs, so we show several methods to include Matplotlib into web sites using low level techniques for two well known web frameworks—Pylons and Django. Last but not the least, we present a number of real world examples of Matplotlib applications.

The core concept of the book is to present how to embed Matplotlib into Python applications, developed using the main GUI libraries: GTK+, Qt 4, and wxWidgets. However, we are by no means limiting ourselves to that. The step-by-step introduction to Matplotlib functions, the advanced details, the example with web frameworks, and several real-life use cases make the book suitable for anyone willing to learn or already working with Matplotlib.

What this book covers

Chapter 1 — Introduction to Matplotlib introduces what Matplotlib is, describing its output formats and the interactions with graphical environments. Several ways to install Matplotlib are presented, along with its dependencies needed to have a correctly configured environment to get along with the book.

Chapter 2 — Getting started with Matplotlib covers the first examples of Matplotlib usage. While still being basic, the examples show important aspects of Matplotlib like how to plot lines, legends, axes labels, axes grids, and how to save the finished plot. It also shows how to configure Matplotlib using its configuration files or directly into the code, and how to work profitable with IPython.

Chapter 3 — Decorate Graphs with Plot Styles and Types discusses the additional plotting capabilities of Matplotlib: lines and points styles and ticks customizations. Several types of plots are discussed and covered: histograms, bars, pie charts, scatter plots, and more, along with the polar representation. It is also explained how to include textual information inside the plot.

Chapter 4 — Advanced Matplotlib examines some advanced (or not so common) topics like the object-oriented interface, how to include more subplots in a single plot or how to generate more figures, how to set one axis (or both) to logarithmic scale, and how to share one axis between two graphs in one plot. A consistent section is dedicated to plotting date information and all that comes with that. This chapter also shows the text properties that can be tuned in Matplotlib and how to use the LaTeX typesetting language. It also presents a section about contour plot and image plotting.

Chapter 5 — Embedding Matplotlib in GTK+ guides us through the steps to embed Matplotlib inside a GTK+ program. Starting from embedding just the Figure and the Navigation toolbar, it will present how to use Glade to design a GUI and then embed Matplotlib into it. It also describes how to dynamically update a Matplotlib plot using the GTK+ capabilities.

Chapter 6 — Embedding Matplotlib in Qt 4 explores how to include a Matplotlib figure into a Qt 4 GUI. It includes an example that uses Qt Designer to develop a GUI and how to use Matplotlib into it. What Qt 4 library provides for a real-time update of a Matplotlib plot is described here too.

Chapter 7 — Embedding Matplotlib in wxWidgets shows what is needed to embed Matplotlib into a wxWidget graphical application. An important example is the one for a real-time plot update using a very efficient technique (borrowed from computer graphics), allowing for a high update rate. WxGlade is introduced, which guides us step-by-step through the process of wxWidgets GUI creation and where to include a Matplotlib plot.

Chapter 8 — Matplotlib for the Web describes how to expose plots generated with Matplotlib on the Web. The first examples start from the lower ground, using CGI and the Apache mod_python module, technologies recommended only for limited or simple tasks. For a full web experience, two web frameworks are introduced, Pylons and Django, and a complete guide for the inclusion of Matplotlib with these frameworks is given.

Chapter 9 — Matplotlib in the Real World takes Matplotlib and brings it into the real world examples field, guiding through several situations that might occur in the real life. The source code to plot the data extracted from a database, a web page, a parsed log file, and from a comma-separated file are described in full detail here. A couple of third-party tools using Matplotlib, NetworkX, and Mpmath, are described presenting some examples of their usage. A considerable section is dedicated to Basemap, a Matplotlib toolkit to draw geographical data.

What you need for this book

In order to be able to have the best experience with this book, you have to start with an already working Python environment, and then follow the advice in Chapter 1 on how to install Matplotlib and its most important dependencies. Some examples require additional tools, libraries, or modules to be installed: consult the distribution or project documentation for installation details.

Python, Matplotlib, and all other tools are cross-platform, so the book examples can be executed on Linux, Windows, or Mac OS X.

The book and the example code was developed using Python 2.5 and Matplotlib 0.98.5.3, but due to recent developments, Python 2.6 (Python 3.x is still not well supported by NumPy, Matplotlib, and several other modules) and Matplotlib 0.99.x can be used as well.

Who this book is for

This book is essentially for Python developers who have a good knowledge of Python; no knowledge of Matplotlib is required. You will be creating 2D plots using Matplotlib in no time at all.

Conventions

In this book, you will find a number of styles of text that distinguish between different kinds of information. Here are some examples of these styles, and an explanation of their meaning.

Code words in text are shown as follows: "This is used for enhanced handling of the `datetime` Python objects."

A block of code is set as follows:

```
In [1]: import matplotlib.pyplot as plt
In [2]: import numpy as np
In [3]: y = np.arange(1, 3)
In [4]: plt.plot(y, 'y');
In [5]: plt.plot(y+1, 'm');
In [6]: plt.plot(y+2, 'c');
In [7]: plt.show()
```

When we wish to draw your attention to a particular part of a code block, the relevant lines or items are set in bold:

```
c[0]*x**deg + c[1]*x**(deg - 1) + ... + c[deg]
```

Any command-line input or output is written as follows:

```
$ easy_install matplotlib-<version>-py<py version>-win32.egg
```

New terms and **important words** are shown in bold. Words that you see on the screen, in menus or dialog boxes for example, appear in the text like this: "There are several aspects we might want to tune in a widget, and this can be done using the **Properties** window."

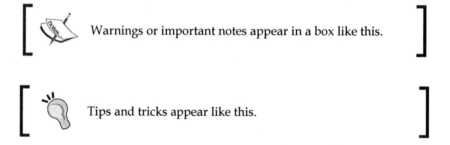

> Warnings or important notes appear in a box like this.

> Tips and tricks appear like this.

Reader feedback

Feedback from our readers is always welcome. Let us know what you think about this book—what you liked or may have disliked. Reader feedback is important for us to develop titles that you really get the most out of.

To send us general feedback, simply send an email to `feedback@packtpub.com`, and mention the book title via the subject of your message.

If there is a book that you need and would like to see us publish, please send us a note in the **SUGGEST A TITLE** form on www.packtpub.com or email suggest@packtpub.com.

If there is a topic that you have expertise in and you are interested in either writing or contributing to a book on, see our author guide on www.packtpub.com/authors.

Customer support

Now that you are the proud owner of a Packt book, we have a number of things to help you to get the most from your purchase.

Downloading the example code for the book

Visit http://www.packtpub.com/files/code/7900_Code.zip to directly download the example code.

The downloadable files contain instructions on how to use them.

Errata

Although we have taken every care to ensure the accuracy of our content, mistakes do happen. If you find a mistake in one of our books—maybe a mistake in the text or the code—we would be grateful if you would report this to us. By doing so, you can save other readers from frustration, and help us to improve subsequent versions of this book. If you find any errata, please report them by visiting http://www.packtpub.com/support, selecting your book, clicking on the **let us know** link, and entering the details of your errata. Once your errata are verified, your submission will be accepted and the errata added to any list of existing errata. Any existing errata can be viewed by selecting your title from http://www.packtpub.com/support.

Piracy

Piracy of copyright material on the Internet is an ongoing problem across all media. At Packt, we take the protection of our copyright and licenses very seriously. If you come across any illegal copies of our works, in any form, on the Internet, please provide us with the location address or web site name immediately so that we can pursue a remedy.

Please contact us at copyright@packtpub.com with a link to the suspected pirated material.

We appreciate your help in protecting our authors, and our ability to bring you valuable content.

Questions

You can contact us at questions@packtpub.com if you are having a problem with any aspect of the book, and we will do our best to address it.

1

Introduction to Matplotlib

A picture is worth a thousand words.

We all know that images are a powerful form of communication. We often use them to understand a situation better or to condense pieces of information into a graphical representation.

Just to give a couple of examples on how helpful they can be, let's consider the scientific and performance analysis fields. In order to clearly identify the bottlenecks, it is very important to be able to visualize data when analyzing performance information. Similarly, taking a quick glance at a graph drawn for a scientific experiment can give a scientist a better understanding of the results, something which is harder to achieve by looking only at the raw data.

Python is an interpreted language with a strong core functions basis and a powerful modular aspect which allows us to expand the language with external modules that offer new functionalities.

Modules reflect the Unix philosophy:

Do one thing, do it well.

So the result is that we have an extensible language with tools to accomplish a single task in the best possible way. Modules are often organized in *packages*. A package is a structured collection of modules that have the same purpose. One example of a package is **Matplotlib**.

Matplotlib is a Python package for 2D plotting that generates production-quality graphs. It supports interactive and non-interactive plotting, and can save images in several output formats (PNG, PS, and others). It can use multiple window toolkits (GTK+, wxWidgets, Qt, and so on) and it provides a wide variety of plot types (lines, bars, pie charts, histograms, and many more). In addition to this, it is highly customizable, flexible, and easy to use.

The dual nature of Matplotlib allows it to be used in both interactive and non-interactive scripts. It can be used in scripts without a graphical display, embedded in graphical applications, or on web pages. It can also be used interactively with the Python interpreter or **IPython**.

In this chapter, we will introduce Matplotlib, learn what it is, and what it can do. Later on, we will see what tools and Python modules are needed to have the best experience with Matplotlib and how to get them installed on our system, be it Linux, Windows, or Mac OS X.

The topics we are going to cover are:

- Introduction to Matplotlib
- Output formats and backends
- Dependencies
- How to install Matplotlib

Merits of Matplotlib

The idea behind Matplotlib can be summed up in the following motto as quoted by John Hunter, the creator and project leader of Matplotlib:

> *Matplotlib tries to make easy things easy and hard things possible.*

We can generate high quality, publication-ready graphs with minimal effort (sometimes we can achieve this with just one line of code or so), and for elaborate graphs, we have at hand a powerful library to support our needs.

Matplotlib was born in the scientific area of computing, where **gnuplot** and **MATLAB** were (and still are) used a lot.

With the entrance of Python into scientific toolboxes, an example of a workflow to process some data might be similar to this: "Write a Python script to parse data, then pass the data to a gnuplot script to plot it". Now with Matplotlib, we can write a single script to parse and plot data, with a lot more flexibility (that gnuplot doesn't have) and consistently using the same programming language.

We have to think of plotting not just as the final step in working with our data, but as an important way of getting visual feedback during the process. Here, the interactive capabilities of Matplotlib will come and rescue us.

Matplotlib was modeled on MATLAB, because graphing was something that MATLAB did very well. The high degree of compatibility between them made many people move from MATLAB to Matplotlib, as they felt like home while working with Matplotlib.

But what are the points that built the success of Matplotlib? Let's look at some of them:

- **It uses Python**: Python is a very interesting language for scientific purposes (it's interpreted, high-level, easy to learn, easily extensible, and has a powerful standard library) and is now used by major institutions such as NASA, JPL, Google, DreamWorks, Disney, and many more.

- **It's open source, so no license to pay**: This makes it very appealing for professors and students, who often have a low budget.

- **It's a real programming language**: The MATLAB language (while being Turing-complete) lacks many of the features of a general-purpose language like Python.

- **It's much more complete**: Python has a lot of external modules that will help us perform all the functions we need to. So it's the perfect tool to acquire data, elaborate the data, and then plot the data.

- **It's very customizable and extensible**: Matplotlib can fit every use case because it has a lot of graph types, features, and configuration options.

- **It's integrated with LaTeX markup**: This is really useful when writing scientific papers.

- **It's cross-platform and portable**: Matplotlib can run on Linux, Windows, Mac OS X, and Sun Solaris (and Python can run on almost every architecture available).

In short, Python became very common in the scientific field, and this success is reflected even on this book, where we'll find some mathematical formulas. But don't be concerned about that, we will use nothing more complex than high school level equations.

Matplotlib web sites and online documentation

The official Matplotlib presence on the Web is made up of two web sites:

- The SourceForge project page at `http://sourceforge.net/projects/matplotlib/`

- The main web site at `http://matplotlib.sourceforge.net/`

The SourceForge page contains, in particular, information about the development of Matplotlib, such as the released source code tarballs and binary packages, the SVN repository location, the bug tracking system, and so on. SourceForge also hosts some mailing lists for Matplotlib which are used for developers' discussions and users support.

On the main web site, we can find several important pieces of information about the Matplotlib package itself. For example:

- It contains a very attractive gallery with a huge number of examples of what Matplotlib can do

- The official documentation of Matplotlib is also present on this web site

The official documentation for Matplotlib is extensive. It covers in detail, all the submodules and the methods exposed by them, including all of their arguments. There are too many function arguments to cover in this book, so we are presenting only the most common ones here. In case of any doubts or questions, the official documentation is a good place to start your research or to look for an answer.

We encourage you to take a look at the gallery — it's inspiring!

Output formats and backends

The aim of Matplotlib is to generate graphs. So, we need a way to actually *view* these images or even to *save* them to files. We're going to look at the various output formats available in Matplotlib and the graphical user interfaces (GUIs) supported by the library.

Output formats

Given its scientific roots (that means several different needs), Matplotlib has a lot of output formats available, which can be used for articles/books and other print publications, for web pages, or for any other reason we can think of. Let's first differentiate the output formats into two distinct categories:

- **Raster images**: These are the classic images we can find on the Web or used for pictures. The most well known raster file formats are PNG, JPG, and BMP. They are widespread and well supported. The format of these images is like a matrix, with rows and columns, and at every matrix cell we have a pixel description (containing information such as colors). This format is said to be *resolution-dependent*, because the size of the matrix (the number of rows and columns) is determined when the image is created. An important parameter for raster images is the **DPI** (**dots-per-inch**) value. Once the image dimensions are decided (length and width, in inches), the DPI value specifies the detail level of the image. Hence, higher the DPI value, higher is the quality of the image (because for the same inch we get more dots). Scaling operations such as zooming or resizing can result in a loss of quality, because the image contains only a limited amount of information.

- **Vector images:** As opposed to raster images, vector images contain a *description* of the image in the form of mathematical equations and geometrical primitives (for example, points, lines, curves, polygons, or shapes). We can think of this format as a series of directives to plot the image: "Draw a point here, draw another point there, draw a line between those two points" and so on. Given this descriptive format, these images are said to be *resolution-independent*, because it's the image interpreter that replots the image at the requested resolution using the instructions in it. Typical examples of vector image usage are typesetting and CAD (architectural or mechanical parts drawings).

Of course, Matplotlib supports both the categories, particularly with the following output formats:

Format	Type	Description
EPS	Vector	Encapsulated PostScript.
JPG	Raster	Graphic format with lossy compression method for photographic output.
PDF	Vector	**Portable Document Format (PDF)**.
PNG	Raster	**Portable Network Graphics (PNG)**, a raster graphics format with a lossless compression method (more adaptable to line art than JPG).
PS	Vector	Language widely used in publishing and as printers jobs format.
SVG	Vector	**Scalable Vector Graphics (SVG)**, XML based.

PS or EPS formats are particularly useful for plots inclusion in LaTeX documents, the main scientific articles format since decades.

Backends

In the previous section, we saw the file output formats—they are also called **hardcopy backends** as they create something (a file on disk).

A backend that displays the image on screen is called a **user interface backend**.

The backend is that part of Matplotlib that works behind the scenes and allows the software to target several different output formats and GUI libraries (for screen visualization).

In order to be even more flexible, Matplotlib introduces the following two layers structured (only for GUI output):

- **The renderer**: This actually does the drawing
- **The canvas**: This is the destination of the figure

The standard renderer is the **Anti-Grain Geometry** (**AGG**) library, a high performance rendering engine which is able to create images of publication level quality, with anti-aliasing, and subpixel accuracy. AGG is responsible for the beautiful appearance of Matplotlib graphs.

The canvas is provided with the GUI libraries, and any of them can use the AGG rendering, along with the support for other rendering engines (for example, GTK+).

Let's have a look at the user interface toolkits and their available renderers:

Backend	Description
GTKAgg	GTK+ (The GIMP ToolKit GUI library) canvas with AGG rendering.
GTK	GTK+ canvas with GDK rendering. GDK rendering is rather primitive, and doesn't include anti-aliasing for the smoothing of lines.
GTKCairo	GTK+ canvas with Cairo rendering.
WxAgg	wxWidgets (cross-platform GUI and tools library for GTK+, Windows, and Mac OS X. It uses native widgets for each operating system, so applications will have the look and feel that users expect on that operating system) canvas with AGG rendering.
WX	wxWidgets canvas with native wxWidgets rendering.
TkAgg	Tk (graphical user interface for Tcl and many other dynamic languages) canvas with AGG rendering.

Backend	Description
QtAgg	Qt (cross-platform application framework for desktop and embedded development) canvas with AGG rendering (for Qt version 3 and earlier).
Qt4Agg	Qt4 canvas with AGG rendering.
FLTKAgg	FLTK (cross-platform C++ GUI toolkit for UNIX/Linux (X11), Microsoft Windows, and Mac OS X) canvas with Agg rendering.

Here is the list of renderers for file output:

Renderer	File type
AGG	`.png`
PS	`.eps` or `.ps`
PDF	`.pdf`
SVG	`.svg`
Cairo	`.png`, `.ps`, `.pdf`, `.svg`
GDK	`.png`, `.jpg`

The renderers mentioned in the previous table can be used directly in Matplotlib, when we want *only* to save the resulting graph into a file (without any visualization of it), in any of the formats supported.

We have to pay attention when choosing which backend to use. For example, if we don't have a graphical environment available, then we have to use the AGG backend (or any other file). If we have installed only the GTK+ Python bindings, then we can't use the WX backend.

About dependencies

As mentioned earlier, Matplotlib has its origin in scientific fields, so it is commonly used to plot huge datasets. Python's native support for long lists becomes impractical for such sizes, so Matplotlib needs better support for arrays.

NumPy, the de facto standard Python module for numerical elaborations, provides support for high performance operations even with big mathematical data types such as arrays or matrices—along with many other mathematical functions that can be useful to Matplotlib users.

NumPy has to be available to use Matplotlib.

Once we have chosen the set of **user interfaces (UIs)** we prefer, then we need to install the Python bindings for them. Here is a summarizing list:

User Interface (UI)	Binding	Version	Description
FLTK	pyFLTK	1.0 or higher	pyFLTK provides Python wrappers for the FLTK widgets library for use with FLTKAgg backend.
GTK+	PyGTK	2.2 or higher	PyGTK provides Python wrappers for the GTK+ widgets library to use it with the GTK or GTKAgg backend. It is recommended to use a version higher than 2.12, for a correct memory management.
Qt	PyQt or PyQt4	3.1 or higher and for Qt4, 4.0 or higher	PyQt or PyQt4 provides Python wrappers for the Qt toolkit and is required by the Matplotlib QtAgg and Qt4Agg backends. The library is widely used on Linux and Windows.
Tk	PyTK	8.3 or higher	Python wrapper for Tcl or Tk widgets library is used in TkAgg backend.
Wx	wxPython	2.6 or higher, or 2.8 or higher	wxPython provides Python wrappers for the wxWidgets library for use with the WX and WXAgg backends. It is widely used on Linux, Mac OS X, and Windows.

Another important tool, in particular for interactive usage, is IPython. It's an interactive Python shell with a lot of useful features, such as history, commands repeating, and others. It already has a **Matplotlib mode** in it. We'll be using IPython in this book, so it is recommended to install it.

Some of the tools that are needed by Matplotlib are already shipped with it (in the source code as well as in the binary distributions). Here is the list of those tools:

- **AGG (version 2.4)**: This is the Anti-Grain Geometry rendering engine. The local copy of the library is linked with the Matplotlib code in a static way. So, there's no need to install it (as a shared library).

- **pytz (version 2007g or higher)**: This is used for handling the time zone for datetime Python objects. It will be installed if it's not already present in the system. It can be overridden using setup.cfg.

- **python-dateutil (version1.1 or higher)**: This is used for enhanced handling of the datetime Python objects. It needs to be installed if it's not already present in the system and can be overridden using setup.cfg.

Build dependencies

The following tools are needed if we're going to install Matplotlib from the source:

- **Python**: Currently, only Python 2.x is supported (no Python 3 yet)
- **NumPy**: Version 1.1 or higher
- **libpng**: Version 1.1 or higher is needed to load or save PNG images (Windows users can skip this requirement)
- **FreeType**: Version 1.4 or higher is needed for reading **TrueType** font files (Windows users can skip this requirement)

 libpng and FreeType for Windows users are already packaged in the Matplotlib Windows installer.

Installing Matplotlib

There are several ways to install Matplotlib on our system:

- Using packages from a Linux distribution
- Using binary installers (for Windows and Mac OS X only)
- Using packaged Python distributions that contain Matplotlib in the toolbox proposed
- From the source code

We will look at each option in detail. We assume that Python, NumPy, and the optional build and runtime dependencies are already installed in the system (in order to install them, refer to their installation guides).

Installing Matplotlib on Linux

The advantage of using a Linux distribution is that several programs and libraries are already prepared by the distribution developers and made available (in a package format) to users. All we have to do is use the right tool and install the package.

In the following table, we will present some of the common Linux distributions package names for Matplotlib and the tools we can use to install the package:

Distribution	Package name	Installer tool
Debian or Ubuntu	`python-matplotlib`	Synaptic (graphical)
(and all other Debian derivatives)		apt-get or aptitude (command line)
Fedora	`python-matplotlib`	PackageKit (graphical)
		yum or rpm (command line)
openSUSE	`python-matplotlib`	YaST (graphical)
		zipper or rpm (command line)

Installing Matplotlib on Windows

Before we can install Matplotlib, we have to satisfy its main dependencies. So, we have to download:

- Installers for Python, which are available in the **DOWNLOAD** section of `http://www.python.org/`

- Installers for NumPy, which are available in the **Download** section of `http://www.scipy.org/`

Once we've got the above packages correctly installed, we can go to the main project page of Matplotlib on SourceForge at `http://sourceforge.net/projects/matplotlib/`. In the **Files** section, we can find the relative versions of the binary packages for the Python that we have just installed (2.4, 2.5, or 2.6).

Installing Matplotlib on Mac OS X

The procedure to install Matplotlib correctly on Mac OS X is similar to that of Windows.

First of all, we need to download:

- Installers for Python, which are available in the **DOWNLOAD** section of `http://www.python.org/` (the one already available in Mac OS X fives problem when using Matplotlib)

- Installers for NumPy, which are available in the **Download** section of `http://www.scipy.org/` or can be retrieved directly from `http://pythonmac.org/`

At this point, once they are correctly installed, we can download the binary installer from the download area of Matplotlib SourceForce page at `http://sourceforge.net/projects/matplotlib/` or we can retrieve the version available at `http://pythonmac.org/`.

Installing Matplotlib using packaged Python distributions

There are some packaged distributions of Python that contain Matplotlib in them, along with many other tools, such as IPython, NumPy, SciPy, and so on. These distributions will set up all the necessary things we need so that we can use Matplotlib on our machine. Some of the distributions are as follows:

- **Enthought Python Distribution** (EPD): This package is available for Windows, Mac OS X, and Red Hat. We can download it from `http://www.enthought.com/products/epd.php`.

- **Python(x,y)**: This package is available for Windows and Ubuntu at `http://www.pythonxy.com/`.

- **Sage**: This package is available for Linux at `http://www.sagemath.org/`.

These are mainly scientific distributions that install a lot of tools we don't directly need or use, but they have the advantage of making it easy to get Python, NumPy, and Matplotlib installed and working on our system.

Installing Matplotlib from source code

There are two ways of obtaining the Matplotlib source code. They are:

- Downloading it from the source code tarballs available in the download area of Matplotlib SourceForge project page at `http://sourceforge.net/projects/matplotlib/`.

- Retrieving it from the Subversion (SVN) repository. This is the place where development takes place, so use it only if you know what you're doing.

If we decided to go with SVN, we can follow the instructions available in the **Develop** section of `http://sourceforge.net/projects/matplotlib/`.

If we are going to use the source code tarball, we will have to unpack it, go into the created source directory, and execute the following commands:

```
$ python setup.py build
$ sudo python setup.py install
```

These commands will build and then install Matplotlib. We will need administrative privileges to install it into the system directories (hence the `sudo` command in this Linux example).

Many aspects of the installation can be tuned using `setup.cfg`, a file shipped with the source code and used at build and install time. We can use it to customize the build process, such as changing the default backend, or choosing whether to install the optional libraries or not.

If we want to install Matplotlib from source on Windows, the **Files** section of Matplotlib SourceForge page contains handy `egg` files which we can download (choosing the Python version of interest) and then install using `setuptools` command. The following command will install Matplotlib on your machine:

```
$ easy_install matplotlib-<version>-py<py version>-win32.egg
```

Egg files are also available for Mac OS X, and we can use them in the same way as described above.

Testing our installation

To ensure we have correctly installed Matplotlib and its dependencies, a very simple test can be carried out in the following manner:

```
$ python
Python 2.5.4 (r254:67916, Feb 18 2009, 03:00:47)
[GCC 4.3.3] on linux2
Type "help", "copyright", "credits" or "license" for more information.
>>> import numpy
>>> print numpy.__version__
1.2.1
>>> import matplotlib
>>> print matplotlib.__version__
0.98.5.3
```

If there's no error while executing this, then we are done.

Summary

In this chapter, we have covered the following areas:

- What is Matplotlib and what are its main key points
- The several file output formats and graphical user interfaces (GUIs) that are supported
- The packages required by Matplotlib, and the ones needed for the GUI bindings
- Installing and testing Matplotlib on a Linux, Windows, or Mac OS X system, in multiple ways

At this point, we only have a general idea of what Matplotlib is, along with the package correctly installed in our system. So let's go and start using Matplotlib!

2
Getting Started with Matplotlib

In the previous chapter, we have given a brief introduction to Matplotlib. We now want to start using it for real—after all, that's what you are reading this book for.

In this chapter, we will:

- Explore the basic plotting capabilities of Matplotlib for single or multiple lines
- Add information to the plots such as legends, axis labels, and titles
- Save a plot to a file
- Describe the interaction with IPython
- Customize Matplotlib, both through configuration files and Python code

Let's start looking at some graphs.

First plots with Matplotlib

One of the strong points of Matplotlib is how quickly we can start producing plots out of the box. Here is our first example:

```
$ ipython
In [1]: import matplotlib.pyplot as plt
In [2]: plt.plot([1, 3, 2, 4])
Out[2]: [<matplotlib.lines.Line2D object at 0x2544f10>]
In [3]: plt.show()
```

This code snippet gives the output shown in the following screenshot:

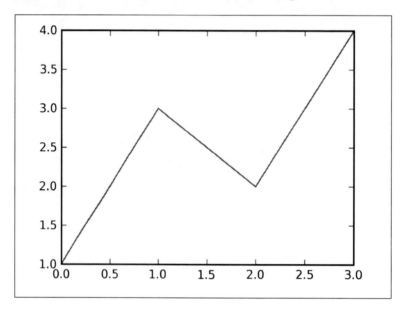

As you can see, we are using IPython. This will be the case throughout the book, so we'll skip the command execution line (and the heading) as you can easily recognize IPython output.

Let's look at each line of the previous code in detail:

```
In [1]: import matplotlib.pyplot as plt
```

This is the preferred format to import the main Matplotlib submodule for plotting, `pyplot`. It's the best practice and in order to avoid pollution of the global namespace, it's strongly encouraged to never import like:

```
from <module> import *
```

The same import style is used in the official documentation, so we want to be consistent with that.

```
In [2]: plt.plot([1, 3, 2, 4])
```

This code line is the actual plotting command. We have specified only a list of values that represent the vertical coordinates of the points to be plotted. Matplotlib will use an implicit horizontal values list, from 0 (the first value) to N-1 (where N is the number of items in the list).

If you remember from high school, the vertical values represent the Y-axis while the horizontal values are the X-axis, and what we do is called "to plot Y against X".

```
In [3]: plt.show()
```

This command actually opens the window containing the plot image.

Of course, we can also explicitly specify both the lists:

```
In [1]: import matplotlib.pyplot as plt
In [2]: x = range(6)
In [3]: plt.plot(x, [xi**2 for xi in x])
Out[3]: [<matplotlib.lines.Line2D object at 0x2408d10>]
In [4]: plt.show()
```

that results in the following screenshot:

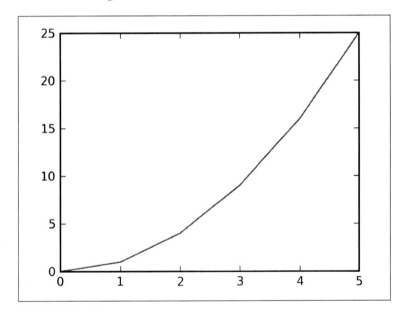

As we can see, the line shown in the previous screenshot has several edges, while we might want a smoother parabola. So, we can start introducing the interaction with NumPy with one of its most used functions, arange(), and highlighting the difference with range():

- range(i, j, k) is a Python built-in function that generates a sequence of integers from i to j with an increment of k (both, the initial value and the step are optional).

- arange(x, y, z) is a part of NumPy, and it generates a sequence of elements (with data type determined by parameter types) from x to y with a spacing z (with the same optional parameters as that of the previous function).

So we can use arange() to generate a finer range:

```
In [1]: import matplotlib.pyplot as plt
In [2]: import numpy as np
In [3]: x = np.arange(0.0, 6.0, 0.01)
In [4]: plt.plot(x, [x**2 for x in x])
Out[4]: [<matplotlib.lines.Line2D object at 0x2f2ef10>]
In [5]: plt.show()
```

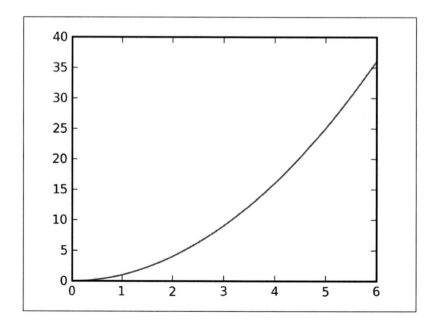

Multiline plots

It's fun to plot a line, but it's even more fun when we can plot more than one line on the same figure. This is really easy with Matplotlib as we can simply plot all the lines that we want before calling show(). Have a look at the following code and screenshot:

```
In [1]: import matplotlib.pyplot as plt
In [2]: x = range(1, 5)
In [3]: plt.plot(x, [xi*1.5 for xi in x])
Out[3]: [<matplotlib.lines.Line2D object at 0x2076ed0>]
In [4]: plt.plot(x, [xi*3.0 for xi in x])
Out[4]: [<matplotlib.lines.Line2D object at 0x1e544d0>]
In [5]: plt.plot(x, [xi/3.0 for xi in x])
Out[5]: [<matplotlib.lines.Line2D object at 0x20864d0>]
In [6]: plt.show()
```

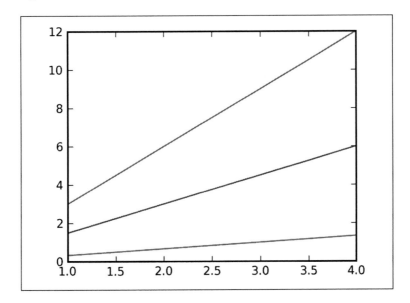

Note how Matplotlib automatically chooses different colors for each line — green for the first line, blue for the second line, and red for the third one (from top to bottom).

Can you tell why a float value was used in line [5]? Try it yourself with an integer one and you'll see. The answer is that if divided by 3 (that is, by using an integer coefficient), the result will also be an integer. So you'll see a line plot like "stairs".

`plot()` supports another syntax useful in this situation. We can plot multiline figures by passing the X and Y values list in a single `plot()` call:

```
In [1]: import matplotlib.pyplot as plt
In [2]: x = range(1, 5)
In [3]: plt.plot(x, [xi*1.5 for xi in x], x, [xi*3.0 for xi in x], x,
[xi/3.0 for xi in x])
Out[3]:
[<matplotlib.lines.Line2D object at 0x1d4bed0>,
 <matplotlib.lines.Line2D object at 0x1d56fd0>,
 <matplotlib.lines.Line2D object at 0x1d5d3d0>]
In [4]: plt.show()
```

The preceding code simply rewrites the previous example with a different syntax.

While list comprehensions are a very powerful tool, they can generate a little bit of confusion in these simple examples. So we'd like to show another feature of the `arange()` function of NumPy:

```
In [1]: import matplotlib.pyplot as plt
In [2]: import numpy as np
In [3]: x = np.arange(1, 5)
In [4]: plt.plot(x, x*1.5, x, x*3.0, x, x/3.0)
Out[4]:
[<matplotlib.lines.Line2D object at 0x15d5d10>,
 <matplotlib.lines.Line2D object at 0x15ddf90>,
 <matplotlib.lines.Line2D object at 0x15e4390>]
In [5]: plt.show()
```

Here, we take advantage of the NumPy `array` objects returned by `arange()`.

The multiline plot is possible because, by default, the `hold` property is enabled (consider it as a declaration to preserve all the plotted lines on the current figure instead of replacing them at every `plot()` call). Try this simple example and see what happens:

```
In [1]: import matplotlib.pyplot as plt
In [2]: plt.interactive(True)# enable interactive mode, in case it was
not
In [3]: plt.hold(False)  # empty window will pop up
In [4]: plt.plot([1, 2, 3])
Out[4]: [<matplotlib.lines.Line2D object at 0x19ea1d0>]
In [5]: plt.plot([2, 4, 6])
Out[5]: [<matplotlib.lines.Line2D object at 0x19e8cd0>]
```

Since `hold` is not enabled, each `plot()` command overwrites the current figure.

A brief introduction to NumPy arrays

In the previous section, we've mentioned NumPy `array` objects (in relation to `arange()`), but they deserve a proper introduction because we will be using them throughout this book.

Python lists are extremely flexible and really handy, but when dealing with a large number of elements or to support scientific computing, they show their limits.

One of the fundamental aspects of NumPy is providing a powerful N-dimensional array object, `ndarray`, to represent a collection of items (all of the same type).

Creating an `array` (an object of type `ndarray`) is simple:

```
In [1]: import numpy as np
In [2]: x = np.array([1, 2, 3])
In [3]: x
Out[3]: array([1, 2, 3])
```

We can pass a list or a tuple to `array()` and in return, we have an `array` object.

We can treat this array as if it was a list; we can slice it or select one of its elements using the standard Python syntax:

```
In [4]: x[1:]
Out[4]: array([2, 3])
In [5]: x[2]
Out[5]: 3
```

As we have already seen, we can operate on the whole array (this kind of operation is common in MATLAB):

```
In [6]: x*2
Out[6]: array([2, 4, 6])
```

This code snippet returns a new array with the elements of x multiplied by 2; if we were working with a list, we would have had to use a list comprehension:

```
In [7]: l = [1, 2, 3]
In [8]: [2*li for li in l]
Out[8]: [2, 4, 6]
```

We can work with more arrays and make them interact:

```
In [9]: a = np.array([1, 2, 3])
In [10]: b = np.array([3, 2, 1])
In [11]: a+b
Out[11]: array([4, 4, 4])
```

We can also create multidimensional arrays:

```
In [12]: M = np.array([[1, 2, 3], [4, 5, 6]])
In [13]: M[1,2]
Out[13]: 6
```

Another important function—the one that we already met, is `arange()`:

```
In [14]: range(6)
Out[14]: [0, 1, 2, 3, 4, 5]
In [15]: np.arange(6)
Out[15]: array([0, 1, 2, 3, 4, 5])
```

It mimics the `range()` function from the core Python but it returns a NumPy `array`.

Grid, axes, and labels

Now we can learn about some features that we can add to plots, and some features to control them better.

Adding a grid

In the previous images, we saw that the background of the figure was completely blank. While it might be nice for some plots, there are situations where having a reference system would improve the comprehension of the plot—for example with multiline plots. We can add a grid to the plot by calling the `grid()` function; it takes one parameter, a Boolean value, to enable (if `True`) or disable (if `False`) the grid:

```
In [1]: import matplotlib.pyplot as plt
In [2]: import numpy as np
In [3]: x = np.arange(1, 5)
In [4]: plt.plot(x, x*1.5, x, x*3.0, x, x/3.0)
Out[4]:
[<matplotlib.lines.Line2D object at 0x8fcc20c>,
 <matplotlib.lines.Line2D object at 0x8fcc50c>,
 <matplotlib.lines.Line2D object at 0x8fcc84c>]
In [5]: plt.grid(True)
In [6]: plt.show()
```

We can see the grid in the following screenshot, as a result of executing the preceding code:

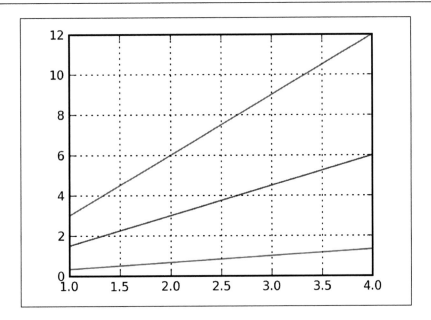

Handling axes

You might have noticed that Matplotlib automatically sets the limits of the figure
to precisely contain the plotted datasets. However, sometimes we want to set the
axes limits ourself (defining the scale of the chart). Let's take the first multiline plot.
Wouldn't it be better to have more spaces between lines and borders? We can achieve
this with the following code:

```
In [1]: import matplotlib.pyplot as plt
In [2]: import numpy as np
In [3]: x = np.arange(1, 5)
In [4]: plt.plot(x, x*1.5, x, x*3.0, x, x/3.0)
Out[4]:
[<matplotlib.lines.Line2D object at 0x2a00d10>,
 <matplotlib.lines.Line2D object at 0x2a05f90>,
 <matplotlib.lines.Line2D object at 0x2a0f390>]
In [5]: plt.axis()  # shows the current axis limits values
Out[5]: (1.0, 4.0, 0.0, 12.0)
In [6]: plt.axis([0, 5, -1, 13])  # set new axes limits
Out[6]: [0, 5, -1, 13]
In [7]: plt.show()
```

We can see in the following screenshot that we now have more space around the lines:

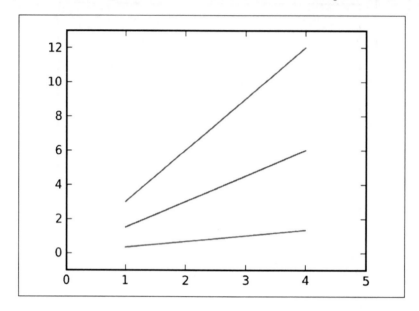

If we execute `axis()` without parameters, it returns the actual axis limits.

There are two ways to pass parameters to `axis()`: by a list of four values or by keyword arguments.

The list of values, that's the whole set of four values of keyword arguments [xmin, xmax, ymin, ymax], allows us to specify at the same time, the minimum and maximum limits respectively for the X-axis and the Y-axis. We can use the specific keyword arguments, for example:

```
plt.axis(xmin=NNN, ymax=NNN)
```

If we wish to set only some of these limits (in the previous line, we set only the minimum value for X-axis and the maximum value for Y-axis).

We can also control the limits for each axis separately using `xlim()` and `ylim()` functions. Let's take the previous code before calling the `axis()` function, and change it in the following way:

```
In [1]: import matplotlib.pyplot as plt
In [2]: import numpy as np
In [3]: x = np.arange(1, 5)
In [4]: plt.plot(x, x*1.5, x, x*3.0, x, x/3.0)
Out[4]:
```

```
[<matplotlib.lines.Line2D object at 0x9f9320c>,
 <matplotlib.lines.Line2D object at 0x9f9350c>,
 <matplotlib.lines.Line2D object at 0x9f9384c>]
In [5]: plt.xlim()
Out[5]: (1.0, 4.0)
In [6]: plt.ylim()
Out[6]: (0.0, 12.0)
```

We obtain the current X and Y limits at line [5] and [6].

Also for `xlim()` and `ylim()`, we can pass a list of two values (for example, `xlim([xmin, xmax])`), or use the keyword arguments.

Adding labels

Now that we know how to manage the axes dimensions, another important piece of information to add to a plot is the axes labels, since they usually specify what kind of data we are plotting.

By referring to the first image that we have seen under the *First plots with Matplotlib* section of this chapter, we can now add labels using these new functions:

```
In [1]: import matplotlib.pyplot as plt
In [2]: plt.plot([1, 3, 2, 4])
Out[2]: [<matplotlib.lines.Line2D object at 0x26f8f10>]
In [3]: plt.xlabel('This is the X axis')
Out[3]: <matplotlib.text.Text object at 0x26e9110>
In [4]: plt.ylabel('This is the Y axis')
Out[4]: <matplotlib.text.Text object at 0x26e9cd0>
In [5]: plt.show()
```

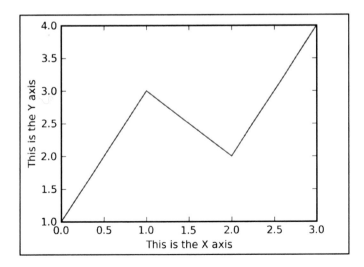

Note how we have defined the labels between the `plot()` call and the actual `show()` of the image. During this interval, many annotations are possible, and labels are just an example.

Titles and legends

We are about to introduce two other important plot features—titles and legends.

Adding a title

Just like in a book or a paper, the title of a graph describes what it is:

```
In [1]: import matplotlib.pyplot as plt
In [2]: plt.plot([1, 3, 2, 4])
Out[2]: [<matplotlib.lines.Line2D object at 0xf54f10>]
In [3]: plt.title('Simple plot')
Out[3]: <matplotlib.text.Text object at 0xf4b850>
In [4]: plt.show()
```

Matplotlib provides a simple function, `plt.title()`, to add a title to an image, as shown in the previous code. The following screenshot displays the output of the previous example:

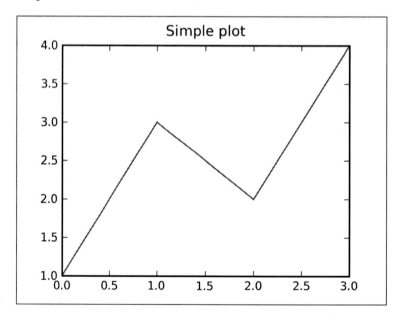

Adding a legend

The last thing we need to see to complete a basic plot is a **legend**.

Legends are used to explain what each line means in the current figure. Let's take the multiline plot example again, and extend it with a legend:

```
In [1]: import matplotlib.pyplot as plt
In [2]: import numpy as np
In [3]: x = np.arange(1, 5)
In [4]: plt.plot(x, x*1.5, label='Normal')
Out[4]: [<matplotlib.lines.Line2D object at 0x2ca6f50>]
In [5]: plt.plot(x, x*3.0, label='Fast')
Out[5]: [<matplotlib.lines.Line2D object at 0x2cabf50>]
In [6]: plt.plot(x, x/3.0, label='Slow')
Out[6]: [<matplotlib.lines.Line2D object at 0x2cb33d0>]
In [7]: plt.legend()
Out[7]: <matplotlib.legend.Legend object at 0x2cb3750>
In [8]: plt.show()
```

The output of this code snippet is shown here:

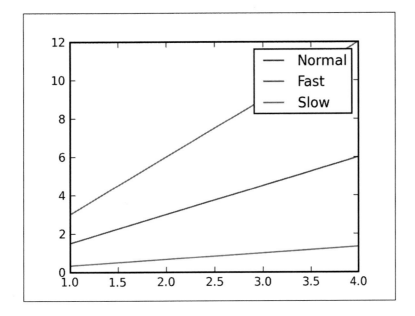

We added an extra keyword argument, label, to the plot() call. This keyword argument provides the information required to compose the text of the legend. Since keyword arguments must come after non-keyword arguments, we have to plot each line in separate plot() calls that include the label argument. Now, calling the legend() function with no argument will show that information in the legend box.

 If any label argument is set to the literal string _nolegend_-, then that line is excluded from the legend.

Alternatively, we could specify the labels of the lines (as mentioned in their respective label arguments), as a list of strings to the legend() call. Thus, the relevant code would appear like this:

```
In [4]: plt.plot(x, x*1.5)
In [5]: plt.plot(x, x*3.0)
In [6]: plt.plot(x, x/3.0)
In [7]: plt.legend(['Normal', 'Fast', 'Slow'])
```

But still, this solution is not the optimum one because of the following reasons:

- It's the plot() command that knows what the line represents, so that information should be there.
- We have to remember the order of lines plotted because the legend() parameters are matched with the lines as they are plotted.

We have to consider plotting as a continuous process, performing the fine-tuning of the result every time it's needed. In the previous screenshot, we can see that the legend is placed on top of a part of one line, and it would be more optimized to have it in the unused space on the upper-left corner. The legend() function allows us to select several locations, which can be specified as an optional argument (or with the keyword argument, loc). The following table gives us the various positions at which the legend could be placed along with the equivalent codes for these positions.

String	Code
best	0
upper right	1
upper left	2
lower left	3
lower right	4
right	5

String	Code
center left	6
center right	7
lower center	8
upper center	9
center	10

We can specify either the location string or the code value.

Alternatively, we can specify the location as a two-elements tuple of coordinates where (0, 1) is the top-left, (0.5, 0.5) is the center, and so on. You can even go outside the plot area, for example, loc=(-0.1, 0.9). Note that in this case, the loc argument specifies the position of the lower-left corner of the legend, so you should adjust the coordinates according to that.

An interesting functionality is the **auto-legend positioning** — setting loc='best', Matplotlib automatically tries to find the the optimal legend position. Another nice argument we'd like to mention is ncol; this argument specifies how many columns to use to layout the legend items.

A complete example

Let's now group together all that we've seen so far and create a complete example as follows:

```
In [1]: import matplotlib.pyplot as plt
In [2]: import numpy as np
In [3]: x = np.arange(1, 5)
In [4]: plt.plot(x, x*1.5, label='Normal')
Out[4]: [<matplotlib.lines.Line2D object at 0x2ab5f50>]
In [5]: plt.plot(x, x*3.0, label='Fast')
Out[5]: [<matplotlib.lines.Line2D object at 0x2ac5210>]
In [6]: plt.plot(x, x/3.0, label='Slow')
Out[6]: [<matplotlib.lines.Line2D object at 0x2ac5650>]
In [7]: plt.grid(True)
In [8]: plt.title('Sample Growth of a Measure')
Out[8]: <matplotlib.text.Text object at 0x2aa8890>
In [9]: plt.xlabel('Samples')
Out[9]: <matplotlib.text.Text object at 0x2aa6150>
In [10]: plt.ylabel('Values Measured')
Out[10]: <matplotlib.text.Text object at 0x2aa6d10>
In [11]: plt.legend(loc='upper left')
Out[11]: <matplotlib.legend.Legend object at 0x2ac5c50>
In [12]: plt.show()
```

A very nice looking plot can be obtained with just a bunch of commands. The plot obtained from the previous code snippet looks like this:

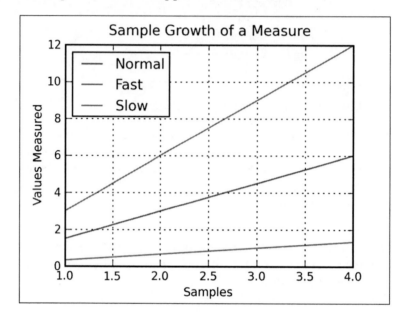

Saving plots to a file

Saving a plot to a file is an easy task. The following example shows how:

```
In [1]: import matplotlib.pyplot as plt
In [2]: plt.plot([1, 2, 3])
Out[2]: [<matplotlib.lines.Line2D object at 0x22a2f10>]
In [3]: plt.savefig('plot123.png')
```

Just a call to savefig() with the filename as the parameter, and we can find the saved plot in the current directory.

```
$ file plot123.png
plot123.png: PNG image, 800 x 600, 8-bit/color RGBA, non-interlaced
```

The file format is based on the filename extension (so in the previous example, we saved a PNG image).

Two values govern the resulting image size in pixels—the figure size and the DPI.

Here, we can see the default values for Matplotlib:

```
In [1]: import matplotlib as mpl
In [2]: mpl.rcParams['figure.figsize']
Out[2]: [8.0, 6.0]
In [3]: mpl.rcParams['savefig.dpi']
Out[3]: 100
```

So, an 8x6 inches figure with 100 DPI results in an 800x600 pixels image (as seen in the previous example).

When an image is displayed on the screen, the length units are ignored, and simply the pixels are displayed. When printed (or used in a document), the size and DPI are used to determine how to scale the image.

 The image sizes are expressed in inches, while all other properties are expressed in points such as line width, or font size.

We can set the DPI value when saving by passing the additional keyword argument `dpi` to `savefig()`. This is explained with the help of the following line of code:

```
In [4]: plt.savefig('plot123_2.png', dpi=200)
```

This code generates a file like this:

$ file plot123_2.png

plot123_2.png: PNG image, 1600 x 1200, 8-bit/color RGBA, non-interlaced

This file is double the size of the first one (since we've doubled the DPI).

If we need to plot to a file without any display available, then the Agg backend is the one we should use:

```
In [1]: import matplotlib as mpl
In [2]: mpl.use('Agg')    #before importing pyplot
In [3]: import matplotlib.pyplot as plt
In [4]: plt.plot([1,2,3])
Out[4]: [<matplotlib.lines.Line2D object at 0x23f5410>]
In [5]: plt.savefig('plot123_3.png')
```

The execution of this code would result in:

$ file plot123_3.png

plot123_3.png: PNG image, 800 x 600, 8-bit/color RGBA, non-interlaced

Agg is limited to the `.png` output format, but it's the best renderer available. We can also use the PS, PDF, or SVG backends for non-interactive plotting.

An interesting feature of savefig() is its ability to receive an open file object (such as the standard output) instead of a filename. This is particularly useful in the context of web servers, where we may be streaming an output over a network.

We might be also interested in the keyword argument transparent, which if set to True will generate a file with a transparent background. This could be useful if, for example, we're going to include that image in a web page which has a colored background.

Interactive navigation toolbar

If you have tried some of the book examples proposed so far, then you may have already noticed the interactive navigation toolbar (because when using matplotlib. pyplot, the toolbar is enabled by default for every figure), but in any case, here is a screenshot of the window:

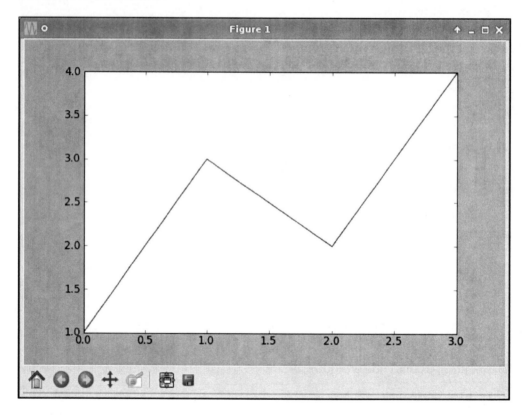

This window pops up with the following code, when executed in IPython:

```
In [1]: import matplotlib as mpl
In [2]: mpl.use('GTKAgg')  # to use GTK UI
In [3]: import matplotlib.pyplot as plt
In [4]: plt.plot([1, 3, 2, 4])
Out[4]: [<matplotlib.lines.Line2D object at 0x909b04c>]
In [5]: plt.show()
```

It's worth taking the time to learn more about this window, since it provides basic elaboration and manipulation functions for interactive plotting.

First of all, note how passing the mouse over the figure area results in the mouse pointer's coordinates being shown in the bottom-right corner of the window.

At the bottom of the window, we can find the navigation toolbar. A description of each of its buttons (from left to right) follows:

Button	Description
	Click on this button to go back to the default (first) view of your data. The net result is to revert all defined views (created using other buttons).
	Click on these buttons to traverse back and forward between the previously defined views. Consider these two buttons and the home one just like the buttons in a web browser: Home takes you back to the first view, while the back and forward buttons navigate between the views defined during this session (they have no effect if nothing has been done so far).
	We can use this button in two different modes: **pan** and **zoom**. Click on this button to enable it, and move the mouse into the figure area. The two views are described as follows: • **Pan**: Click on the left mouse button and hold it to pan the figure, dragging it to a new position. Once we're happy with the position, release the mouse button. While panning, if we press (or hold) the *x* or *y* key, then the panning is limited to the selected axis. • **Zoom**: Click on the right mouse button and hold it to zoom the figure, dragging it to a new position. Movement to the right or to the left generates a proportional zoom in or out of the X-axis of the figure. The same holds for the up or down movement of the Y-axis. The point where we click the mouse remains still so that we are able to zoom around a given point in the figure. The *x* and *y* keys work in the same way as mentioned earlier, but now we can press the *Ctrl* key to preserve the aspect ratio.

Button	Description
	Enabling this mode, we can draw a rectangle on the figure (hold the left mouse button while drawing it), and the view will be zoomed to that rectangle.
	When we click on this button, a window pops up that allows us to configure the various spaces that surround the figure (left, right, up, button, between).
	Click on this button, and a **save file** dialog will pop up that allows us to save the current figure.

When a mode is enabled, its name appears in the bottom-right part of the window (together with the mouse pointer position on the figure).

There are even a series of keyboard shortcuts to enable these functions. They are:

Keyboard shortcut	Command
h or *r* or *home*	Home or Reset
c or left arrow or *backspace*	Back
v or right arrow	Forward
p	Pan or Zoom
o	Zoom-to-rectangle
s	Save
f	Toggle fullscreen
hold *x*	Constrain pan or zoom to x-axis
hold *y*	Constrain pan or zoom to y-axis
hold *ctrl*	Preserve aspect ratio
g	Toggle grid
l	Toggle y-axis scale (log or linear)

IPython support

We have already used IPython throughout the chapter, and we saw how useful it is. Therefore, we want to give it a better introduction.

Matplotlib tends to defer drawing till the end, since it's an expensive operation, and updating the plot at every property change would slow down the execution.

That's fine for batch operations, but when we're working with the Python shell, we want to see updates at every command we type. Easy to say, but difficult to implement.

Most GUI libraries need to control the main loop of execution of Python, thus preventing any further interaction (that is, you can't type while viewing the image). The only GUI that plays nice with Python's standard shell is **Tkinter**.

 Tkinter is the standard Python interface to the Tk GUI library.

So you might want to set the backend property to TkAgg and interactive to True when using the Python interpreter interactively.

IPython uses a smart method to handle this situation—it spawns a thread to execute GUI library code in, and uses another thread to handle user command input.

To activate this feature for Matplotlib, simply pass the -pylab option to the IPython command line. The -pylab option enables a special Matplotlib support mode in IPython that reads the Matplotlib configuration file looking for the backend, activating the proper GUI threading model if required. It also sets the Matplotlib interactive mode, so that show() commands won't block the interactive shell.

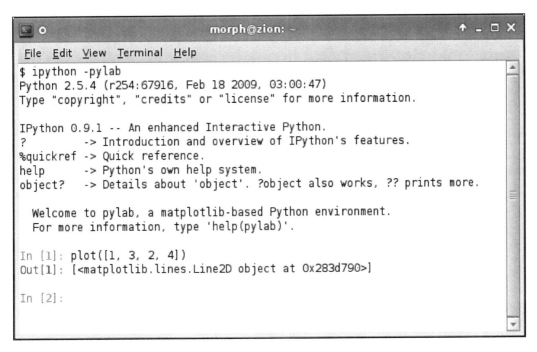

After entering the `plot()` command, the image window opens automatically, and we are still able to type commands in the IPython console to change the plot

In this mode, we do not need to import any modules (because they are already imported through the `-pylab` mode), and IPython enables the interactive mode so that every command triggers a figure update.

Controlling the interactive mode

The term *Interactive* in the Matplotlib sense specifies when the figure is updated. If we are in interactive mode, then the figure is redrawn on every plot command. If we are not in interactive mode, a figure *state* is updated on every plot command, but the figure is actually drawn only when an explicit call to `draw()` or `show()` is made.

In IPython, `-pylab` mode automatically enables interactive mode, but there are other ways to control it.

First, there is the `interactive: True` flag in the `matplotlibrc` file. Also, the `interactive` property is available in the `rcParams` dictionary.

```
In [1]: import matplotlib as mpl
In [2]: mpl.rcParams['interactive']
Out[2]: True
```

we can also change it using a Matplotlib function:

```
In [3]: mpl.interactive(False)
In [4]: mpl.rcParams['interactive']
Out[4]: False
```

Here are the functions available in `-pylab` mode (provided by `pylab` module) to manage interactive mode:

- `isinteractive()`: Returns `True` or `False`, the value of `interactive` property
- `ion()`: Enables interactive mode
- `ioff()`: Disables interactive mode
- `draw()`: Forces a figure canvas redraw

Remember that `draw()` is an expensive operation, in particular, for big figures. So there are situations where it's better to temporarily disable the interactive mode while executing some commands and to re-enable it after them. It's a wise choice even for batch executions.

Suppressing functions output

Some commands print some information about their execution to the output. Given the complexity or the quantity of input, the output can be very long, and in particular during interactive sessions, we'd like to suppress it.

With IPython, we just need to append a semicolon at the end of the line to suppress the command output.

```
In [1]: import matplotlib.pyplot as plt
In [2]: plt.plot([1, 2])
Out[2]: [<matplotlib.lines.Line2D object at 0x26abfd0>]
In [3]: plt.plot([2, 1]);
In [4]:
```

We can see that at line [2] we got an output from `plot()`, while on line [3], which is using the semicolon, the output is suppressed.

Configuring Matplotlib

In order to have the best experience with any program, we have to configure it to our own preferences; the same holds true for Matplotlib.

Matplotlib provides for massive configurability of plots, and there are several places to control the customization:

- **Global machine configuration file**: This is used to configure Matplotlib for all the users of the machine.

- **User configuration file**: A separate file for each user, where they can choose their own settings, overwriting the global configuration file (note that it will be used by that used any time the given user execute a Matplotlib-related code).

- **Configuration file in the current directory**: Used for specific customization to the current script or program. This is particularly useful in situations when different programs have different needs, and using an external configuration file is better than hardcoding those settings in the code.

- **Python code in the current script or program or interactive session**: To fine-tune settings only for that execution; this overwrites every configuration file.

On a Linux system, the global configuration file is located at `/etc/matplotlibrc`, while the user configuration file is located in the users' home directory at `$HOME/.matplotlib/matplotlibrc`.

On a Windows system, the user configuration file is located at `C:\Documents and Settings\yourname\.matplotlib` (there's no global configuration file).

With these files and Matplotlib functions, we can control every property of your plots such as image size, colors, lines width, legends, and so on.

Configuration files contain many useful parameters to allow you to tweak your setup, so we'll take a look at some of them. They share the same syntax so we can apply what we'll learn to any of them.

Let's reinforce the fact that configuration is done at various layers. Matplotlib has a set of default configuration parameters that can be customized with this precedence order (from the most specific to the most general):

- Matplotlib functions in Python code
- `matplotlibrc` file in the current directory
- User `matplotlibrc` file
- Global `matplotlibrc` file

We only need to change the settings we want to: all the others will maintain the default values.

Configuration files

On a Debian system, `/etc/matplotlibrc` is the same configuration file shipped with an upstream tarball. It contains every possible configuration item (commented with a "#" character, if not currently set) along with a description of its purpose and usage. A look at that file will give you an idea of how much can be customized in Matplotlib.

Since there are a lot of configuration settings, let's look at some of the ones that might be particularly interesting. One of the most important settings (and probably the first we would like to set up) is the `backend`:

```
backend     : TkAgg
```

`TkAgg` is the backend that should work without any additional dependency, since it uses Tkinter (available with Python itself). For the same reason, it is the default backend on some systems (such as Debian or Ubuntu).

Here are some other settings:

Setting	Description
numerix	Specifies the numerical library to use. Nowadays, the one to use is numpy, but on older systems we can find Numeric or numarray.
interactive	Specifies to enable the interactive mode (boolean).
line.linewidth	Specifies the default line width (in points) used on plots.
line.linecolor	Specifies the default line color used on plots.
figure.figsize	Specifies the figure sizes, in inches.
savefig.dpi	Specifies the DPI when saving to file.
savefig.edgecolor	Specifies the edge color when saving to file.
savefig.facecolor	Specifies the face color when saving to file.

Configuring through the Python code

Matplotlib provides a way to change the settings for the current session, be it a script or program or an interactive session with the Python interpreter or IPython.

Let's first see how we can view the parameters currently set:

```
$ ipython
In [1]: import matplotlib as mpl
In [2]: mpl.rcParams
Out[2]:
{'agg.path.chunksize': 0,
 'axes.axisbelow': False,
 'axes.edgecolor': 'k',
 'axes.facecolor': 'w',
```

matplotlib.rcParams is a handy dictionary, global to the whole matplotlib module, which contains default configuration settings (overridden by matplotlibrc files, if present). We can modify this dictionary directly with code like this:

```
mpl.rcParams['<param name>'] = <value>
```

For example, with the following command, we set the figure size to 4x3 inches:

```
In [3]: mpl.rcParams['figure.figsize'] = (4, 3)
```

Matplotlib has a couple of useful functions to modify configuration parameters:

- `matplotlib.rcdefaults()`: Restores Matplotlib's default configuration parameters values
- `matplotlib.rc()`: Sets multiple settings in a single command

For example, we can set the same property to more than one group (In this case, `figure` and `savefig` groups):

```
mpl.rc(('figure', 'savefig'), facecolor='r')
```

This is equivalent to:

```
mpl.rcParam['figure.facecolor'] = 'r'
mpl.rcParam['savefig.facecolor'] = 'r'
```

This command sets `facecolor` to red for both the displayed image (`figure`) and the saved one (`savefig`). We can also set more parameters for the same group:

```
mpl.rc('line', linewidth=4, linecolor='b')
```

This line of code is equivalent to the following:

```
mpl.rcParam['line.linewidth'] = 4
mpl.rcParam['line.linecolor'] = 'b'
```

This code sets the line width to four points and line color to blue.

Related to `rc` settings, there is the module `matplotlib.rcsetup` that contains the default Matplotlib parameter values and some validation functions to prevent spurious values from being used in a setting.

Selecting backend from code

Matplotlib has another configuration function, to select the backend to use at runtime, `matplotlib.use()`:

```
In [1]: import matplotlib as mpl
In [2]: mpl.use('Agg') # to render to file, or to not use a graphical
display
In [3]: mpl.use('GTKAgg')  # to render to a GTK UI window
```

Please note that the function `matplotlib.use()` must be called right after importing `matplotlib` for the first time, in particular **before** importing `pylab` or `pyplot` (or `matplotlib.backends`), or else it won't work.

Summary

If you've arrived here, now you know:

- How to create single or multiline plots handling the axes limits
- How to add information to the plot such as legends, labels, and titles
- How to save plots to a file for reuse
- How to use the toolbar that the interactive window provides
- Why IPython is so useful in collaboration with Matplotlib
- How to customize Matplotlib to your needs (both from configuration files and from Python code)

But we have only scratched the surface of what Matplotlib can do. We'll see much more in the next chapter!

3

Decorate Graphs with Plot Styles and Types

So far, we have only seen a glimpse of Matplotlib's potential, and we want to see more—that's exactly what this chapter aims at.

We saw plain lines, but Matplotlib can do a lot more. In this chapter, we will explore:

- Line style customization—changing how the lines are drawn
- Point style customization—changing how we plot points on the graph
- Axes tick customization—changing how we draw ticks on the axes
- The several plots types available in Matplotlib such as histograms, bars, error bars, pie charts, scatter plots, and so on
- Polar charts, in case we need to plot relationships better expressed in terms of angles and radii
- Inserting textual information in our plots

Let's start with line and marker customizations.

Markers and line styles

In the previous chapter, all the plots were made of points with lines joining them. The points are the pairs (x,y) from the X and Y input lists we pass to plot(); lines are the straight segments connecting any two adjacent points.

Points are almost invisible, if not for the edges in the graph. However, they are the real generators of the plot because points mark positions. As a result, they are called *markers* in Matplotlib terminology.

By default, Matplotlib draws markers as a single dot and lines as straight thin segments; there are situations where we would like to change either the marker style (to clearly identify them in the plot) or the line style (so that the line appears dashed, for example).

`plot()` supports an optional third argument that contains a format string for each pair of X, Y arguments in the form of:

```
plt.plot(X, Y, '<format>', ...)
```

There are three levels of customization:

- Colors
- Line styles
- Marker styles

Each of them can be represented by a given set of characters that can be concatenated into a single format string.

We are now going to see them one-by-one.

Control colors

We've already seen that in a multiline plot, Matplotlib automatically chooses different colors for different lines. We are also free to choose them by ourselves:

```
In [1]: import matplotlib.pyplot as plt
In [2]: import numpy as np
In [3]: y = np.arange(1, 3)
In [4]: plt.plot(y, 'y');
In [5]: plt.plot(y+1, 'm');
In [6]: plt.plot(y+2, 'c');
In [7]: plt.show()
```

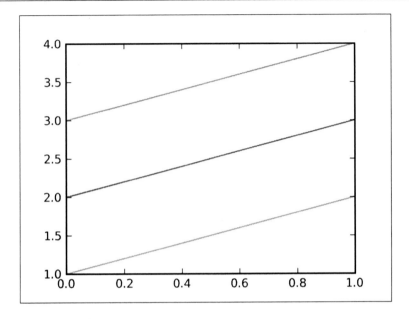

In the preceding code, we specify color as the last argument — the `<format>` argument (in this case with an implicit X-axis) — to draw yellow, magenta, and cyan lines (from bottom to top).

Here is a table of the abbreviations used to select colors:

Color abbreviation	Color Name
b	blue
c	cyan
g	green
k	black
m	magenta
r	red
w	white
y	yellow

There are several ways to specify colors, other than by color abbreviations:

- The full color name, such as `yellow`, as specified in the Color name column of the previous table
- Hexadecimal string (the same format as in HTML code) such as `#FF00FF`
- RGB or RGBA tuples, for example, `(1, 0, 1, 1)`
- Grayscale intensity, in string format such as `'0.7'`

Specifying styles in multiline plots

We appreciated the flexibility of the plot() function in multiline plots—specifying all the lines in a single function call. So, we expect the same for formatting.

Indeed, the plot() syntax can be expanded as:

```
plt.plot(x1, y1, fmt1, x2, y2, fmt2, ...)
```

Where we specify the (X_i, Y_i) pairs, along with the relative formatting strings.

Thus, we can rewrite the previous example in a more compact way:

```
In [1]: import matplotlib.pyplot as plt
In [2]: import numpy as np
In [3]: y = np.arange(1, 3)
In [4]: plt.plot(y, 'y', y+1, 'm', y+2, 'c');
In [5]: plt.show()
```

and obtain the same image as shown previously.

Control line styles

All the lines seen until now are proper ones without any dots or dashes. Matplotlib allows us to use different line styles, for example:

```
In [1]: import matplotlib.pyplot as plt
In [2]: import numpy as np
In [3]: y = np.arange(1, 3)
In [4]: plt.plot(y, '--', y+1, '-.', y+2, ':');
In [5]: plt.show()
```

This code snippet generates a blue dashed line, a green dash-dotted line, and a red dotted line, as shown in the next screenshot:

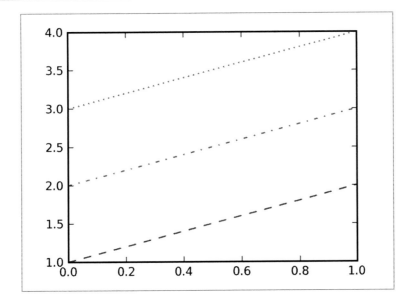

All the available styles are listed in the following table:

Style abbreviation	Style
-	solid line
- -	dashed line
- .	dash-dot line
:	dotted line

Now, we can see the default format string for a single line plot is `'b-'`.

Control marker styles

Markers are, by default, drawn as point markers. They are just a location on the figure where segments join.

Matplotlib provides a lot of customization options for markers. The following table contains a list of the available styles:

Marker abbreviation	Marker style
.	Point marker
,	Pixel marker
o	Circle marker

Marker abbreviation	Marker style
v	Triangle down marker
^	Triangle up marker
<	Triangle left marker
>	Triangle right marker
1	Tripod down marker
2	Tripod up marker
3	Tripod left marker
4	Tripod right marker
s	Square marker
p	Pentagon marker
*	Star marker
h	Hexagon marker
H	Rotated hexagon marker
+	Plus marker
x	Cross (x) marker
D	Diamond marker
d	Thin diamond marker
|	Vertical line (vline symbol) marker
_	Horizontal line (hline symbol) marker

Let's look at some of them:

```
In [1]: import matplotlib.pyplot as plt
In [2]: import numpy as np
In [3]: y = np.arange(1, 3, 0.2)
In [4]: plt.plot(y, 'x', y+0.5, 'o', y+1, 'D', y+1.5, '^', y+2, 's');
In [5]: plt.show()
```

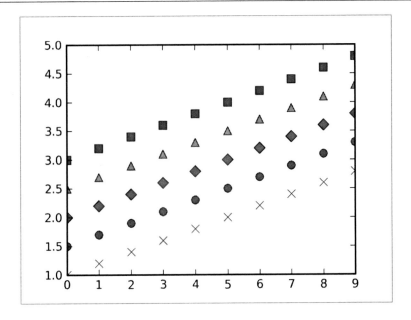

In the preceding code, we did not specify any color, so the default sequence is used (blue, green, red, cyan, and magenta). There is no style for lines, so there is no line at all; we have to explicitly indicate the line format to use if we specify a marker's style.

In the following example, we try to group up all the customization available for colors, lines, and markers in the following way:

```
In [1]: import matplotlib.pyplot as plt
In [2]: import numpy as np
In [3]: y = np.arange(1, 3, 0.3)
In [4]: plt.plot(y, 'cx--', y+1, 'mo:', y+2, 'kp-.');
In [5]: plt.show()
```

As we can see in the next screenshot, the preceding code snippet results in a cyan dashed line with crosses as markers, a magenta line with circles as markers, and a black line with pentagons as markers.

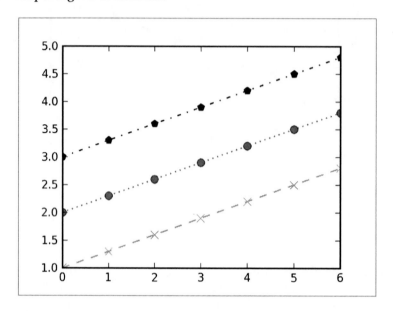

Finer control with keyword arguments

Format strings are really useful, but they have some drawbacks. For example, they don't allow us to specify different colors for lines and markers, as we saw in the previous example.

`plot()` is a really rich function, and there are some keyword arguments to configure colors, markers, and line styles:

Keyword argument	Description
`color` or `c`	Sets the color of the line; accepts any Matplotlib color format.
`linestyle`	Sets the line style; accepts the line styles seen previously.
`linewidth`	Sets the line width; accepts a float value in points.
`marker`	Sets the line marker style.
`markeredgecolor`	Sets the marker edge color; accepts any Matplotlib color format.
`markeredgewidth`	Sets the marker edge width; accepts float value in points.
`markerfacecolor`	Sets the marker face color; accepts any Matplotlib color format.
`markersize`	Sets the marker size in points; accepts float values.

With them, we can now plot a blue line in a dot-dash style with red markers having black edges and all of the markers being bigger than their default width:

```
In [1]: import matplotlib.pyplot as plt
In [2]: import numpy as np
In [3]: y = np.arange(1, 3, 0.3)
In [4]: plt.plot(y, color='blue', linestyle='dashdot', linewidth=4,
marker='o', markerfacecolor='red', markeredgecolor='black',
markeredgewidth=3, markersize=12);
In [5]: plt.show()
```

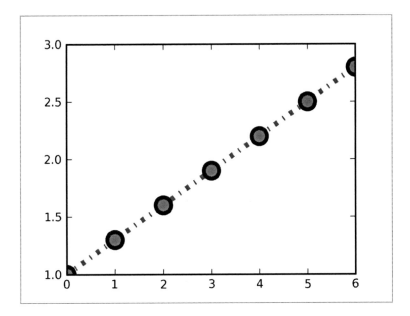

Well, the previous screenshot is not one of the prettiest graphs that Matplotlib can generate, but it shows how many configuration options we have at hand.

Another possibility offered by keyword arguments is that if we plot multiple lines, the arguments are applied to all of them. Let's say that we want to plot two lines in green, so we can call:

```
plt.plot(x1, y1, x2, y2, color='green')
```

and the color is applied to both the lines.

There's a lot to experiment with markers and line styles, and your imagination is the only limit.

Handling X and Y ticks

We have seen X and Y ticks in every plot but we haven't yet noticed their presence explicitly.

Vertical and horizontal ticks are those little segments on the axes, usually coupled with axes labels, used to give a reference system on the graph (they are, for example, the origin of the grid lines).

Matplotlib provides two basic functions to manage them—xticks() and yticks(). They behave in the same way, so the description for one function will apply to the other too.

Executing with no arguments, the tick function returns the current ticks' locations and the labels corresponding to each of them:

```
locs, labels = plt.xticks()
```

The arguments (in the form of lists) that we can pass to the function are:

- Locations of the ticks
- Labels to draw at these locations (if necessary)

Let's try to explain it with an example:

```
In [1]: import matplotlib.pyplot as plt
In [2]: x = [5, 3, 7, 2, 4, 1]
In [3]: plt.plot(x);
In [4]: plt.xticks(range(len(x)), ['a', 'b', 'c', 'd', 'e', 'f']);
In [5]: plt.yticks(range(1, 8, 2));
In [6]: plt.show()
```

In this code snippet, we used xticks() to specify both, locations and labels and yticks() to only show ticks at odd numbered locations.

The previous example gives us the following output:

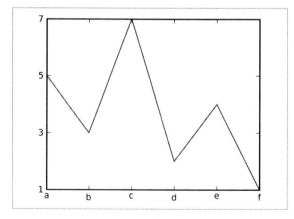

Plot types

In all the images that we have encountered so far, we have only plotted lines. Matplotlib has a lot of other plot formats, and we are about to see many of them. We want to introduce first a really nice graph that helps to choose the best chart for the kind of comparison and data we want to show:

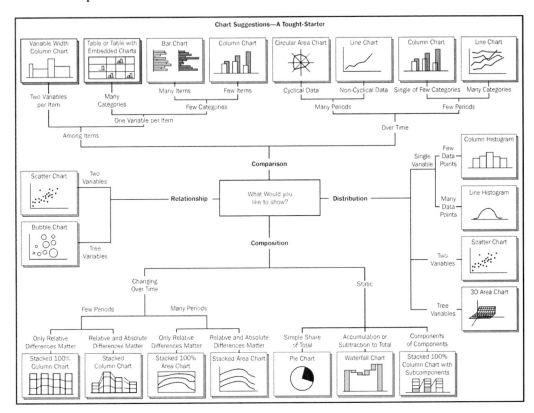

Histogram charts

Histogram charts are a graphical display of frequencies, represented as bars. They show what portion of the dataset falls into each category, usually specified as non-overlapping intervals. Matplotlib calls those categories *bins*.

We will use NumPy `random.randn()` to obtain an array of random numbers in a Gaussian distribution and then plot them in a histogram format using `hist()` function:

```
In [1]: import matplotlib.pyplot as plt
In [2]: import numpy as np
In [3]: y = np.random.randn(1000)
```

```
In [4]: plt.hist(y);
In [5]: plt.show()
```

The output of this code snippet is displayed in the next screenshot:

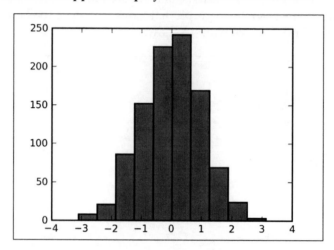

Histogram plots group up values into bins of values. By default, `hist()` uses a `bin` value of 10 (so only ten categories, or bars, are computed), but we can customize it, either by passing an additional parameter, for example, in `hist(y, <bins>)`, or using the `bin` keyword argument as `hist(y, bin=<bins>)`.

Replotting the previous dataset, but with `bin=25`:

```
In [6]: plt.hist(y, 25);
In [7]: plt.show()
```

This results in a set of finer grained bars, as shown in the following screenshot:

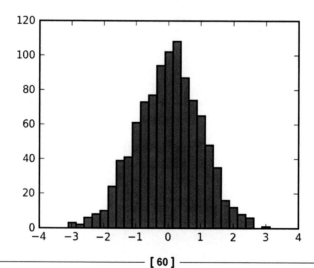

Error bar charts

In experimental sciences, we know that all the measurements that we take lack perfect precision. This leads to repeating the measurements, which results in obtaining a set of values. The expected result is that all those measures group up *around the true value* that we want to measure.

The representation of this distribution of data values is done by plotting a single data point, (commonly) the mean value of dataset, and an *error bar* to represent the overall distribution of data. This helps us to get a general idea of how accurate a measurement is (or how far the reported value could be from the error-free value).

Using the `errorbar()` function, Matplotlib allows us to create such a graph type.

Let's take a look at the next example:

```
In [1]: import matplotlib.pyplot as plt
In [2]: import numpy as np
In [3]: x = np.arange(0, 4, 0.2)
In [4]: y = np.exp(-x)
In [5]: e1 = 0.1 * np.abs(np.random.randn(len(y)))
In [6]: plt.errorbar(x, y, yerr=e1, fmt='.-');
In [7]: plt.show()
```

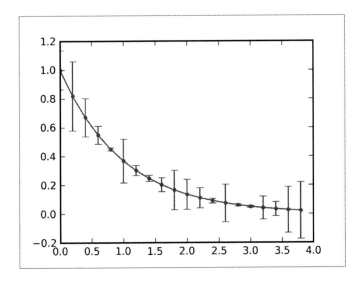

We just plotted x versus y with error deltas as vertical error bars, as specified by the `yerr` keyword argument. There is an equivalent argument, `xerr`, to draw horizontal error bars.

Note that we used a custom format for the line, specified by the `fmt` argument. The interesting formatting arguments are:

- `fmt`: This is the plot format for lines. If `None`, then only the error bars are plotted with no line connecting them.

- `ecolor`: This accepts any Matplotlib color and specifies the color of the error bars. If `None`, then the marker color is used.

- `elinewidth`: This specifies the line width of the error bars. If `None`, then the line width is used.

- `capsize`: This specifies the size of the cap of the error bars in pixels.

We can also specify both `yerr` and `xerr` together:

```
In [8]: e2 = 0.1 * np.abs(np.random.randn(len(y)))
In [9]: plt.errorbar(x, y, yerr=e1, xerr=e2, fmt='.-', capsize=0);
In [10]: plt.show()
```

In this code, we have used the `capsize` argument as well.

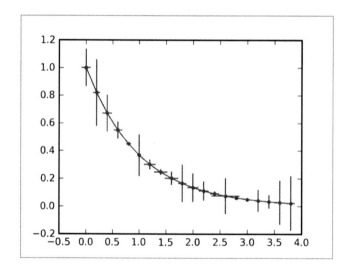

As we can see, for each point we can have four different errors, that is, one for each direction: -x, +x, -y, and +y.

The error bars described in the previous example are called **symmetrical** error bars, as their negative error is equal in value to the positive error (so error bar is symmetrical to the point where it's drawn). There is another type of error bar, which is **asymmetrical** error bar.

To draw asymmetrical error bars, we have to pass two lists (or a 2D array) of values to `yerr` and/or `xerr`—the first list is for negative errors while the second list is for positive errors.

```
In [11]: plt.errorbar(x, y, yerr=[e1, e2], fmt='.-');
In [12]: plt.show()
```

In this code snippet, -y is `e1` and +y is `e2`.

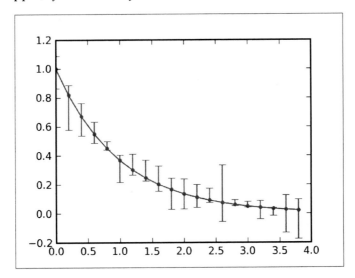

Bar charts

Bar charts display rectangular bars (either vertical or horizontal) with their length proportional to the values they represent. They are commonly used to visually compare two or more values.

The `bar()` function is used to generate bar charts in Matplotlib. The function expects two lists of values: the X coordinates that are the positions of the bar's left margin and the heights of the bars:

```
In [1]: import matplotlib.pyplot as plt
In [2]: plt.bar([1, 2, 3], [3, 2, 5]);
In [3]: plt.show()
```

As we can see in the following screenshot, the left margin of the bars start at the points specified in the first list, while their heights are the values of the second list.

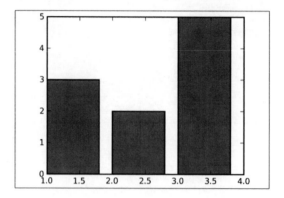

Matplotlib sets, the bar width to 0.8 by default (`width` is also the name of the keyword argument to change that value), so we see nice separated bars. As usual, everything is scaled and auto-adjusted to perfectly fit the figure area.

We can say that a bar is contained in a box starting from the left-bottom corner, specified by the value on the first list, with height specified by the value on the second list. The width of the bar is either the default value or the one we specify using the `width` argument.

To recap, the box has these dimensions (with a rather free notation, we hope you allow us), expressed in clockwise direction, starting from left or bottom — left, left + height, left + height + width, left + width.

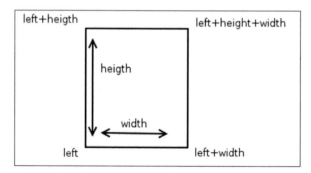

A list of the most useful keyword arguments is as follows:

- `width`: The width of the bars
- `color`: The color of the bars
- `xerr`, `yerr`: The error bars on the bar chart (yes, `bar()` supports error bars)
- `bottom`: The bottom coordinates of the bars

Let's see an example where we create a bar chart from a dictionary. We will use the dictionary values as bar heights and as parameters to `yticks()`, while the dictionary keys are used as `xtick()` locations and labels of the bars.

```
In [1]: import matplotlib.pyplot as plt
In [2]: import numpy as np
In [3]: dict = {'A': 40, 'B': 70, 'C': 30, 'D': 85}
In [4]: for i, key in enumerate(dict): plt.bar(i, dict[key]);
In [5]: plt.xticks(np.arange(len(dict))+0.4, dict.keys());
In [6]: plt.yticks(dict.values());
In [7]: plt.show()
```

In this example, note how:

- We add bars one-by-one by calling `bar()` each time and not by passing two lists of values to a single `bar()` call (line [4]).

- As we know that the bar's width is 0.8, we used `0.4` (the half) to place the label at the middle of bars (line [5]).

- `yticks()` contain only the height of the bars, so only they are used as ticks without intermediate values. Due to this, the resulting graph displays the plotted values more clearly.

The output of the previous code is displayed in the following screenshot:

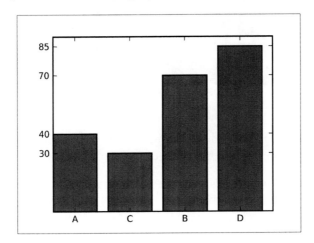

We will now try a more complex example where we will use three sets of bars — the second one with an error bar in it, managing carefully the locations of the `xticks`.

```
In [1]: import matplotlib.pyplot as plt
In [2]: import numpy as np
In [3]: data1 = 10*np.random.rand(5)
In [4]: data2 = 10*np.random.rand(5)
In [5]: data3 = 10*np.random.rand(5)
In [6]: e2 = 0.5 * np.abs(np.random.randn(len(data2)))
In [7]: locs = np.arange(1, len(data1)+1)
In [8]: width = 0.27
In [9]: plt.bar(locs, data1, width=width);
In [10]: plt.bar(locs+width, data2, yerr=e2, width=width,
color='red');
In [11]: plt.bar(locs+2*width, data3, width=width, color='green') ;
In [12]: plt.xticks(locs + width*1.5, locs);
In [13]: plt.show()
```

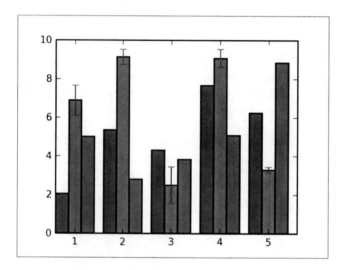

In the previous screenshot, we can see that the bar group colors are blue, red, and green (the usual sequence), while the color of the error bar is blue.

Note the width variable usage: first, we used it to specify the width of each bar to be the same, then we made the subsequent bar series start at multiples of width (so that the previous bar ends where the current one begins, packing the bars together); last, we used it to place the xticks in the middle of the "group of three bars"—multiplying by 1.5 (equal to 3/2), we obtain to place it in the middle of the group.

A similar function provided by Matplotlib is barh() that plots horizontal bars (instead of vertical, as bar() does). Moreover, there are other types of bar charts; for example, up or down, stacked, candlestick bars, and so on. You can go through the Matplotlib documentation and enjoy experimenting with them.

Pie charts

Pie charts are circular representations, divided into sectors (also called *wedges*). The arc length of each sector is proportional to the quantity we're describing. It's an effective way to represent information when we are interested mainly in comparing the wedge against the whole pie, instead of wedges against each other.

Matplotlib provides the pie() function to plot pie charts from an array X. Wedges are created proportionally, so that each value x of array X generates a wedge proportional to x/sum(X).

Please note that if sum(X) is less than 1, then the pie is drawn using X values directly and no normalization is done, resulting in a pie with discontinuity.

Pie charts look best if the figure and axes are in a square format (if not, with the common rectangular figure, they look like ellipses).

In the next example, we are going to plot a simple pie, using the legend keyword argument to give names to the wedges:

```
In [1]: import matplotlib.pyplot as plt
In [2]: plt.figure(figsize=(3,3));
In [3]: x = [45, 35, 20]
In [4]: labels = ['Cats', 'Dogs', 'Fishes']
In [5]: plt.pie(x, labels=labels);
In [6]: plt.show()
```

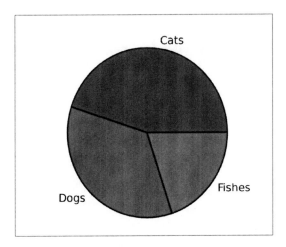

We can see from the previous screenshot that the color progression in wedges is the same as that of lines—the first wedge is colored in blue, the second in green, and the third in red.

The sum of the array x is 100, but we can specify any values for wedges, and Matplotlib will adapt the pie to them accordingly.

There are some interesting keyword arguments we can use to customize pie charts:

- `explode`: If specified, it's an array of the same length as that of x. Each of its values specify the radius fraction with which to offset the wedge from the center of the pie.
- `colors`: This is a list of Matplotlib colors, cyclically used to color the wedges.
- `labels, labeldistance`: This is a list of labels, one for each of the X values. `labeldistance` is the radial distance at which the labels are drawn.
- `autopct, pctdistance`: This formatting string or function is used to label wedges with their numeric values. `pctdstance` is the ratio between the center of the pie and the start of the text.
- `shadow`: This draws a shadow for wedges or pie.

Let's put some of them together and see the result:

```
In [1]: import matplotlib.pyplot as plt
In [2]: plt.figure(figsize=(3,3));
In [3]: x = [4, 9, 21, 55, 30, 18]
In [4]: labels = ['Swiss', 'Austria', 'Spain', 'Italy', 'France',
'Benelux']
In [5]: explode = [0.2, 0.1, 0, 0, 0.1, 0]
In [6]: plt.pie(x, labels=labels, explode=explode, autopct='%1.1f%%');
In [7]: plt.show()
```

We can observe in the next screenshot that the color progression in wedges is the same as that of lines—blue, green, red, cyan, magenta, and yellow. We can also see that the wedges are drawn from the horizontal axis, starting from the right side, and moving counterclockwise.

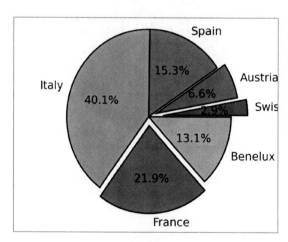

Scatter plots

Scatter plots display values for two sets of data. The data visualization is done as a collection of points not connected by lines. Each of them has its coordinates determined by the value of the variables (one variable determines the X position, the other the Y position).

A scatter plot is often used to identify potential association between two variables, and it's often drawn before working on a fitting regression function. It gives a good visual picture of the correlation, in particular for nonlinear relationships.

Matplotlib provides the `scatter()` function to plot X versus Y unidimensional array of the same length as scatter plot.

Let's show an example, again by using the `randn()` NumPy function to generate our datasets (so no correlation can be searched here).

```
In [1]: import matplotlib.pyplot as plt
In [2]: import numpy as np
In [3]: x = np.random.randn(1000)
In [4]: y = np.random.randn(1000)
In [5]: plt.scatter(x, y);
In [6]: plt.show()
```

The output of the previous code is as shown:

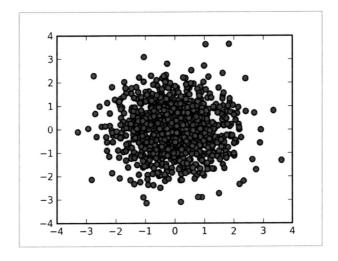

We can decorate the chart by using some of the following keyword arguments:

- s: This stands for the size of the markers in pixel*pixel. It can be a single value (to be used for all the points) or an array of the same size of X and Y (so that each point will have its own size).

- c: This is the points color. It can be a single value or a list of colors (that will be cycled on the points plotted) eventually of the same size of X and Y. The values can be the Matplotlib color codes or even numbers mapped to colors using color maps.

- marker: This specifies the marker to use to plot the points; the available values are:

Marker value	Description
s	Square
o	Circle
^	Triangle up
v	Triangle down
>	Triangle right
<	Triangle left
d	Diamond
p	Pentagon
h	Hexagon
8	Octagon
+	Plus
x	Cross

We can now apply some of them to the next example, where we specify a different size and color for each point of the previous dataset.

```
In [7]: size = 50*np.random.randn(1000)
In [8]: colors = np.random.rand(1000)
In [9]: plt.scatter(x, y, s=size, c=colors);
In [10]: plt.show()
```

On executing this code snippet, we get the output as:

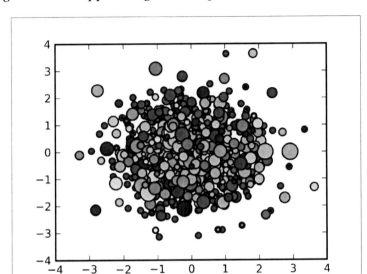

Polar charts

Polar plots use a completely different coordinate system, so we have dedicated a separate section to them.

For all the previous images, we used the Cartesian system — two perpendicular lines meet at a point (the *origin* of axes) with precise axes directions to determine positive and negative values on both, the X and Y axes.

A polar system is a two-dimensional coordinate system, where the position of a point is expressed in terms of a radius and an *angle*. This system is used where the relationship between two points is better expressed using those information.

As mentioned earlier, there are two coordinates — the radial and the angular coordinates. The radial coordinate, represented as r, denotes the point distance from a central point (called *pole*, equivalent to the origin on Cartesian systems). On the other hand, the angular coordinate, represented as theta, denotes the angle required to reach the point from the 0° ray (also known as *polar axis*, equivalent to the X-axis in Cartesian systems).

The angular coordinate can be expressed either in radians or in degrees. Though, Matplotlib uses degrees.

The `polar()` Matplotlib function plots polar charts. Its parameters are two lists (of the same length)—`theta` for the angular coordinates and `r` for the radial coordinates. It's the corresponding function of `plot()` for polar charts, so it can take multiple `theta` and `r`, along with the formatting strings.

Here is an example of what we can do in polar coordinates:

```
In [1]: import matplotlib.pyplot as plt
In [2]: import numpy as np
In [3]: theta = np.arange(0., 2., 1./180.)*np.pi
In [4]: plt.polar(3*theta, theta/5);
In [5]: plt.polar(theta, np.cos(4*theta));
In [6]: plt.polar(theta, [1.4]*len(theta));
In [7]: plt.show()
```

The output is as shown:

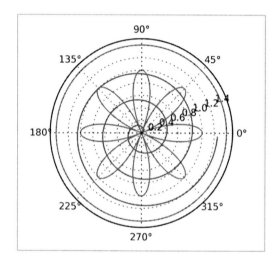

Note the following points in the previous example:

- At line [3], we define `theta` to be an array of 360 values, equally spaced between 0 and 2Π.

- At line [4], we draw a spiral.

- At line [5], we draw a *polar rose*, a pretty function that resembles a flower.

- Lastly, at line [6], we draw a circular line. In a polar system, to draw a circle we just need to keep `r` constant (in this case, we set it to `1.4`).

Navigation Toolbar with polar plots

The navigation toolbar (the bar displayed at the bottom of the window shown in interactive mode that we had treated in Chapter 2, *Getting Started with Matplotlib*) behaves a little differently with polar plots, particularly with the pan and zoom functions. The radial coordinate labels can be dragged using the left mouse button, while the radial scale can be zoomed in and out using the right mouse button.

Control radial and angular grids

There are two functions to control the radial and the angular grids: rgrid() and thetagrid() functions respectively.

rgrids(), when called with no arguments, returns two arrays–the radial grid lines (the dashed concentric circles around the pole) and the tick labels (the numbers all plotted in a row at the circle's positions).

The arguments we can pass are:

- radii: The radial distances at which the grid lines should be drawn.
- labels: The labels to display at radii grid. By default, the values from radii would be used, but if not None, then it has to be of the same length as that of radii.
- angle: The angle at which the labels are displayed (by default it's 22.5°).

The given tick's labels are printed at the specified radii location. The only required argument is radii. labels which becomes radii values if not specified. If labels for angle() is not specified, then its default values are used.

thetagrids() behaves similar to rgrids() when called with no arguments: the current radial lines (the dashed lines that connect the pole to the labels) and labels are returned.

The arguments we can pass are:

- angles: The location where to draw the labels, which are the only required arguments.
- labels: Specifies the labels to be printed at given angles. If None, then the angles values are used, or else the array must be of the same length of angles.
- frac: The polar axes radius fraction at which we want the label to be drawn (1 is the edge, 1.1 is outside, and 0.9 is inside).

Let's plot an example to show both of them:

```
In [1]: import matplotlib.pyplot as plt
In [2]: import numpy as np
In [3]: theta = np.arange(0., 2., 1./180.)*np.pi
In [4]: r = np.abs(np.sin(5*theta) - 2.*np.cos(theta))
In [5]: plt.polar(theta, r);
In [6]: plt.thetagrids(range(45, 360, 90));
In [7]: plt.rgrids(np.arange(0.2, 3.1, .7), angle=0);
In [8]: plt.show()
```

Using the `rgrids()` and `thetagrids()`, this code snippet generates a nice line resembling a butterfly as shown:

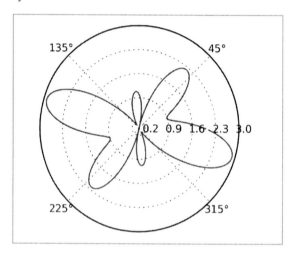

Text inside figure, annotations, and arrows

We are going to introduce additional features to allow even more plot decorations.

Text inside figure

We already saw how to use `xlabel()`, `ylabel()`, and `title()` to add text *around* the figure, but we can do something more, namely, add text *inside* the figure.

The `text()` function does that—writes a string (`text`) at an arbitrary position (specified by (x, y)):

```
plt.text(x, y, text)
```

Let's plot the sine function, and add a note that says `sin(0)` is equal to `0`.

```
In [1]: import matplotlib.pyplot as plt
In [2]: import numpy as np
In [3]: x = np.arange(0, 2*np.pi, .01)
In [4]: y = np.sin(x)
In [5]: plt.plot(x, y);
In [6]: plt.text(0.1, -0.04, 'sin(0)=0');
In [7]: plt.show()
```

The output of this code snippet is shown in the following screenshot:

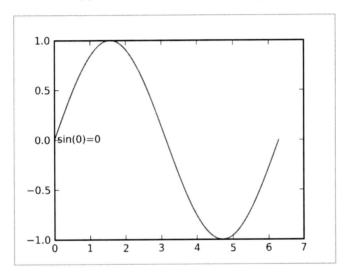

The location specified in the `text()` function is in *data* coordinates, and it's relative to the data currently plotted. There's a similar function, `figtext()`, that draws a given string at a position in *figure* coordinates. It takes a couple of values between 0 and 1 where (0,0) is the lower-left corner, and (1,1) is the upper-right corner.

Annotations

The `text()` function places text at a given position on the plot, but often, what we really want is to *annotate* some features of a graph.

The `annotate()` function provides functionality to make annotation easy. In annotation, we have to consider two points — the graph point we want to annotate (represented by an `xy` keyword argument) and the plot position where we want to place the annotation text (represented by `xytext`). Both are expressed in an (x,y) format in data coordinate positions.

Moreover, there is an additional argument to specify the arrow properties, that's the fundamental difference between `text()` and `annotate()`. We connect the annotation text to the annotated point with an arrow.

Let's see an example of the usage of `annotate()`:

```
In [1]: import matplotlib.pyplot as plt
In [2]: y = [13, 11, 13, 12, 13, 10, 30, 12, 11, 13, 12, 12, 12, 11,
12]
In [3]: plt.plot(y);
In [4]: plt.ylim(ymax=35);
In [5]: plt.annotate('this spot must really\nmean something',
xy=(6, 30), xytext=(8, 31.5), arrowprops=dict(facecolor='black',
shrink=0.05));
In [6]: plt.show()
```

The output of this code snippet is as shown:

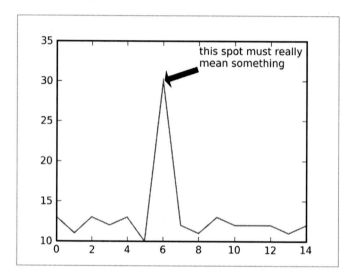

A note about the `shrink` property—it is used to make some space from the points passed as a parameter and the arrow tip and base. If this property is not specified, then the arrow would exactly connect the two points—`xy` and `xytext`. This looks visually unpleasant. Some interesting arguments are:

- `width`: The width of the arrow in points
- `frac`: The fraction of the arrow length occupied by the head
- `headwidth`: The width of the base of the arrow head in points
- `shrink`: Moves the tip and the base of the arrow some percent away from the annotated point and text, in percentage (so 0.05 is equal to 5%)

Also note that we had to use `ylim()` to adjust the Y limits, as `annotate()` does not do it automatically.

Arrows

We have just learned about the arrows of `annotate()`, but it is also possible to use arrows elsewhere in other plots.

Matplotlib provides an `arrow()` function. It takes the coordinates of the arrow origin (x,y), and the delta distance (dx, xy), the distance at which the head is to be placed. This implies that the arrow starts at (x,y) and ends at $(x + dx, y + dy)$:

```
plt.arrow(x, y, dx, dy)
```

Sadly, this function is quite hard to use and presents several difficulties.

We can use a small trick here. Reuse `annotate()` without text to only create an arrow. `annotate()` uses a different object under the hood, and is much more powerful and graphically attractive.

On such an arrow, there are two possible types of customization—the connection and the arrow styles.

The connection style (represented by the `connectionstyle` keyword argument) describes how the two points are connected. The available connection styles are:

Name	Attributes (= default values)
angle	angleA=90, angleB=0, rad=0.0
angle3	angleA=90, angleB=0
arc	angleA=0, angleB=0, armA=None, armB,=None, rad=0.0
arc3	rad=0.0

They are rather specific to Bezier curves, but the following examples will clarify this a bit.

The arrow style (represented by the `arrowstyle` keyword argument) describes how the arrow will be drawn. The available arrow styles are:

Name	Attributes
-	None
->	head_length=0.4, head_width=0.2
-[	WidthB=1.0, lengthB=0.2, angleB=None
<-	head_length=0.4, head_width=0.2

Name	Attributes
`<->`	head_length=0.4, head_width=0.2
`fancy`	head_length=0.4, head_width=0.4, tail_width=0.4
`simple`	head_length=0.5, head_width=0.5, tail_width=0.2
`wedge`	tail_width=0.3, shrink_factor=0.5

Let's see some examples.

```
In [1]: import matplotlib.pyplot as plt
In [2]: plt.axis([0, 10, 0, 20]);
In [3]: arrstyles = ['-', '->', '-[', '<-', '<->', 'fancy', 'simple',
'wedge']
In [4]: for i, style in enumerate(arrstyles):
   ...:
                plt.annotate(style, xytext=(1, 2+2*i), xy=(4, 1+2*i),
arrowprops=dict(arrowstyle=style));
In [5]: connstyles=["arc", "arc,angleA=10,armA=30,rad=15",
"arc3,rad=.2", "arc3,rad=-.2", "angle", "angle3"]
In [6]: for i, style in enumerate(connstyles):
                plt.annotate("", xytext=(6, 2+2*i), xy=(8, 1+2*i), arr
owprops=dict(arrowstyle='->', connectionstyle=style));
   ...:
In [7]: plt.show()
```

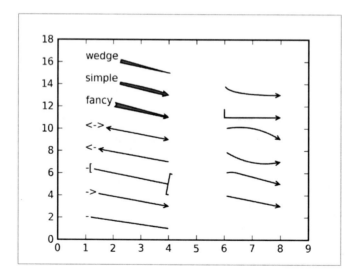

In the first series of the example, we used the annotation text, but only to show what arrow style we were using. To get an arrow alone, we should use a form such as:

```
plt.annotate("", ...)
```

This form was used in the second series.

Needless to say, all these options can be used even when we really need to annotate a plot.

Summary

Our Matplotlib toolbox has now grown to a considerable size. Let's recap what we've just seen in this chapter:

- How we can customize the markers and lines representation
- How we can adjust the visualization of ticks on plot axes
- How we can use different plot types — histograms, error bars, bars, pies, scatters charts, and so on
- How we can generate polar charts, and the peculiarities they have
- How we can *describe* the plots, either by adding text or annotating (using text and arrows) the plot, and how we can draw arrows alone

Matplotlib still has a lot to show us, in particular, for advanced users and purposes. The next chapter will introduce the object-oriented world of Matplotlib, and much more.

4
Advanced Matplotlib

We are about to explore some advanced aspects of Matplotlib. The topics that we are going to cover in detail are:

- Matplotlib's object-oriented interface
- Subplots and multiple figures
- Additional and shared axes
- Logarithmic scaled axes
- Date plotting with ticks formatting and locators
- Text properties, fonts, LaTeX typewriting
- Contour plots and image plotting

The basis for all of these topics is the object-oriented interface, so we will learn about that first.

Object-oriented versus MATLAB styles

So far in this book, we have seen a lot of examples, and in all of them we used the `matplotlib.pyplot` module to create and manipulate the plots, but this is not the only way to make use of the Matplotlib plotting power.

There are three ways to use Matplotlib:

- `pyplot`: The module used so far in this book
- `pylab`: A module to merge Matplotlib and NumPy together in an environment closer to MATLAB
- Object-oriented way: The Pythonic way to interface with Matplotlib

Let's first elaborate a bit about the `pyplot` module: `pyplot` provides a MATLAB-style, procedural, state-machine interface to the underlying object-oriented library in Matplotlib.

A **state machine** is a system with a global status, where each operation performed on the system changes its status.

`matplotlib.pyplot` is stateful because the underlying engine keeps track of the current figure and plotting area information, and plotting functions change that information. To make it clearer, we did not use any object references during our plotting we just issued a `pyplot` command, and the changes appeared in the figure.

At a higher level, `matplotlib.pyplot` is a collection of commands and functions that make Matplotlib behave like MATLAB (for plotting).

This is really useful when doing interactive sessions, because we can issue a command and see the result immediately, but it has several drawbacks when we need something more such as low-level customization or application embedding.

If we remember, Matplotlib started as an alternative to MATLAB, where we have at hand both numerical and plotting functions. A similar interface exists for Matplotlib, and its name is `pylab`.

`pylab` (do you see the similarity in the names?) is a companion module, installed next to `matplotlib` that merges `matplotlib.pyplot` (for plotting) and `numpy` (for mathematical functions) modules in a single namespace to provide an environment as near to MATLAB as possible, so that the transition would be easy.

We and the authors of Matplotlib discourage the use of `pylab`, other than for proof-of-concept snippets. While being rather simple to use, it teaches developers the wrong way to use Matplotlib, so we intentionally do not present it in this book.

The third way to use Matplotlib is through the **object-oriented** interface (**OO**, from now on). This is the most powerful way to write Matplotlib code because it allows for complete control of the result however it is also the most complex. This is the Pythonic way to use Matplotlib, and it's highly encouraged when *programming* with Matplotlib rather than working interactively. We will use it a lot from now on as it's needed to go down deep into Matplotlib.

Please allow us to highlight again the preferred style that the authors of this book, and the authors of Matplotlib want to enforce: a bit of `pyplot` will be used, in particular for convenience functions, and the remaining plotting code is either done with the OO style or with `pyplot`, with `numpy` explicitly imported and used for numerical functions.

In this preferred style, the initial imports are:

```
import matplotlib.pyplot as plt
import numpy as np
```

In this way, we know exactly which module the function we use comes from (due to the module prefix), and it's exactly what we've always done in the code so far.

Now, let's present the same piece of code expressed in the three possible forms which we just described.

First, we present it in the same style that we have used in the previous chapters, pyplot only:

```
In [1]: import matplotlib.pyplot as plt
In [2]: import numpy as np
In [3]: x = np.arange(0, 10, 0.1)
In [4]: y = np.random.randn(len(x))
In [5]: plt.plot(x, y)
Out[5]: [<matplotlib.lines.Line2D object at 0x1fad810>]
In [6]: plt.title('random numbers')
In [7]: plt.show()
```

The preceding code snippet results in:

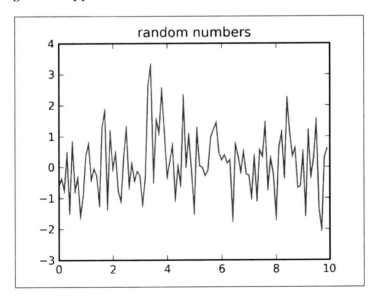

Now, let's see how we can do the same thing using the `pylab` interface:

```
$ ipython -pylab
. . .
In [1]: x = arange(0, 10, 0.1)
In [2]: y = randn(len(x))
In [3]: plot(x, y)
Out[3]: [<matplotlib.lines.Line2D object at 0x4284dd0>]
In [4]: title('random numbers')
In [5]: show()
```

Note that:

```
ipython -pylab
```

is not the same as running `ipython` and then:

```
from pylab import *
```

This is because `ipython`'s-`pylab` switch, in addition to importing everything from `pylab`, also enables a specific `ipython` threading mode so that both the interactive interpreter and the plot window can be active at the same time.

Finally, lets make the same chart by using OO style, but with some `pyplot` convenience functions:

```
In [1]: import matplotlib.pyplot as plt
In [2]: import numpy as np
In [3]: x = np.arange(0, 10, 0.1)
In [4]: y = np.random.randn(len(x))
In [5]: fig = plt.figure()
In [6]: ax = fig.add_subplot(111)
In [7]: l, = plt.plot(x, y)
In [8]: t = ax.set_title('random numbers')
In [9]: plt.show()
```

As we can see, the `pylab` code is the simplest, and `pyplot` is in the middle, while the OO is the most complex or verbose.

As the Python Zen teaches us, "Explicit is better than implicit" and "Simple is better than complex" and those statements are particularly true for this example: for simple interactive sessions, `pylab` or `pyplot` are the perfect choice because they hide a lot of complexity, but if we need something more advanced, then the OO API makes clearer where things are coming from, and what's going on. This expressiveness will be appreciated when we will embed Matplotlib inside GUI applications.

From now on, we will start presenting our code using the OO interface mixed with some `pyplot` functions.

A brief introduction to Matplotlib objects

Before we can go on in a productive way, we need to briefly introduce which Matplotlib objects compose a figure.

Let's see from the higher levels to the lower ones how objects are nested:

Object	Description
FigureCanvas	Container class for the Figure instance
Figure	Container for one or more Axes instances
Axes	The rectangular areas to hold the basic elements, such as lines, text, and so on

Our first (simple) example of OO Matplotlib

In the previous pieces of code, we had transformed this:

```
...
In [5]: plt.plot(x, y)
Out[5]: [<matplotlib.lines.Line2D object at 0x1fad810>]
...
```

into:

```
...
In [7]: l, = plt.plot(x, y)
...
```

The new code uses an explicit reference, allowing a lot more customizations.

As we can see in the first piece of code, the plot() function returns a list of Line2D instances, one for each line (in this case, there is only one), so in the second code, l is a reference to the line object, so every operation allowed on Line2D can be done using l.

For example, we can set the line color with:

```
l.set_color('red')
```

Instead of using the keyword argument to plot(), so the line information can be changed after the plot() call.

Subplots

In the previous section, we have seen a couple of important functions without introducing them. Let's have a look at them now:

- `fig = plt.figure()`: This function returns a `Figure`, where we can add one or more `Axes` instances.

- `ax = fig.add_subplot(111)`: This function returns an `Axes` instance, where we can plot (as done so far), and this is also the reason why we call the variable referring to that instance `ax` (from `Axes`). This is a common way to add an `Axes` to a `Figure`, but `add_subplot()` does a bit more: it adds a **subplot**. So far we have only seen a `Figure` with one `Axes` instance, so only one *area* where we can draw, but Matplotlib allows more than one.

`add_subplot()` takes three parameters:

fig.add_subplot(numrows, numcols, fignum)

where:

- `numrows` represents the number of rows of subplots to prepare
- `numcols` represents the number of columns of subplots to prepare
- `fignum` varies from `1` to `numrows*numcols` and specifies the current subplot (the one used now)

Basically, we describe a matrix of `numrows*numcols` subplots that we want into the `Figure`; please note that `fignum` is `1` at the upper-left corner of the `Figure` and it's equal to `numrows*numcols` at the bottom-right corner. The following table should provide a visual explanation of this:

numrows=2, numcols=2, fignum=1	numrows=2, numcols=2, fignum=2
numrows=2, numcols=2, fignum=3	numrows=2, numcols=2, fignum=4

Some usage examples are:

```
ax = fig.add_subplot(1, 1, 1)
```

Where we want a `Figure` with just a single plot area (like in all the previous examples).

```
ax2 = fig.add_subplot(2, 1, 2)
```

Here, we define the plot's matrix as made of two subplots in two different rows, and we want to work on the second one (`fignum=2`).

An interesting feature is that we can specify these numbers as a single parameter *merging* the numbers in just one string (as long as all of them are less than 10). For example:

```
ax2 = fig.add_subplot(212)
```

which is equivalent to:

```
ax2 = fig.add_subplot(2, 1, 2)
```

A simple example can clarify a bit:

```
In [1]: import matplotlib.pyplot as plt
In [2]: fig = plt.figure()
In [3]: ax1 = fig.add_subplot(211)
In [4]: ax1.plot([1, 2, 3], [1, 2, 3]);
In [5]: ax2 = fig.add_subplot(212)
In [6]: ax2.plot([1, 2, 3], [3, 2, 1]);
In [7]: plt.show()
```

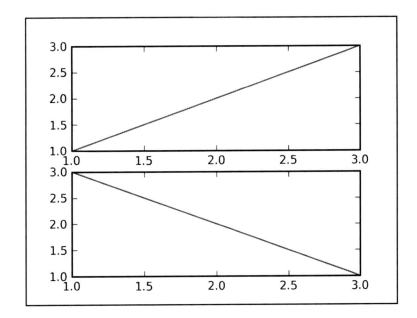

We will use a simple naming convention for the variables that we are using. For example, we call all the Axes instance variables ax, and if there is more than one variable in the same code, then we add numbers at the end, for example, ax1, ax2, and so on.

This will allow us to make changes to the Axes instance after it's created, and in the case of multiple Axes, it will allow us to modify any of them after their creation.

The same applies for multiple figures.

Multiple figures

Matplotlib also provides the capability to draw not only multiple Axes inside the same Figure, but also multiple figures.

We can do this by calling figure() multiple times, keeping a reference to the Figure object and then using it to add as many subplots as needed in exactly the same way as having a single Figure.

We can now see a code with two calls to figure():

```
In [1]: import matplotlib.pyplot as plt
In [2]: fig1 = plt.figure()
In [3]: ax1 = fig1.add_subplot(111)
In [4]: ax1.plot([1, 2, 3], [1, 2, 3]);
In [5]: fig2 = plt.figure()
In [6]: ax2 = fig2.add_subplot(111)
In [7]: ax2.plot([1, 2, 3], [3, 2, 1]);
In [8]: plt.show()
```

This code snippet generates two windows with one line each:

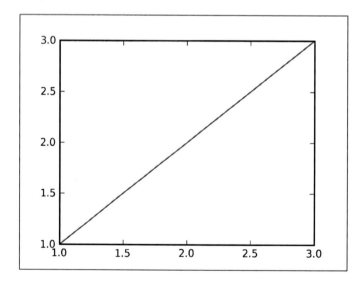

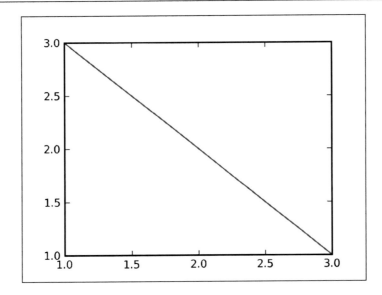

Note how the Axes instances are generated by calling the add_subplot() method on the two different Figure instances.

As a side note, when using pylab or pyplot, we can call figure() with an integer parameter to access a previously created Figure: figure(1) returns a reference to the first Figure, figure(2) to the second one, and so on.

Additional Y (or X) axes

There are situations where we want to plot two sets of data on the same image. In particular, this is the case when for the same X variable, we have two datasets (consider the situation where we take two measurements at the same time, and we want to plot them together to spot some relationships).

Matplotlib can do it:

```
In [1]: import matplotlib.pyplot as plt
In [2]: import numpy as np
In [3]: x = np.arange(0., np.e, 0.01)
In [4]: y1 = np.exp(-x)
In [5]: y2 = np.log(x)
In [6]: fig = plt.figure()
In [7]: ax1 = fig.add_subplot(111)
In [8]: ax1.plot(x, y1);
In [9]: ax1.set_ylabel('Y values for exp(-x)');
```

```
In [10]: ax2 = ax1.twinx()    # this is the important function
In [11]: ax2.plot(x, y2, 'r');
In [12]: ax2.set_xlim([0, np.e]);
In [13]: ax2.set_ylabel('Y values for ln(x)');
In [14]: ax2.set_xlabel('Same X for both exp(-x) and ln(x)');
In [15]: plt.show()
```

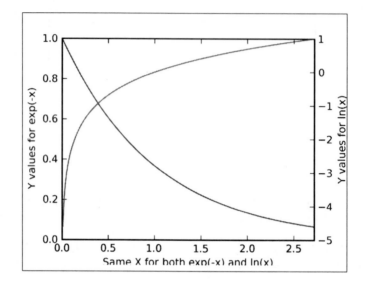

What's really happening here is that two different Axes instances are placed such that one is on top of the other. The data for y1 will go in the first Axes instance, and the data for y2 will go in the second Axes instance.

The twinx() function does the trick: it creates a second set of axes, putting the new ax2 axes at the exact same position of ax1, ready to be used for plotting.

This is the reason why we had to set the red color for the second line: the plot information was reset so that line would have been blue, as if it was part of a completely new figure.

We can see that by using ax1 and ax2 for referring to Axes instances, we are able to modify the information (in this case, the axes labels) for both of them. Of course, since X is shared between the two, we have to call set_xlabel() for just one Axes instance.

Using two different Axes also allows us to have different scales for the two plots.

The complementary function, twiny(), allows us to share the Y-axis with two different X-axes.

Logarithmic axes

Another interesting feature of Matplotlib is the possibility to set the axes scale to a logarithmic one. We can independently set the X, the Y, or both axes to a logarithmic scale.

Let's see an example where both subplots and the logarithmic scale are put together:

```
In [1]: import matplotlib as mpl
In [2]: mpl.rcParams['font.size'] = 10.
In [3]: import matplotlib.pyplot as plt
In [4]: import numpy as np
In [5]: x = np.arange(0., 20, 0.01)
In [6]: fig = plt.figure()
In [7]: ax1 = fig.add_subplot(311)
In [8]: y1 = np.exp(x/6.)
In [9]: ax1.plot(x, y1);
In [10]: ax1.grid(True)
In [11]: ax1.set_yscale('log')
In [12]: ax1.set_ylabel('log Y');
In [13]: ax2 = fig.add_subplot(312)
In [14]: y2 = np.cos(np.pi*x)
In [15]: ax2.semilogx(x, y2);
In [16]: ax2.set_xlim([0, 20]);
In [17]: ax2.grid(True)
In [18]: ax2.set_ylabel('log X');
In [19]: ax3 = fig.add_subplot(313)
In [20]: y3 = np.exp(x/4.)
In [21]: ax3.loglog(x, y3, basex=3);
In [22]: ax3.grid(True)
In [23]: ax3.set_ylabel('log X and Y');
In [24]: plt.show()
```

The output of the preceding code is as follows:

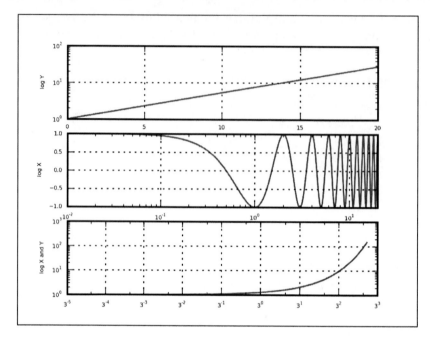

Note how the characters in this image are smaller than those in the other plots. This is because we had to reduce the font size to avoid the labels and plots overlapping with each other.

`semilogx()` (and the twin function `semilogy()`) is a commodity function that merges `plot()` and `ax.set_xscale('log')` functions in a single call. The same holds for `loglog()`, which makes a plot with log scaling on both X and Y axes.

The default logarithmic base is 10, but we can change it with the `basex` and `basey` keyword arguments for their respective axes. The functions `set_xscale()` or `set_yscale()` are more general as they can also be applied to polar plots, while `semilogx()`, `semilogy()`, or `loglog()` work for lines and scatter plots.

Share axes

With `twinx()`, we have seen that we can plot two `Axes` on the same plotting area sharing one axis. But what if we want to draw more than two plots sharing an axis? What if we want to plot on different `Axes` in the same figure, still sharing that axis? Some areas where we might be interested in such kind of graphs are:

- **Financial data** — comparing the evolution of some economic indicators over the same time

- **Hardware testing** — plotting the electrical signals received at each pin of a parallel or serial port

- **Health status** — showing the development of some medical information in a given time frame (such as blood pressure, beating heart rate, weight, and so on)

 Note that while having the same unit measure on the shared axis, the other is free to have any unit; this is very important as it allows us to group up heterogeneous information.

Matplotlib makes it very easy to share an axis (for example, the X one) on different Axes instances, for example, pan and zoom actions on one graph are automatically replayed to all the others.

```
In [1]: import matplotlib as mpl
In [2]: mpl.rcParams['font.size'] = 11.
In [3]: import matplotlib.pyplot as plt
In [4]: import numpy as np
In [5]: x = np.arange(11)
In [6]: fig = plt.figure()
In [7]: ax1 = fig.add_subplot(311)
In [8]: ax1.plot(x, x);
In [9]: ax2 = fig.add_subplot(312, sharex=ax1)
In [10]: ax2.plot(2*x, 2*x);
In [11]: ax3 = fig.add_subplot(313, sharex=ax1)
In [12]: ax3.plot(3*x, 3*x);
In [13]: plt.show()
```

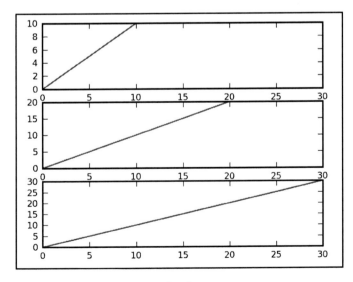

Again, we have to use a smaller font for texts. When printed, it looks like a standard subplot image. However, if you run the code on `ipython`, then you'll observe that when zooming, panning, or performing other similar activities on a subplot, all the others will be modified too, according to the same transformation.

As we can expect, there are a couple of keyword arguments; `sharex` and `sharey`, and it's also possible to specify both of them together. In particular, this is useful when the subplots show data with the same units of measure.

Plotting dates

Sooner or later, we all have had the need to plot some information over time, be it for the bank account balance each month, the total web site accesses for each day of the year, or one of many other reasons.

Matplotlib has a plotting function ad hoc for dates, `plot_date()` that considers data on X, Y, or both axes, as dates, labeling the axis accordingly.

As usual, we now present an example, and we will discuss it later:

```
In [1]: import matplotlib as mpl
In [2]: import matplotlib.pyplot as plt
In [3]: import numpy as np
In [4]: import datetime as dt
In [5]: dates = [dt.datetime.today() + dt.timedelta(days=i) \
   ...: for i in range(10)]
In [6]: values = np.random.rand(len(dates))
In [7]: plt.plot_date(mpl.dates.date2num(dates), values, linestyle='-');
In [8]: plt.show()
```

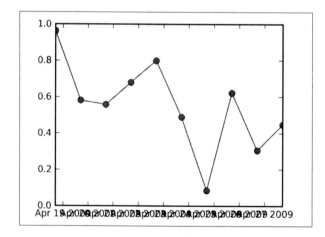

First, a note about `linestyle` keyword argument: without it, there's no line connecting the markers that are displayed alone.

We created the `dates` array using `timedelta()`, a `datetime` function that helps us define a date interval—10 days in this case. Note how we had to convert our date values using the `date2num()` function. This is because Matplotlib represents dates as float values corresponding to the number of days since 0001-01-01 UTC.

Also note how the X-axis labels, the ones that have data values, are badly rendered.

Matplotlib provides ways to address the previous two points—date formatting and conversion, and axes formatting.

Date formatting

Commonly, in Python programs, dates are represented as `datetime` objects, so we have to first convert other data values into `datetime` objects, sometimes by using the `dateutil` companion module, for example:

```
import datetime
date = datetime.datetime(2009, 03, 28, 11, 34, 59, 12345)
```

or

```
import dateutil.parser
datestrings = ['2008-07-18 14:36:53.494013','2008-07-20
14:37:01.508990', '2008-07-28 14:49:26.183256']
dates = [dateutil.parser.parse(s) for s in datestrings]
```

Once we have the `datetime` objects, in order to let Matplotlib use them, we have to convert them into floating point numbers that represent the number of days since 0001-01-01 00:00:00 UTC.

To do that, Matplotlib itself provides several helper functions contained in the `matplotlib.dates` module:

- `date2num()`: This function converts one or a sequence of `datetime` objects to float values representing days since 0001-01-01 00:00:00 UTC (the fractional parts represent hours, minutes, and seconds)

- `num2date()`: This function converts one or a sequence of float values representing days since 0001-01-01 00:00:00 UTC to `datetime` objects (or a sequence, if the input is a sequence)

- `drange(dstart, dend, delta)`: This function returns a date range (a sequence) of float values in Matplotlib date format; `dstart` and `dend` are `datetime` objects while delta is a `datetime.timedelta` instance

Usually, what we will end up doing is converting a sequence of `datetime` objects into a Matplotlib representation, such as:

```
dates = list of datetime objects
mpl_dates = matplotlib.dates.date2num(dates)
```

`drange()` can be useful in situations like this one:

```
import matplotlib as mpl
from matplotlib import dates
import datetime as dt
date1 = dt.datetime(2008, 9, 23)
date2 = dt.datetime(2009, 4, 12)
delta = dt.timedelta(days=10)
dates = mpl.dates.drange(date1, date2, delta)
```

where `dates` will be a sequence of floats starting from `date1` and ending at `date2` with a `delta` timestamp between each item of the list.

Axes formatting with axes tick locators and formatters

As we have already seen, the X labels on the first image are not that nice looking. We would expect Matplotlib to allow a better way to label the axis, and indeed, there is.

The solution is to change the two parts that form the axis ticks—**locators** and **formatters**. Locators control the tick's position, while formatters control the formatting of labels. Both have a *major* and *minor* mode: the major locator and formatter are active by default and are the ones we commonly see, while minor mode can be turned on by passing a relative locator or formatter function (because minors are turned off by default by assigning `NullLocator` and `NullFormatter` to them).

While this is a general tuning operation and can be applied to all Matplotlib plots, there are some specific locators and formatters for date plotting, provided by `matplotlib.dates`:

- `MinuteLocator`, `HourLocator`, `DayLocator`, `WeekdayLocator`, `MonthLocator`, `YearLocator` are all the locators available that place a tick at the time specified by the name, for example, `DayLocator` will draw a tick at each day. Of course, a minimum knowledge of the date interval that we are about to draw is needed to select the best locator.

- `DateFormatter` is the tick formatter that uses `strftime()` to format strings.

The default locator and formatter are `matplotlib.ticker.AutoDateLocator` and `matplotlib.ticker.AutoDateFormatter`, respectively. Both are set by the `plot_date()` function when called. So, if you wish to set a different locator and/or formatter, then we suggest to do that after the `plot_date()` call in order to avoid the `plot_date()` function resetting them to the default values.

Let's group all this up in an example:

```
In [1]: import matplotlib as mpl
In [2]: import matplotlib.pyplot as plt
In [3]: import numpy as np
In [4]: import datetime as dt
In [5]: fig = plt.figure()
In [6]: ax2 = fig.add_subplot(212)
In [7]: date2_1 = dt.datetime(2008, 9, 23)
In [8]: date2_2 = dt.datetime(2008, 10, 3)
In [9]: delta2 = dt.timedelta(days=1)
In [10]: dates2 = mpl.dates.drange(date2_1, date2_2, delta2)
In [11]: y2 = np.random.rand(len(dates2))
In [12]: ax2.plot_date(dates2, y2, linestyle='-');
In [13]: dateFmt = mpl.dates.DateFormatter('%Y-%m-%d')
In [14]: ax2.xaxis.set_major_formatter(dateFmt)
In [15]: daysLoc = mpl.dates.DayLocator()
In [16]: hoursLoc = mpl.dates.HourLocator(interval=6)
In [17]: ax2.xaxis.set_major_locator(daysLoc)
In [18]: ax2.xaxis.set_minor_locator(hoursLoc)
In [19]: fig.autofmt_xdate(bottom=0.18) # adjust for date labels
display
In [20]: fig.subplots_adjust(left=0.18)
In [21]: ax1 = fig.add_subplot(211)
In [22]: date1_1 = dt.datetime(2008, 9, 23)
In [23]: date1_2 = dt.datetime(2009, 2, 16)
In [24]: delta1 = dt.timedelta(days=10)
In [25]: dates1 = mpl.dates.drange(date1_1, date1_2, delta1)
In [26]: y1 = np.random.rand(len(dates1))
In [27]: ax1.plot_date(dates1, y1, linestyle='-');
In [28]: monthsLoc = mpl.dates.MonthLocator()
In [29]: weeksLoc = mpl.dates.WeekdayLocator()
In [30]: ax1.xaxis.set_major_locator(monthsLoc)
In [31]: ax1.xaxis.set_minor_locator(weeksLoc)
In [32]: monthsFmt = mpl.dates.DateFormatter('%b')
In [33]: ax1.xaxis.set_major_formatter(monthsFmt)
In [34]: plt.show()
```

The result of executing the previous code snippet is as shown:

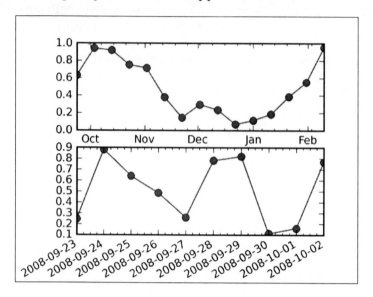

We drew the subplots in reverse order to avoid some minor overlapping problems.

`fig.autofmt_xdate()` is used to nicely format date tick labels. In particular, this function rotates the labels (by using `rotation` keyword argument, with a default value of 30°) and gives them more room (by using `bottom` keyword argument, with a default value of 0.2).

We can achieve the same result, at least for the additional spacing, with:

```
fig = plt.figure()
fig.subplots_adjust(bottom=0.2)
ax = fig.add_subplot(111)
```

This can also be done by creating the `Axes` instance directly with:

```
ax = fig.add_axes([left, bottom, width, height])
```

while specifying the explicit dimensions.

The `subplots_adjust()` function allows us to control the spacing around the subplots by using the following keyword arguments:

- `bottom`, `top`, `left`, `right`: Controls the spacing at the bottom, top, left, and right of the subplot(s)

- `wspace`, `hspace`: Controls the horizontal and vertical spacing between subplots

We can also control the spacing by using these parameters in the Matplotlib configuration file:

```
figure.subplot.<position> = <value>
```

Custom formatters and locators

Even if it's not strictly related to date plotting, tick formatters allow for custom formatters too:

```
...
import matplotlib.ticker as ticker
...
def format_func(x, pos):
    return <a transformation on x>
...
formatter = ticker.FuncFormatter(format_func)
ax.xaxis.set_major_formatter(formatter)
...
```

The function `format_func` will be called for each label to draw, passing its value and position on the axis. With those two arguments, we can apply a transformation (for example, divide x by 10) and then return a value that will be used to actually draw the tick label.

Here's a general note on `NullLocator`: it can be used to remove axis ticks by simply issuing:

```
ax.xaxis.set_major_locator(matplotlib.ticker.NullLocator())
```

Text properties, fonts, and LaTeX

Matplotlib has excellent text support, including mathematical expressions, TrueType font support for raster and vector outputs, newline separated text with arbitrary rotations, and Unicode.

We have total control over every text property (font size, font weight, text location, color, and so on) with sensible defaults set in the `rc` configuration file. Specifically for those interested in mathematical or scientific figures, Matplotlib implements a large number of TeX math symbols and commands to support mathematical expressions anywhere in the figure.

We already saw some text functions, but the following list contains all the functions which can be used to insert text with the `pyplot` interface, presented along with the corresponding API method and a description:

Pyplot function	API method	Description
`text()`	`mpl.axes.Axes.text()`	Adds text at an arbitrary location on the Axes
`xlabel()`	`mpl.axes.Axes.set_xlabel()`	Adds an axis label to the X-axis
`ylabel()`	`mpl.axes.Axes.set_ylabel()`	Adds an axis label to the Y-axis
`title()`	`mpl.axes.Axes.set_title()`	Adds a title to the Axes
`figtext()`	`mpl.figure.Figure.text()`	Adds text to the Figure at an arbitrary location
`suptitle()`	`mpl.figure.Figure.suptitle()`	Adds a centered title to the Figure
`annotate()`	`mpl.axes.Axes.annotate()`	Adds an annotation with an optional arrow to the Axes

All of these commands return a `matplotlib.text.Text` instance. We can customize the text properties by passing keyword arguments to the functions or by using `matplotlib.artist.setp()`:

```
t = plt.xlabel('some text', fontsize=16, color='green')
```

We can also do it as:

```
t = plt.xlabel('some text')
plt.setp(t, fontsize=16, color='green')
```

Handling objects allows for several new possibilities; such as setting the same property to all the objects in a specific group. Matplotlib has several convenience functions to return the objects of a plot. Let's take the example of the tick labels:

```
ax.get_xticklabels()
```

This line of code returns a sequence of object instances (the labels for the X-axis ticks) that we can tune:

```
for t in ax.get_xticklabels():
    t.set_fontsize(5.)
```

or else, still using `setp()`:

```
setp(ax.get_xticklabels(), fontsize=5.)
```

It can take a sequence of objects, and apply the same property to all of them.

To recap, all of the properties such as `color`, `fontsize`, `position`, `rotation`, and so on, can be set either:

- At function call using keyword arguments
- Using setp() referencing the Text instance
- Using the modification functions

Fonts

Where there is text, there are also fonts to draw it. Matplotlib allows for several font customizations.

The most complete documentation on this is currently available in the Matplotlib configuration file, /etc/matplotlibrc. We are now reporting that information here.

There are six font properties available for modification:

Property name	Values and description
font.family	This property has five values: • serif (example, Times) • sans-serif (example, Helvetica) • cursive (example, Zapf-Chancery) • fantasy (example, Western) • monospace (example, Courier) Each of these font families has a default list of font names in decreasing order of priority associated with them (as seen in the next table). In addition to these generic font names, font.family may also be an explicit name of a font available on the system.
font.style	This property has three values: normal (or roman), italic, or oblique. The oblique style will be used for italic, if it is not present.
font.variant	This property has two values: normal or small-caps. For TrueType fonts, which are scalable, small-caps is equivalent to using a font size of smaller, or about 83% of the current font size.
font.weight	This property has effectively 13 values—normal, bold, bolder, lighter, 100, 200, 300, ..., 900. normal is the same as 400, and bold is 700. bolder and lighter are relative values with respect to the current weight.

Property name	Values and description
font.stretch	This property has 11 values—ultra-condensed, extra-condensed, condensed, semi-condensed, normal, semi-expanded, expanded, extra-expanded, ultra-expanded, wider, and narrower. This property is not currently implemented. It works if the font supports it, but only few do.
font.size	This property sets the default font size for text, given in points. 12pt is the standard value.

The list of font names, selected by font.family, in the priority search order is:

Property name	Font list
font.serif	Bitstream Vera Serif, New Century Schoolbook, Century Schoolbook L, Utopia, ITC Bookman, Bookman, Nimbus Roman No9 L, Times New Roman, Times, Palatino, Charter, serif
font.sans-serif	Bitstream Vera Sans, Lucida Grande, Verdana, Geneva, Lucid, Arial, Helvetica, Avant Garde, sans-serif
font.cursive	Apple Chancery, Textile, Zapf Chancery, Sand, cursive
font.fantasy	Comic Sans MS, Chicago, Charcoal, Impact, Western, fantasy
font.monospace	Bitstream Vera Sans Mono, Andale Mono, Nimbus Mono L, Courier New, Courier, Fixed, Terminal, monospace

The first valid and available (that is, installed) font in each family is the one that will be loaded. If the fonts are not specified, the Bitstream Vera Sans fonts are used by default.

As usual, we can set these values in the configuration file or in the code accessing the rcParams dictionary provided by Matplotlib.

Using LaTeX formatting

If you have ever used LaTeX, you know how powerful it can be at rendering mathematical expressions. Given its root in the scientific field, Matplotlib allows us to embed TeX text in its plots. There are two ways available:

- Mathtext
- Using an external TeX renderer

Mathtext

Matplotlib includes an internal engine to render TeX expression, `mathtext`. The `mathtext` module provides TeX style mathematical expressions using FreeType 2 and the default font from TeX, Computer Modern.

As Matplotlib ships with everything it needs to make `mathtext` work, there is no requirement to install a TeX system (or any other external program) on the computer for it to be used.

The markup character used to signal the start and the end of a `mathtext` string is $; encapsulating a string inside a pair of $ characters will trigger the `mathtext` engine to render it as a TeX mathematical expression.

We should use raw strings (preceding the quotes with an r character) and surround the `mathtext` with dollar signs ($), as in TeX. The use of raw strings is important so that backslashes (used for TeX symbols escaping) are not mangled by the Python interpreter.

Matplotlib accepts TeX equations in any text expressions, so regular text and `mathtext` can be interleaved within the same string.

An example of the kind of text we can generate is:

```
In [1]: import matplotlib.pyplot as plt
In [2]: fig = plt.figure()
In [3]: ax= fig.add_subplot(111)
In [4]: ax.set_xlim([1, 6]);
In [5]: ax.set_ylim([1, 9]);
In [6]: ax.text(2, 8, r"$ \mu \alpha \tau \pi \lambda \omega \tau \
lambda \iota \beta $");
In [7]: ax.text(2, 6, r"$ \lim_{x \rightarrow 0} \frac{1}{x} $");
In [8]: ax.text(2, 4, r"$ a \ \leq \ b \ \leq \ c \ \Rightarrow \ a \
\leq \ c$");
In [9]: ax.text(2, 2, r"$ \sum_{i=1}^{\infty}\ x_i^2$");
In [10]: ax.text(4, 8, r"$ \sin(0) = \cos(\frac{\pi}{2})$");
In [11]: ax.text(4, 6, r"$ \sqrt[3]{x} = \sqrt{y}$");
In [12]: ax.text(4, 4, r"$ \neg (a \wedge b) \Leftrightarrow \neg a
\vee \neg b$");
In [13]: ax.text(4, 2, r"$ \int_a^b f(x)dx$");
In [14]: plt.show()
```

The preceding code snippet results in the following:

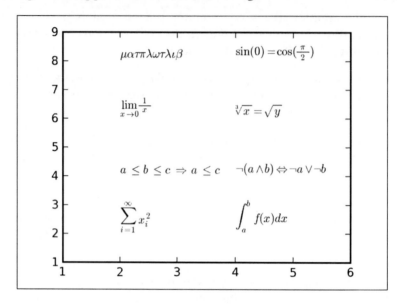

The escape sequence is almost the same as that of LaTeX; consult the Matplotlib and/or LaTeX online documentation to see the full list.

External TeX renderer

Matplotlib also allows to manage all the text layout using an external LaTeX engine. This is limited to Agg, PS, and PDF backends and is commonly needed when we want to create graphs to be embedded into LaTeX documents, where rendering uniformity is really pleasant.

To activate an external TeX rendering engine for text strings, we need to set this parameter in the configuration file:

```
text.usetex : True
```

or use the rcParams dictionary:

```
rcParams['text.usetex'] = True
```

This mode requires LaTeX, dvipng, and Ghostscript to be correctly installed and working. Also note that usually external TeX management is slower than Matplotlib's mathtext and that all the texts in the figure are drawn using the external renderer, not only the mathematical ones.

There are several optimizations and configurations that you will need to do when dealing with TeX, postscripts and so, we invite you to consult an official documentation for additional information.

When the previous example is executed and rendered using an external LaTeX engine, the result is:

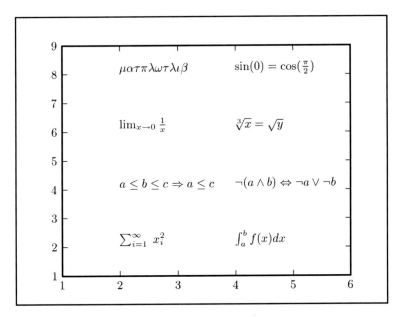

Also, look at how the tick label's text is rendered in the same font as the text in the figure, as in this real world example:

```
In [1]: import matplotlib as mpl
In [2]: import matplotlib.pyplot as plt
In [3]: mpl.rcParams['text.usetex'] = True
In [4]: import numpy as np
In [5]: x = np.arange(0., 5., .01)
In [6]: y = [np.sin(2*np.pi*xx) * np.exp(-xx) for xx in x]
In [7]: plt.plot(x, y, label=r'$\sin(2\pi x)\exp(-x)$');
In [8]: plt.plot(x, np.exp(-x), label=r'$\exp(-x)$');
In [9]: plt.plot(x, -np.exp(-x), label=r'$-\exp(-x)$');
In [10]: plt.title(r'$\sin(2\pi x)\exp(-x)$ with the two asymptotes
$\pm\exp(-x)$');
In [11]: plt.legend();
In [12]: plt.show()
```

The preceding code snippet results in a sinusoidal line contained in two asymptotes:

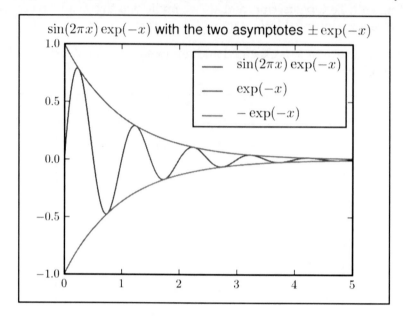

Contour plots and image plotting

We will now discuss the features Matplotlib provides to create contour plots and display images.

Contour plots

Contour lines (also known as *level lines* or *isolines*) for a function of two variables are curves where the function has constant values. Mathematically speaking, it's a graph image that shows:

```
f(x, y) = L
```

with L constant. Contour lines often have specific names beginning with iso- (from Greek, meaning equal) according to the nature of the variables being mapped.

There are a lot of applications of contour lines in several fields such as meteorology (for temperature, pressure, rain precipitation, wind speed), geography, oceanography, cartography (elevation and depth), magnetism, engineering, social sciences, and so on.

The absolutely most common examples of contour lines are those seen in weather forecasts, where lines of isobars (where the atmospheric pressure is constant) are drawn over the terrain maps. In particular, those are *contour maps* because contour lines are drawn above a map in order to add specific information to it.

The density of the lines indicates the *slope* of the function. The gradient of the function is always perpendicular to the contour lines, and when the lines are close together, the length of the gradient is large and the variation is steep.

Here is a contour plot from a random number matrix:

```
In [1]: import matplotlib.pyplot as plt
In [2]: import numpy as np
In [3]: matr = np.random.rand(21, 31)
In [4]: cs = plt.contour(matr)
In [5]: plt.show()
```

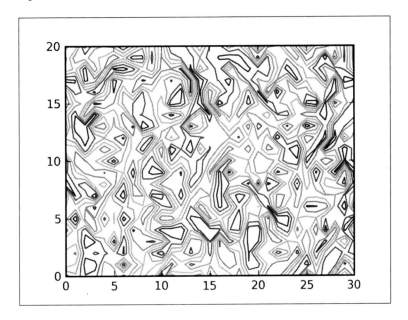

where the contour lines are colored from blue to red in a scale from the lower to the higher values.

The `contour()` function draws contour lines, taking a 2D array as input (a list of list notations). In this case, it's a matrix of 21x31 random elements. The number of level lines to draw is chosen automatically, but we can also specify it as an additional parameter, `N`:

```
contour(matrix, N)
```

The previous line of code tells us to draw N automatically chosen level lines.

There is also a similar function that draws a *filled* contours plot, `contourf()`:

```
In [6]: csf = plt.contourf(matr)
In [7]: plt.colorbar();
In [8]: plt.show()
```

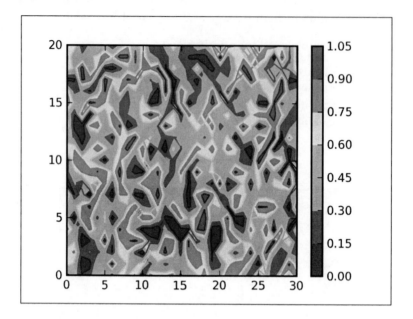

`contourf()` fills the spaces between the contours lines with the same color progression used in the `contour()` plot: dark blue is used for low value areas, while red is used for high value areas, fading in between for the intermediate values.

Contour colors can be changed using a **colormap**, a set of colors used as a lookup table by Matplotlib when it needs to select more colors, specified using the `cmap` keyword argument.

We also added a `colorbar()` call to draw a color bar next to the plot to identify the ranges the colors are assigned to. In this case, there are a few bins where the values can fall because `rand()` NumPy function returns values between 0 and 1.

Labeling the level lines is important in order to provide information about what levels were chosen for display; `clabel()` does this by taking as input a contour instance, as returned by a previous `contour()` call:

```
In [1]: import matplotlib.pyplot as plt
In [2]: import numpy as np
In [3]: x = np.arange(-2, 2, 0.01)
```

```
In [4]: y = np.arange(-2, 2, 0.01)
In [5]: X, Y = np.meshgrid(x, y)
In [6]: ellipses = X*X/9 + Y*Y/4 - 1
In [7]: cs = plt.contour(ellipses)
In [8]: plt.clabel(cs);
In [9]: plt.show()
```

Here, we draw several ellipses and then call `clabel()` to display the selected levels. We used the NumPy `meshgrid()` function to get the coordinate matrices, X and Y, from the two coordinate vectors, x and y. The output of this code is shown in the following image:

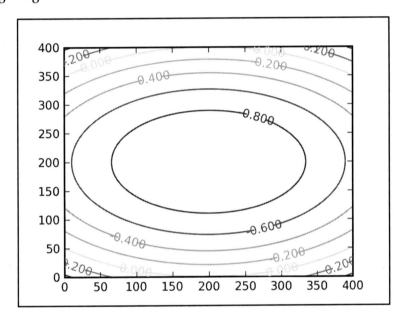

Image plotting

Matplotlib also has basic image plotting capabilities provided by the functions: `imread()` and `imshow()`.

`imread()` reads an image from a file and converts it into a NumPy array; `imshow()` takes an array as input and displays it on the screen:

```
import matplotlib.pyplot as plt
f = plt.imread('/path/to/image/file.ext')
plt.imshow(f)
```

Matplotlib can only read PNG files natively, but if the **Python Imaging Library** (usually known as **PIL**) is installed, then this library will be used to read the image and return an array (if possible).

Note that when working with images, the origin is in the upper-left corner. This can be changed using the origin keyword argument, origin='lower' (which is the only other acceptable value, in addition to the default 'upper'), which will set the origin on the lower-left corner. We can also set it as a configuration parameter, and the key name is image.origin.

Just note that once the image is an array, we can do all the transformations we like.

imshow() can plot any 2D sets of data and not just the ones read from image files. For example, let's take the ellipses code we used for contour plot and see what imshow() draws:

```
In [1]: import matplotlib.pyplot as plt
In [2]: import numpy as np
In [3]: x = np.arange(-2, 2, 0.01)
In [4]: y = np.arange(-2, 2, 0.01)
In [5]: X, Y = np.meshgrid(x, y)
In [6]: ellipses = X*X/9 + Y*Y/4 - 1
In [7]: plt.imshow(ellipses);
In [8]: plt.colorbar();
In [9]: plt.show()
```

This example creates a full spectrum of colors starting from deep blue of the image center, slightly turning into green, yellow, and red near the image corners:

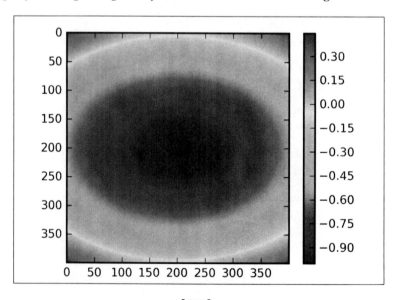

Summary

We've come a long way even in this chapter, so let's recap the arguments
we touched:

- Object-oriented interfaces and the relationship with `pyplot` and `pylab`
- How to draw subplots and multiple figures
- How to manipulate axes so that they can be shared between subplots or can be shared between two plots
- Logarithmic scaled axes
- How to plot dates, and tune tick formatters and locators
- Text properties, fonts, and LaTeX typewriting both with the internal engine `mathtext` and with an external renderer
- Contour plots and image plotting

With the information that we have gathered so far, we are ready to extract Matplotlib from a pure script or interactive usage inside the Python interpreter and learn how we can embed this library in a GUI Python application.

5
Embedding Matplotlib in GTK+

We have seen a lot of examples so far, and we are now pretty productive with Matplotlib and the IPython interpreter.

While this is very handy for interactive plotting, experimenting with datasets, trying different visualization of the same data, and so on, there will be cases where we want an application to acquire, parse, and then, display our data.

In this chapter, we will present some examples of how to embed Matplotlib in applications (quite simple ones) that use GTK+ as the graphical interface library. While doing this, we will show how using the Matplotlib API to program these examples is the best way to achieve this goal.

We will see the following in detail:

- How to embed a Matplotlib Figure into a GTK+ window
- How to embed both, Matplotlib Figure and a navigation toolbar into a GTK+ window
- What does GTK+ provide to update a Matplotlib graph in real-time
- How we can use Glade to design a GUI for GTK+ and then embed Matplotlib into it

A brief introduction to GTK+

Let's first clarify that this is not a course in GTK+ programming, so we are not going to get into the specifics of GTK+, but we will show how to embed Matplotlib inside simple GTK+ application examples. If you find it interesting, then you're encouraged to explore GTK+ in more depth.

We are now going to give a brief, high-level presentation of what GTK+ is. But we will give additional details about specific functionalities of GTK+ as and when we encounter them while describing the code we present.

GTK+ is a highly usable, feature-rich toolkit used to develop graphical user interfaces with a cross-platform compatibility and an easy-to-use API.

GTK+ was initially developed as a widget set for the **GNU Image Manipulation Program (GIMP)**—the name comes from GIMP ToolKit—but then it became bigger and it's now the base for the **GNOME** desktop environment along with many other applications.

The GTK+ library has been developed for over ten years and has reached a high level of stability and performance. While being the library traditionally used to develop nice GUI applications for Linux, it has been ported to several platforms: Linux, Windows, and Mac OS. It is also being made available on mobile platforms.

Getting slightly more specific, GTK+ has a wide collection of core widgets available, for example: windows, buttons, trees, menus, combo boxes, toolbars, dialog windows, and many others.

GTK+ mainly relies on another library, **GLib,** that provides fundamental algorithms and language constructs (such as thread support, lists, arrays, hash tables, trees, and so on) which are commonly used, thus avoiding code duplication.

Another important library for GTK+ is **GObject**. The name comes from the contraction of **GLib Object System**, and it aims to provide a flexible and easy-to-map object-oriented framework to C. It contains a generic type system, a collection of fundamental type implementations (such as integers and so forth), and a signal system that can serve as a powerful notification system. Thus, it provides the object system used by GTK+.

Together with the Glade GUI builder, they provide a very powerful application development environment.

The GTK+ library is written in C, but it has several bindings to many popular programming languages, and this makes it quite an attractive library for application development. This list also includes Python with the PyGTK project.

PyGTK is a binding for the GTK+ library, which allows us to easily create GUI programs using Python and the GTK+ library, which provides all the graphical elements.

Joining Python and GTK+ allows us to develop a truly multiplatform application which is able to run unmodified on several platforms.

Introduction to GTK+ signal system

GTK+ is an event-driven toolkit, which means it is always sleeping in a loop function and waiting for events to occur, and then passes control to the appropriate function. Examples of events are a click on a button, a menu item activation, the ticking of a checkbox, and so forth.

This passing of control is done using the idea of *signals*. Note that, although the terminology is almost identical, GTK+ signals are not the same as the Unix system signals and are not implemented using them.

When an *event*, such as the press of a mouse button occurs, the appropriate signal is emitted by the widget that received the click. This is one of the most important parts of GTK+ work. There are signals that all the widgets inherit, such as `destroy`, and there are signals that are widget specific such as `toggled` on a toggle button.

To let the signal framework be functional, we need to set up a **signal handler** to catch those signals and call the appropriate function.

We can do this by using a `GtkWidget` method (inherited from the GObject class): `connect()`. The generic form for `connect()` is:

```
handler = widget.connect(signal_name, func, func_params)
```

where:

- `handler` is an optional (we can call `widget.connect()` directly) reference to the signal handler that can be used to disconnect or block the handler
- `widget` is the `GtkWidget` object that emits the signal named `signal_name` that we want to catch
- `func` is a reference to the function we will call upon receiving a signal
- `func_params` are optional parameters we can pass to `func`

The function `func` is a *callback* function: the name comes from the fact that we do not call this function directly, instead it is called by the GTK+ events manager when an event occurs.

The general form for a GTK+ signal's callback function is:

```
def callback_func(widget, callback_data)
```

where `widget` is a reference to the widget that emitted the signal, and `callback_data` is an optional reference to `func_params` object defined in the `connect()` method.

If the callback function is an object method, then as usual, the `self` object needs to be the first parameter.

Embedding a Matplotlib figure in a GTK+ window

We can now start to describe how to embed a Matplotlib `Figure` into a GTK+ window as we walk through the code. We will present a simple example, and describe it step-by-step, highlighting the important parts of the code, in particular the GTK+ related ones.

Note again, we are not going to explain the GTK+ functionalities completely, and it is left to the reader to read further if he/she is interested.

Let's start:

```
import gtk
from matplotlib.figure import Figure
import numpy as np
```

These are the usual imports along with the `gtk` module, which is required to access the GTK+ library functions. Once imported, the `gtk` module also takes care of GTK+ environment initialization.

It is also common to find this type of import:

```
import pygtk
pygtk.require('2.0')
import gtk
```

It's useful to differentiate between multiple copies of PyGTK that might be installed on our system. The `require()` function specifies that we need version 2.0, which covers all the versions with major number 2.

```
from matplotlib.backends.backend_gtkagg \
    import FigureCanvasGTKAgg as FigureCanvas
```

This line of code imports Matplotlib's `FigureCanvasGTKAgg` class, which is needed to let a `Figure` object be rendered using the `GTKAgg` backend.

`FigureCanvasGTKAgg` is based on the `FigureCanvasBase` class (that is backend-independent) and adds the logic needed to use GTK+ renderer upon it; in fact, this is also a `gtk.DrawingArea` object, a GTK+ widget.

```
win = gtk.Window()
```

This creates the GTK+ main window — the window that will contain all other widgets. We can consider it as the window where the users will have the main interactions.

Rather than creating a window of 0x0 size, without children and with no specific dimensions, GTK+ sets it to 200x200 by default, so you can still manipulate it.

Note that after this command, the window is not displayed yet, as we have to explicitly pass the execution control to GTK+, and we will do it only at the very end of the example.

```
win.connect("destroy", gtk.main_quit)
```

We connect the signal `destroy`, emitted by the GTK+ main window (because we invoked the `connect()` method of the `win` object), when the user closes the window to the function `gtk.main_quit()` that causes the GTK+ window and the main program with it, to quit.

Another common code snippet for the previously mentioned `connect()` method is:

```
win.connect('destroy', lambda x: gtk.main_quit())
```

But we feel that the version we have proposed is clearer and nicer.

Going on:

```
win.set_default_size(600, 400)
```

This line of code sets the GTK+ main window's height and width, in pixels.

```
win.set_title("Matplotlib Figure in a GTK+ Window")
```

This is the window title, not the `Figure` one; it's the string set at the GUI level, such as Firefox, or OpenOffice.org Writer, which appears at the top of the window.

```
fig = Figure(figsize=(5, 4), dpi=100)
ax = fig.add_subplot(111)
x = np.arange(0,2*np.pi,.01)
y = np.sin(x**2)*np.exp(-x)
ax.plot(x, y)
```

This is the Matplotlib code used to generate a plot. There should be nothing new here.

```
canvas = FigureCanvas(fig)
```

With this command, we associate the `Figure` object (that is backend-independent) to the `FigureCanvas` (that we recall to be `FigureCanvasGTKAgg`), so now we have a widget that's able to draw a `Figure` using GTK+ primitives.

```
win.add(canvas)
```

We now add that new widget to the GTK+ main window using the add() method.

```
win.show_all()
```

This is used to show all the widgets that are attached to the main window (in this case, we have only one widget, the FigureCanvas).

```
gtk.main()
```

We now start the GTK+ main loop.

The main loop is the GTK+ event processing code where the library sleeps while continuously checking if an event has occurred, and whether it was a signal, a timeout, or an I/O notification.

Now that we have introduced the main loop, we can clarify what the gtk.main_quit() function does: it simply lets GTK+ exit from the loop, causing the application to quit.

Let's now display the whole program so that we can have a global look at the code:

```
# gtk module
import gtk

# matplotlib Figure object
from matplotlib.figure import Figure
# numpy functions for image creation
import numpy as np

# import the GtkAgg FigureCanvas object, that binds Figure to
# GTKAgg backend. In this case, this is a gtk.DrawingArea
from matplotlib.backends.backend_gtkagg \
   import FigureCanvasGTKAgg as FigureCanvas

# instantiate the GTK+ window object
win = gtk.Window()
# connect the 'destroy' signal to gtk.main_quit function
win.connect("destroy", gtk.main_quit)
# define the size of the GTK+ window
win.set_default_size(600, 400)
# set the window title
win.set_title("Matplotlib Figure in a GTK+ Window")

# matplotlib code to generate the plot
fig = Figure(figsize=(5, 4), dpi=100)
ax = fig.add_subplot(111)
```

```
x = np.arange(0,2*np.pi, .01)
y = np.sin(x**2)*np.exp(-x)
ax.plot(x, y)

# we bind the figure to the FigureCanvas, so that it will be
# drawn using the specific backend graphic functions
canvas = FigureCanvas(fig)
# add that widget to the GTK+ main window
win.add(canvas)

# show all the widget attached to the main window
win.show_all()
# start the GTK+ main loop
gtk.main()
```

When this example is executed, the following window is generated:

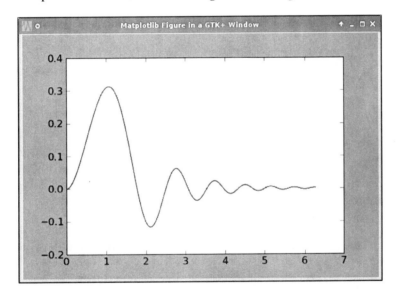

Including a navigation toolbar

The navigation toolbar that is always present when doing interactive plotting might also be useful when embedding Matplotlib in a GUI application, since it already contains many functions to manipulate the plot.

So what we'll be doing here is modifying the previous code to also add the Matplotlib navigation toolbar into the GTK+ window application.

We will show only the additional code that has been added, and then again present the whole program:

```
from matplotlib.backends.backend_gtkagg \
    import NavigationToolbar2GTKAgg as NavigationToolbar
```

This line of code imports the `NavigationToolbar2GTKAgg` class that draws the navigation toolbar.

```
vbox = gtk.VBox()
win.add(vbox)
```

Here, we instantiate a `gtk.VBox` object and add it to the main window. A `gtk.VBox` is a container that organizes its child widgets into a single column, it's a **vertical box**, as the name implies.

Now that we have more than one widget to add to the main window, we cannot simply do:

```
win.add(canvas)
```

Instead, we need to do some more operations:

```
vbox.pack_start(canvas)
toolbar = NavigationToolbar(canvas, win)
vbox.pack_start(toolbar, expand=False, fill=False)
```

Here, we use the `pack_start()` function to inject the Matplotlib objects into the `VBox` instance. The `pack_start()` method adds an object to the box, starting from the top of the box. The widget is packed after any other child in the next available position from the beginning of the box.

In the first call, we added the `Figure` canvas to the `VBox`. In the second call, where we want to add the navigation toolbar, we used additional parameters to `pack_start()`:

- `expand`: This controls whether or not the widget should consume all of the space available when the container and the children are shown. Note that the extra space is shared between all the widgets with `expand=True`. In the navigation toolbar case, it's set to `False`, so the dimensions don't change, and all the extra space allocated to the box can be given to the Matplotlib `Figure` (the only other widget in the `VBox`).

- `fill`: This controls whether the extra space granted with the `expand` parameter is actually allocated to the widget (extending its dimensions) or is just used as padding. If `expand=False`, then `fill` has no meaning. In the navigation toolbar case, we set it to `False` to maintain the widget's original size (we added it for clarity reasons, even though it's not needed, as explained earlier).

- padding: Though this argument is not used here, it's still available to specify the padding space around the widget in pixels.

Here is the complete source code:

```
#!/usr/bin/python

# gtk module
import gtk

# matplotlib Figure object
from matplotlib.figure import Figure
# numpy functions for image creation
import numpy as np

# import the GtkAgg FigureCanvas object, that binds Figure to GTKAgg
backend.
# In this case, this is a gtk.DrawingArea
from matplotlib.backends.backend_gtkagg \
   import FigureCanvasGTKAgg as FigureCanvas
# import the NavigationToolbar GTKAgg widget
from matplotlib.backends.backend_gtkagg \
   import NavigationToolbar2GTKAgg as NavigationToolbar

# instantiate the GTK+ window object
win = gtk.Window()
# connect the 'destroy' signal to gtk.main_quit function
win.connect("destroy", gtk.main_quit)
# define the size of the GTK+ window
win.set_default_size(600,400)
# set the window title
win.set_title("Matplotlib Figure in a GTK+ Window With
NavigationToolbar")

# create a vertical container for widgets
vbox = gtk.VBox()
# and add it to the main GTK+ window
win.add(vbox)

 # matplotlib code to generate the plot
fig = Figure(figsize=(5, 4), dpi=100)
ax = fig.add_subplot(111)
x = np.arange(0,2*np.pi,.01)
y = np.sin(x**2)*np.exp(-x)
ax.plot(x,y)
```

```
# we bind the figure to the FigureCanvas,so that it will be drawn
# using the specific backend graphic functions
canvas = FigureCanvas(fig)
# add the Figure widget as the first one on the box container
vbox.pack_start(canvas)
# instantiate the NavigationToolbar as bind to the Figure
# and the main GTK+ window
toolbar = NavigationToolbar(canvas, win)
# add the NavigationToolbar to the box container
vbox.pack_start(toolbar, expand=False, fill=False)

# show all the widgets attached to the main window
win.show_all()
# start the GTK+ main loop
gtk.main()
```

The output of this program results in the next screenshot:

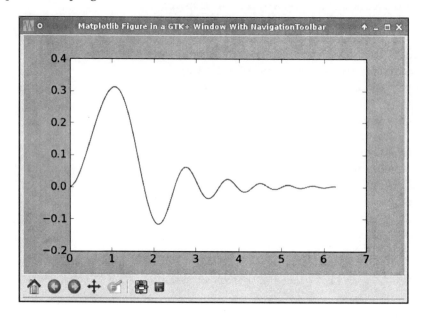

Real-time plots update

We have all heard a lot about real-time these days and the possibility to always have fresh results as things change is becoming more important everyday. So the ability to update our graphs as soon as data comes in or changes is a really interesting feature for those applications (scientific mainly) where we deal with *real-time* streams of data.

Embedding our graphs in a GTK+ window allows us to use some additional sophisticated mechanisms provided by its underlying libraries, and one of these is the ability to simulate a real-time update of our plot.

To design our example in a slightly more realistic way, we decided to take the plotting data from a real source: our CPU (Central Processing Unit, the processor on our machine) usage, during a 30 second period, taking a sample every second.

In a modern operating system, there are several processes always running together with the user programs. Each of these processes participate for a given slice of the total CPU usage.

In particular, we will plot four CPU usage indicators:

- **user**: Time consumed by processes executed by the users of the machine
- **nice**: Time consumed by processes executed by the users but with a lower priority
- **system**: Time consumed by system tasks
- **idle**: Time consumed when waiting for something to execute

These four values will tell us how the computer is being used. Note that there are other indicators that we have ignored here: they contribute to only a very minimal part of the global CPU usage, so discarding them introduces an error that we can simply ignore.

As done before, we will describe the code in blocks, and then present the whole code right after it.

Here is the beginning:

```
import gtk
```

We import this module to access the GTK+ library.

```
import gobject
```

This module is needed because it's the binding to the GNOME GLib library, and we need a function from it.

```
from matplotlib.figure import Figure
from matplotlib.backends.backend_gtkagg \
    import FigureCanvasGTKAgg as FigureCanvas
```

These are the classic Matplotlib modules.

```
import time
```

We need to call the `sleep()` function, which is present in the `time` module.

```
import psutil as p
```

`psutil` is a multiplatform module (which can run on Linux, Windows, and Mac OS X) that provides an interface to retrieve information about the running system, such as processes, memory, CPU, and so on. In particular, it has a function to access the CPU usage set of information.

```
def prepare_cpu_usage():
```

We start by creating a function that will retrieve the CPU information and return them in a format we can easily use to generate the plot.

```
    t = p.cpu_times()
```

So at first, we read the CPU usage information by using the function `cpu_times()` from `psutil`.

```
        if hasattr(t, 'nice'):
            return [t.user, t.nice, t.system, t.idle]
        else:
            # special case for Windows, without 'nice' value
            return [t.user, 0, t.system, t.idle]
```

Windows doesn't have the concept of *niced* processes, so we check if the `nice` attribute is present, then returning the whole set of data, else replacing nice with a 0. In this way, we have a code that can run unmodified both on Windows and on Unix-like systems.

```
def get_cpu_usage():
```

We define another function, which will take care of preparing the data for plotting. We take the CPU usage values each second, so we need to know (in seconds) what the percentage of each indicator is compared to the total CPU usage.

```
    global before
```

We use a global variable `before` that contains the CPU usage values of the previous execution.

```
now = prepare_cpu_usage()
```

We then retrieve the current values of CPU usage.

```
delta = [now[i]-before[i] for i in range(len(now))]
```

The values returned by `cpu_times()` of `psutil()` are counters that are always incremented (initialized at machine boot and reset at reboot), so we compute the difference between the current and the previous values for each indicator (that represent the indicator slice in the total CPU usage).

```
total = sum(delta)
```

Then we compute the sum of these differences (that represents the total CPU usage in current time interval).

```
before = now
```

This line of code saves the current values (so that they'll be available when the function will be called the next time).

```
return [(100.0*dt)/total for dt in delta]
```

At the end we return the values that we really need to plot: we compute the percentage of each indicator (take each of them, multiply by 100, and then divide by the sum).

```
def update_draw(*args):
    global i
    result = get_cpu_usage()
    user.append(result[0])
    nice.append(result[1])
    sys.append( result[2])
    idle.append(result[3])
```

This is the first piece of the function we call to update the plot.

We use the global variable `i` to count the number of executions of this function. Then we take the values returned by the `get_cpu_usage()` function, and we append them to their respective lists.

```
l_user.set_data(range(len(user)), user)
l_nice.set_data(range(len(nice)), nice)
l_sys.set_data( range(len(sys)),  sys)
l_idle.set_data(range(len(idle)), idle)
fig.canvas.draw()
```

This is a very important part of the function. Matplotlib returns an object reference after each `plot()` call, which allows us to control the line object. What we don't want to do here is replot the same data at every iteration, but to *update* the line already drawn to reflect the new values as this is much faster and there is no flickering on screen.

Here, we are resetting the lines values, both for X and for Y to the new values: we call `set_data()` for each indicator with a `range()` of the same length as that of the list and the list itself.

After that, we have to explicitly call a `draw()` on the canvas to force Matplotlib's engine to redraw the objects that were updated.

```
i += 1
if i > 30:
    return False
else:
    time.sleep(1)
return True
```

Here, we are controlling the number of repetitions. We are incrementing the counter and checking if we've completed the number of iterations decided. If `False` is returned, then the graph's updates are stopped; else the CPU sleeps for a second and then returns `True`, in order to let this function be executed again.

```
i = 0
before = prepare_cpu_usage()
```

We start now the main part of the code, setting the two global variables we need for updating the algorithm: `i`, to keep track of the number of executions of the updating function, and `before` to compute the percentage of CPU usage.

```
win = gtk.Window()
win.connect("destroy", gtk.main_quit)
win.set_default_size(600, 400)
win.set_title("30 Seconds of CPU Usage Updated in real-time")
```

Nothing new, this is the GTK+ window setup, which was also done in the previous examples.

```
fig = Figure()
ax = fig.add_subplot(111)
ax.set_xlim(0, 30)
ax.set_ylim([0, 100])
ax.set_autoscale_on(False)
```

That's a part of the Matplotlib code: we define the `Figure`, the `Axes` inside it, and then we set the X and Y limits. The intervals are from 0 to 30 for X-axis as these will be the number of seconds during which we plot data, and from 0 to 100 for Y-axis as this is the possible range for percentage.

We also have to stop the automatic axes scaling done by Matplotlib, or else the forced limits would be useless. If we wish to let the Y-axis autoscale, then we will have to add `ax.set_autoscale_on(False)` right after these lines:

```
locator = ax.yaxis.get_major_locator()
ax.set_ylim(locator.autoscale())
```

Continuing with the example code:

```
user, nice, sys, idle = [], [], [], []
l_user, = ax.plot([], user, label='User %')
l_nice, = ax.plot([], nice, label='Nice %')
l_sys,  = ax.plot([], sys,  label='Sys %')
l_idle, = ax.plot([], idle, label='Idle %')
```

Here, we are simply generating placeholder line objects for the real plot of CPU data. Both the axes are empty, but the most important thing is that now we have the handlers for the line objects, and we will use them to *animate* the image (as described earlier).

```
ax.legend()
```

We add a legend to the plot using the labels defined by the previous `plot()` calls.

```
canvas = FigureCanvas(fig)
win.add(canvas)
```

This is the same binding that is done between the Matplotlib `FigureCanvas` and the GTK+ main window.

```
update_draw()
```

We make an explicit call to the updating function: it's a trick to speed up the visualization of the lines on the window.

```
gobject.idle_add(update_draw)
```

We use the `idle_add()` function from the `gobject` module, passing our `update_draw` as a callback function. `idle_add()` sets a function to be called when no other events of a higher priority are running. Since in our application, the GTK+ main loop usually has no other events to process, our function is called almost continuously (but remember, we do `sleep()` in the function).

Will the function be called indefinitely or can we stop it? Here the return value of the callback function becomes important: if the function returns False, the function itself is removed from the list of events to check, so it will not be called again and the animation stops. If the function returns True, then it's kept in the list and will be called again.

If our function had parameters, then we could pass them after the function name in the idle_add() call.

```
win.show_all()
gtk.main()
```

In the end, we have the usual function call to show all the widgets of the GTK+ main window and the one to start the GTK+ main loop.

As promised, here is the full code:

```
# gtk module
import gtk

# binding for GLib
import gobject

# matplotlib Figure object
from matplotlib.figure import Figure
# import the GtkAgg FigureCanvas object, that binds Figure to
# GTKAgg backend. In this case, this is a gtk.DrawingArea
from matplotlib.backends.backend_gtkagg \
    import FigureCanvasGTKAgg as FigureCanvas

# needed for the sleep function
import time

# used to obtain CPU usage information
import psutil as p


def prepare_cpu_usage():
    """Helper function to return CPU usage info"""

    # get the CPU times using psutil module
    t = p.cpu_times()

    # return only the values we're interested in
    if hasattr(t, 'nice'):
```

```
            return [t.user, t.nice, t.system, t.idle]


        else:
            # special case for Windows, without 'nice' value
            return [t.user, 0, t.system, t.idle]



def get_cpu_usage():
    """Compute CPU usage comparing previous and current values"""
    # use the global 'before' variable
    global before

    # take the current CPU usage information
    now = prepare_cpu_usage()
    # compute deltas between current and previous measurements
    delta = [now[i]-before[i] for i in range(len(now))]
    # compute the total (needed for percentages calculation)
    total = sum(delta)
    # save the current measurement to before object
    before = now
    # return the percentage of CPU usage for our 4 categories
    return [(100.0*dt)/total for dt in delta]

def update_draw(*args):
    """Update the graph with current CPU usage values"""

    # use the global 'i' variable
    global i

    # get the CPU usage information
    result = get_cpu_usage()

    # append new data to the datasets
    user.append(result[0])
    nice.append(result[1])
    sys.append( result[2])
    idle.append(result[3])

    # update lines data using the lists with new data
    l_user.set_data(range(len(user)), user)
    l_nice.set_data(range(len(nice)), nice)
    l_sys.set_data( range(len(sys)),  sys)
    l_idle.set_data(range(len(idle)), idle)
```

```
    # force a redraw of the Figure
    fig.canvas.draw()

    # after 30 iteration, exit; else, sleep 1 second
    i += 1
    if i > 30:
        return False
    else:
        time.sleep(1)

    return True

# global var to initialize the loop counter
i = 0
# global var, initialized with the current CPU usage values
before = prepare_cpu_usage()

# instantiate the GTK+ window object
win = gtk.Window()
# connect the 'destroy' signal to gtk.main_quit function
win.connect("destroy", gtk.main_quit)
# define the size of the GTK+ window
win.set_default_size(600, 400)
# set the window title
win.set_title("30 Seconds of CPU Usage Updated in real-time")

# first image setup
fig = Figure()
ax = fig.add_subplot(111)

# set specific limits for X and Y axes
ax.set_xlim(0, 30)
ax.set_ylim([0, 100])

# and disable figure-wide autoscale
ax.set_autoscale_on(False)

# generates first "empty" plots
user, nice, sys, idle = [], [], [], []

l_user, = ax.plot([], user, label='User %')
l_nice, = ax.plot([], nice, label='Nice %')
l_sys,  = ax.plot([] , sys,  label='Sys %')
l_idle, = ax.plot([], idle, label='Idle %')
```

```
# add legend to plot
ax.legend()
# we bind the figure to the FigureCanvas, so that it will be
# drawn using the specific backend graphic functions
canvas = FigureCanvas(fig)
# add that widget to the GTK+ main window
win.add(canvas)

# explicit update the graph (speedup graph visualization)
update_draw()

# exec our "updated" funcion when GTK+ main loop is idle
gobject.idle_add(update_draw)
# show all the widget attached to the main window
win.show_all()

# start the GTK+ main loop
gtk.main()
```

The output of the previous program is as shown:

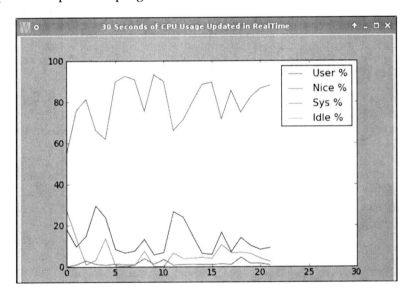

To take this snapshot, we have simulated a high low on this machine. The result is the nice line (green) near the top of the graph that represents 100% of CPU usage. The other indicators are at the bottom of the graph with the user line (in blue) a bit above the idle line (cyan) and the system line (red) is almost at 0%. In Chapter 7, we will present a similar technique to update a plot in real-time, but with a much higher throughput.

Embedding Matplotlib in a Glade application

Glade is a user interface designer that allows to create and edit user interfaces for GTK+ applications.

Glade is used to place GTK+ widgets in a GUI, and change the layout or the properties of each widget. It also allows to add connections between those widgets and the application code.

Glade stores the GUI design in an XML format, and by using `libglade`, Glade XML files can be dynamically loaded in applications developed in several programming languages (Python included).

The example we are going to present is about counting the letters in a file and then plotting the result. If you have ever studied basic cryptography, you were taught that *e* is the most common letter in the English writings — this is your chance to experimentally verify that!

Before presenting and discussing the Python code, we will describe how we have designed the GUI with Glade.

Designing the GUI using Glade

When Glade executable is started (with no `glade` file as parameter), it displays a window to select some settings for the new project; the important thing here is to select the project file format as **Libglade** (at least if we want it to be used in Python code). This option can be changed later, but let's start with the right one.

Now, we are presented with an empty design space that we can populate: the **palette toolbox** contains all the widgets that we can use. Let's start taking a main GTK+ window and keep adding widgets until we reach the desired result. This is really easy as everything is done through drag-and-drop, mouse selection, and so on.

The GUI we have designed for this example appears like this in Glade:

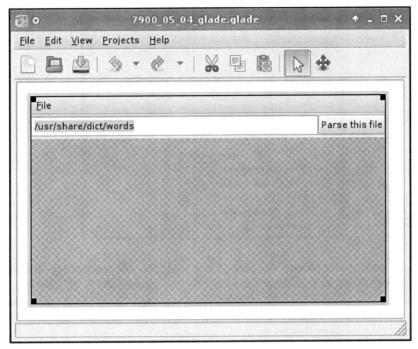

As we can see, there is a large unmanaged area in the GUI: this will be the place where we will embed the Matplotlib `Figure` object directly from the Python code.

To determine the layout of the GUI, we suggest using `VBox`, `HBox`, `Table`, `Alignment`, and other similar widgets as they create groups of widgets that can be resized, moved, and so on—altogether, that will result in a nice user interface.

For example, we used an `Alignment` and an `HBox` to contain and format the text entry and button widgets, and then we used a `VBox` to contain the menu, the `Alignment` set, and the empty area for `Figure`.

As briefly just mentioned, we also included a short menu with two items: a file selector and the quit item.

To have a clear view of all the widget dependencies and locations, Glade provides an **Inspector** window with the widgets hierarchy:

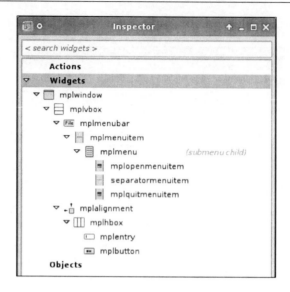

The previous screenshot shows the tree of our widgets. We encourage to choose widget names that are descriptive: for example, we named them all starting with mpl (the common abbreviation for Matplotlib), then we used the widget name, and in case there are more widgets of the same type in the GUI, then we numbered them or clarified the location of the widgets in the window.

There are several aspects we might want to tune for each widget, and this can be done using the **Properties** window:

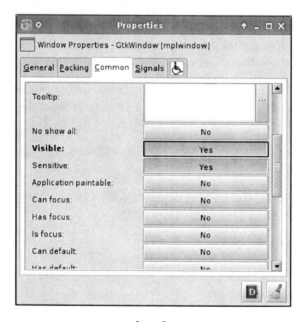

This is the screenshot where we not only set the **Visible** field of the main window to **Yes** (by default it's not shown if we don't set this property, take note for your project too), but we also set the **Expand** property of the **mplbutton** to **No** to limit its dimensions, allowing the **mplentry** widget to use as much space as possible.

Another important configuration to do when designing the interface is defining the signals each widget emits (if any) and the callback functions for them.

This is done in the **Properties** toolbar under the **Signals** tab:

This information will then be used in the Python code to actually set up the signal framework.

It's there that we define the **Handler** name for each signal we want to catch. We suggest a naming convention for these callback functions like the one proposed by Glade itself:

```
on_<widget name>_<signal name>
```

Code to use Glade GUI

We are now able to explore the code that will be used to implement our example:

```python
from __future__ import with_statement
import numpy as np
import gtk
import gtk.glade
```

```
from matplotlib.figure import Figure
from matplotlib.backends.backend_gtkagg \
    import FigureCanvasGTKAgg as FigureCanvas
```

The modules imported are almost the same as before except for the `gtk.glade` module, which is needed to load the Glade XML file to create the GUI and the `with` statement, backported from Python 2.6 to 2.5 and available through `__future__`.

The `with` statement is a nice construct to use when we need to open files: it automatically closes the file object at the end of the statement, and it also handles error conditions without leaving open file objects hanging around.

```
def parse_file(filename):
```

We define a function that we will use to parse the input file.

```
letters = {}
for i in range(97, 122 + 1):
    letters[chr(i)] = 0
```

Here is the `letters` dictionary initialization: we first create an empty dictionary, then we add a key for each lowercase letter of the English alphabet (calling `chr()` on numbers between 97 and 122) with value 0. They represent the occurrences of each letter, so at the beginning, they are of course all 0.

```
with open(filename) as f:
    for line in f:
        for char in line:
            if ord(char.lower()) in range(97, 122 + 1):
                letters[char.lower()] += 1
return letters
```

Here is the parsing code, there is nothing extremely special about it: we access the file using the `with` statement, then for each line of the file, and for each character in the line, we check if it's a letter and in that case, we increment its counter in the dictionary. At the end, we return the `letters` dictionary with the number of occurrences of each letter in the given file.

```
def update_graph(fig_ref, ax_ref, letters_freq):
```

We define another function that we will use to update the Matplotlib plot. We pass as parameters the references to the Matplotlib `Figure` and `Axes`, and also the dictionary containing the letters frequencies.

```
k = sorted(letters_freq.keys())
v = [letters_freq[ki] for ki in k]
```

From that `letters_freq` dictionary, we extract a sorted list of the keys, and then we generate the list of dictionary values ordered by k.

```
ax_ref.clear()
```

We clear the `Axes`, removing all elements from it, to start the new plot from scratch.

```
ax_ref.bar(np.arange(len(k))-0.25, v, width=0.5)
```

Then we draw a set of bars, one for each letter in k, with the heights set to the letter's frequencies. We set the bar width to be `0.5`, so shifting the bar's starting point by 0.25 will center them on the X ticks.

```
ax_ref.set_xlim(xmin=-0.25, xmax=len(k)-0.75)
```

Due to the bar's shift, we have also to adjust the X limits to contain the bars precisely: the minimum is set to `-0.25` because the first bar starts there (the tick is at 0, but half of the bar is on the negative side), while the maximum is set to the tick position (`len(k)-1`), but adding an additional half-bar quantity of `0.25` makes it `-0.75`.

```
ax_ref.set_xticks(range(len(k)))
ax_ref.set_xticklabels(k)
```

We set the ticks at k positions (that will be in the middle of the bars), and the labels are the letters themselves.

```
ax_ref.get_yaxis().grid(True)
```

We enable grid lines only for the Y-axis (enabling grid also for X would only create confusion).

```
fig_ref.canvas.draw()
```

In the end, we force a redraw of plot on the `Figure`.

```
class GladeEventsHandlers:
```

We now define a class to contain the callback functions for the events of the Glade GUI. This is a common practice, and it also allows for a nice trick that we'll see in a bit (but for the trick to work we have to define the callback functions with the exact same name in the Glade GUI, and in this class).

```
def on_mplbutton_clicked(event):
    update_graph(fig, ax, parse_file(entry.get_text()))
```

This is the callback function for the `clicked` event emitted by `mplbutton` object (as the function name should tell). When that event occurs, we call the `update_graph()` function to update the graph line.

```
def on_mplopenmenuitem_activate(event):
```

To facilitate the selection of a file to parse, we added a menu item to open a file selection dialog, and this is the callback function that does it.

```
chooser = gtk.FileChooserDialog("Open..",
            None,
            gtk.FILE_CHOOSER_ACTION_OPEN,
            (gtk.STOCK_CANCEL, gtk.RESPONSE_CANCEL,
            gtk.STOCK_OPEN, gtk.RESPONSE_OK))
```

We instantiate the `FileChooserDialog` dialog object.

```
chooser.set_default_response(gtk.RESPONSE_OK)
res = chooser.run()
```

We set the default response and then start the dialog window to be actually displayed.

```
if res == gtk.RESPONSE_OK:
    entry.set_text(chooser.get_filename())
```

If the result is a click on the **OK** button, then we take the file selected by the user and reset the entry widget text to the path of that file.

```
chooser.destroy()
```

In the end, we destroy the dialog window.

We can now describe the main code of the example:

```
win = gtk.glade.XML('7900_05_04_glade.glade', 'mplwindow')
```

With the method `gtk.glade.XML()`, we instantiate the Glade XML file into the interface that we now can access to get the widgets contained in it and modify them.

```
win.signal_autoconnect(GladeEventsHandlers.__dict__)
```

The `glade` module allows us to connect handlers to the signals defined in the interface. We do this by using the module's dictionary of the `GladeEventsHandlers` class:

```
In [7]: GladeEventsHandlers.__dict__
Out[7]:
{'__doc__': None,
 '__module__': '__main__',
 'on_mplbutton_clicked': <function on_mplbutton_clicked at 0x2272668>,
 'on_mplopenmenuitem_activate': <function on_mplopenmenuitem_activate
at 0x22721b8>}
```

If we take a look at this dictionary, we can see that it contains the name of the signal handlers (that are the methods names), along with their references (the method's memory locations). As we have defined the same handlers' names in Glade, we have a handy way to associate the callback functions references with the handlers defined in the Glade GUI.

```
d = {"on_mplwindow_destroy": gtk.main_quit}
win.signal_autoconnect(d)
```

We can also explicitly define a dictionary and then call `signal_autoconnect()` on it.

```
win.get_widget("mplquitmenuitem").connect("activate", gtk.main_quit)
```

or we can do the usual `connect()` of the signal to the callback function once we have obtained a reference to the widget using the `get_widget()` method of the `gtk.glade.XML` object.

```
window = win.get_widget('mplwindow')
window.set_title("Matplotlib In a Glade GUI - Count letters frequency
in a file")
```

Here, we get a reference to the main GTK+ window's widgets to define the window title.

```
fig = Figure()
ax = fig.add_subplot(111)
```

This is the code to set up the Matplotlib Figure and Axes.

```
entry = win.get_widget("mplentry")
```

We take the reference to the `mplentry` widget as we need it to read the filename from it and to reset that value if we choose another file using the `FileChooserDialog`. We already preset a file for this widget /usr/share/dict/words, a file present on the Debian system (and probably on other Linux distributions) that contains a very long list of English words—a very nice default value for this example.

```
canvas = FigureCanvas(fig)
canvas.show()
canvas.set_size_request(600, 400)
```

We embed the `Figure` object in a canvas, and set its size.

```
place = win.get_widget("mplvbox")
place.pack_start(canvas, True, True)
```

Then we get the reference to a `VBox` widget, and we inject our `FigureCanvas` into the empty area that we had left during our GUI design.

```
gtk.main()
```

At the end, we can start the GTK+ main loop and play with the resulting application.

Here is the whole code in a block:

```
# used to parse files more easily
from __future__ import with_statement

# Numpy module
import numpy as np

# gtk module
import gtk

# module to handle Glade ui
import gtk.glade

# matplotlib Figure object
from matplotlib.figure import Figure
# import the GtkAgg FigureCanvas object, binds Figure to GTKAgg
# In this case, this is also a gtk.DrawingArea
from matplotlib.backends.backend_gtkagg \
    import FigureCanvasGTKAgg as FigureCanvas

def parse_file(filename):
    """Function to parse a text file to extract letters freqs"""

    # dict initialization
    letters = {}

    # lower-case letter ordinal numbers
    for i in range(97, 122 + 1):
        letters[chr(i)] = 0

    # parse the input file
    with open(filename) as f:
        for line in f:
            for char in line:
                # counts only letters
                if ord(char.lower()) in range(97, 122 + 1):
                    letters[char.lower()] += 1
```

```
        return letters
def update_graph(fig_ref, ax_ref, letters_freq):

    """Updates the graph with new letters frequencies"""

    # sort the keys and the values
    k = sorted(letters_freq.keys())
    v = [letters_freq[ki] for ki in k]

    # clean the Axes
    ax_ref.clear()

    # draw a bar chart for letters and their frequencies
    # set the width to 0.5 and shift bars of 0.25, to be centered
    ax_ref.bar(np.arange(len(k))-0.25, v, width=0.5)

    # reset the X limits
    ax_ref.set_xlim(xmin=-0.25, xmax=len(k)-0.75)
    # set the X ticks & tickslabel as the letters
    ax_ref.set_xticks(range(len(k)))

    ax_ref.set_xticklabels(k)
    # enable grid only on the Y axis
    ax_ref.get_yaxis().grid(True)

    # force an image redraw
    fig_ref.canvas.draw()


class GladeEventsHandlers:
    def on_mplbutton_clicked(event):
        """callback for a click on the button"""

        update_graph(fig, ax, parse_file(entry.get_text()))

    def on_mplopenmenuitem_activate(event):
        """callback for activate on the Open menu item"""

        # create a FileChooserDialog window
        chooser = gtk.FileChooserDialog("Open..",
                    None,
                    gtk.FILE_CHOOSER_ACTION_OPEN,
                    (gtk.STOCK_CANCEL, gtk.RESPONSE_CANCEL,
                    gtk.STOCK_OPEN, gtk.RESPONSE_OK))
        chooser.set_default_response(gtk.RESPONSE_OK)
```

```
        # execute the dialog window and get the result
        res = chooser.run()

        # if the result is a click on OK
        if res == gtk.RESPONSE_OK:
            # get file selected and set it to the entry widget
            entry.set_text(chooser.get_filename())

        # distroy the dialog window
        chooser.destroy()

# Main

# parse glade xml file, return an object to access widgets
# contained in the glade file
win = gtk.glade.XML('7900_05_04_glade.glade', 'mplwindow')
# connect the signals with the function in GladeEventsHandlers
# class with a trick...
win.signal_autoconnect(GladeEventsHandlers.__dict__)
# commodity dictionary to easily connect destroy to gtk.main_quit()
d = {"on_mplwindow_destroy": gtk.main_quit}
win.signal_autoconnect(d)
# also connect the menu item Quit to gtk.main_quit() function
win.get_widget("mplquitmenuitem").connect("activate", gtk.main_quit)

# get the main window widget and set its title
window = win.get_widget('mplwindow')
window.set_title("Matplotlib In a Glade GUI - Count letters frequency
in a file")

# matplotlib code to generate an empty Axes
# we define no dimensions for Figure because it will be
# expanded to the whole empty space on main window widget
fig = Figure()
ax = fig.add_subplot(111)

# get the mplentry widget, we will use across callback functions
entry = win.get_widget("mplentry")
# we bind the figure to the FigureCanvas, so that it will be
# drawn using the specific backend graphic functions
canvas = FigureCanvas(fig)
canvas.show()
# define dimensions of the Figure canvas
canvas.set_size_request(600, 400)

# embed the canvas into the empty area left in glade window
place = win.get_widget("mplvbox")
```

```
place.pack_start(canvas, True, True)

# start the GTK+ main loop
gtk.main()
```

Here we can see the screenshot of the running program:

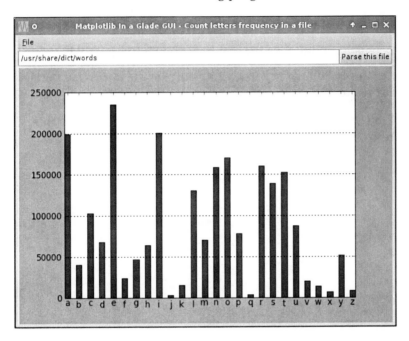

We can see how the vowels, and in particular, the letter *e*, are indeed the most used letters in the example file.

Summary

In this chapter, we presented some examples of how to:

- Embed Matplotlib `Figure` inside a simple GTK+ window
- Add the Matplotlib navigation toolbar
- Plot data in real time
- Use Glade to design the GUI and then embed Matplotlib into it

We kept the examples simple to concentrate only on the important parts, but we encourage our readers to explore further possibilities.

GTK+ is not the only GUI library that can be used. In the coming chapters, we'll see how to use two other important libraries—stay tuned!

6
Embedding Matplotlib in Qt 4

There are several GUI libraries available, and one of the most famous is Qt. In this book, we will use Qt 4, the latest major version of this library. Unless explicitly mentioned, when we write Qt, we are referring to Qt 4.

We will follow the same progression as in the GTK+ chapter, and we will present the same examples, but this time written in Qt.

We believe that this method will allow us to directly compare the libraries, and it has the advantage of not leaving the "How would I write something with library X?" question unanswered.

During this chapter, we will see how to:

- Embed a Matplotlib `Figure` into a Qt widget
- Embed a `Figure` and navigation toolbar into a Qt widget
- Use events to update in real-time a Matplotlib plot
- Use Qt Designer to draw a GUI and then use it with Matplotlib in a simple Python application

We begin by giving an introduction to the library.

Brief introduction to Qt 4 and PyQt4

Qt is a cross-platform application development framework, widely used for graphical programs (GUI) but also for non-GUI tools.

Qt was developed by Trolltech (now owned by Nokia), and it's probably best known for being the foundation of the **K Desktop Environment** (**KDE**) for Linux.

The Qt toolkit is a collection of classes to simplify the creation of programs. Qt is more than just a GUI toolkit; it includes components for abstractions of network sockets, threads, Unicode, regular expressions, SQL databases, SVG, OpenGL, and XML, as well as a fully functional web browser, a help system, a multimedia framework, and a rich collection of GUI widgets.

Qt is available on several platforms, in particular: Unix/Linux, Windows, Mac OS X, and also some embedded devices. As it uses the native APIs of the platform to render the Qt controls, applications developed with Qt have a look and feel which fits the running environment (without looking like *aliens* in it).

Though written in C++, Qt can also be used in several other programming languages, through language bindings available for Ruby, Java, Perl, and also Python with PyQt.

PyQt is a comprehensive set of Python bindings for the Qt framework. PyQt provides bindings for Qt 2 and Qt 3. PyQt4 is a separate set of bindings and covers the Qt 4 series of releases. We will use PyQt4 and references to PyQt should be considered to be referring to PyQt4.

PyQt brings together the Qt C++ cross-platform application framework and the cross-platform interpreted language, Python. An application written in Qt and PyQt often runs unchanged on all the supported platforms.

The Qt components are mapped to several Python submodules (where PyQt4 is the main module), and the most important are:

- The `QtCore` module, which contains the core non-GUI classes (for example, the event loop).

- The `QtGui` module, which contains the majority of the GUI classes.

- `QtOpenGL`, `QtScript` (JavaScript support), `QtSql` (SQL databases support), `QtSvg` (SVG file support), `QtTest` (unit testing support), `QtXml` (XML support), `QtNetwork` (for network programming), and several others. Note how many of these submodules provide functionalities that are already present in Python standard library.

Embedding a Matplotlib figure in a Qt window

We are going to see how to embed a Matplotlib `Figure` into a simple Qt window. We will first walk through the code and describe it, while presenting it as a whole at the end of the section (this presentation style will be used throughout the chapter).

Here is the beginning:

```
import sys
```

The module `sys` contains information and functions used to interact with the Python interpreter. In this case, we need it to access the command-line arguments passed to the Python script.

```
from PyQt4 import QtGui
```

We import the PyQt4 submodule, `QtGui` which contains the biggest part of the GUI classes, for example, all the basic GUI widgets are located in this module.

```
import numpy as np
```

The NumPy module is needed for our example graph.

```
from matplotlib.figure import Figure
```

Import the `Figure` Matplotlib object: this is the backend-independent representation of our plot.

```
from matplotlib.backends.backend_qt4agg \
    import FigureCanvasQTAgg as FigureCanvas
```

Here we import from the `matplotlib.backends.backend_qt4agg` module the `FigureCanvasQTAgg` class, which is the backend-dependent figure canvas; it contains the backend-specific knowledge to render the `Figure` we've drawn to the Qt 4 backend.

Note that `FigureCanvasQTAgg`, other than being a Matplotlib class, is also a `QWidget` — the base class of all user interface objects (it simply represents an empty area). So this means we can treat `FigureCanvasQTAgg` like a pure Qt widget object, using it in the GUI window as we would do with buttons, text areas, and so on.

```
class Qt4MplCanvas(FigureCanvas):
```

We now define a new class, `Qt4MplCanvas`, to render our Matplotlib plot; it inherits from `FigureCanvas`, as well as from `QWidget`. Therefore, it can be used as a Qt element in the main window of our application.

```
def __init__(self):
    self.fig = Figure()
    self.axes = self.fig.add_subplot(111)
    self.x = np.arange(0.0, 3.0, 0.01)
    self.y = np.cos(2*np.pi*self.x)
    self.axes.plot(self.x, self.y)
```

In the `__init__` method, which is called upon class instantiation, we write the code to draw the graph.

```
FigureCanvas.__init__(self, self.fig)
```

We also instantiate the `FigureCanvas`, which is responsible for taking the Matplotlib `Figure` object, and render it in a Qt widget.

```
qApp = QtGui.QApplication(sys.argv)
```

This command creates the Qt application, initialized with the list of arguments given from the command line. This is a required parameter, and it's the reason we imported the `sys` module.

> Every PyQt4 application must create one and only one `QApplication` instance, no matter how many windows compose the application.

`QApplication` manages the GUI application's control flow and main settings. It's the place where the main event loop is executed, processing and dispatching to the widgets all the events coming from the window system and other sources.

It is also responsible for application initialization and finalization, handling most of the system-wide and application-wide settings.

Since `QApplication` handles the entire initialization phase, it must be created before any other objects related to the UI are created.

```
mpl = Qt4MplCanvas()
```

We can now instantiate the `Qt4MplCanvas`. A `QWidget` with no parent (like the one over here) is called a **window**. Consider the *parent* as the object where we want to put the widget; if it's `None`, then it's a main window. Otherwise, if we want to put the widget in a window, then we set the parent as a reference to that window.

```
mpl.show()
```

The `show()` method makes the widget visible on the screen.

```
sys.exit(qApp.exec_())
```

The command `qApp.exec_()` enters the Qt main event loop. Once `exit()` or `quit()` is called, it returns the relevant return code. Until the main loop is started, nothing is displayed on screen.

It's necessary to call this function as the main loop handles all events and signals coming from both the application widgets and from the window system; essentially, no user interaction can take place before it's called.

You may be wondering why there is an underscore in `exec_()`; the reason is simple: `exec()` is a reserved word in Python, thus the addition of the underscore to the `exec()` Qt method.

Wrapping it inside `sys.exit()` allows the Python script to exit with the same return code, informing the environment how the application ended (whether successfully or not).

Here is the complete source code:

```
# for command-line arguments
import sys

# Python Qt4 bindings for GUI objects
from PyQt4 import QtGui

# Numpy functions for image creation
import numpy as np

# Matplotlib Figure object
from matplotlib.figure import Figure
# import the Qt4Agg FigureCanvas object, that binds Figure to
# Qt4Agg backend. It also inherits from QWidget
from matplotlib.backends.backend_qt4agg \
   import FigureCanvasQTAgg as FigureCanvas

class Qt4MplCanvas(FigureCanvas):
    """Class to represent the FigureCanvas widget"""
    def __init__(self):
        # Standard Matplotlib code to generate the plot
        self.fig = Figure()
        self.axes = self.fig.add_subplot(111)
        self.x = np.arange(0.0, 3.0, 0.01)
        self.y = np.cos(2*np.pi*self.x)
        self.axes.plot(self.x, self.y)
        # initialize the canvas where the Figure renders into
        FigureCanvas.__init__(self, self.fig)
```

```
# Create the GUI application
qApp = QtGui.QApplication(sys.argv)
# Create the Matplotlib widget
mpl = Qt4MplCanvas()
# show the widget
mpl.show()
# start the Qt main loop execution, exiting from this script
# with the same return code of Qt application
sys.exit(qApp.exec_())
```

Here is the screenshot from the running application:

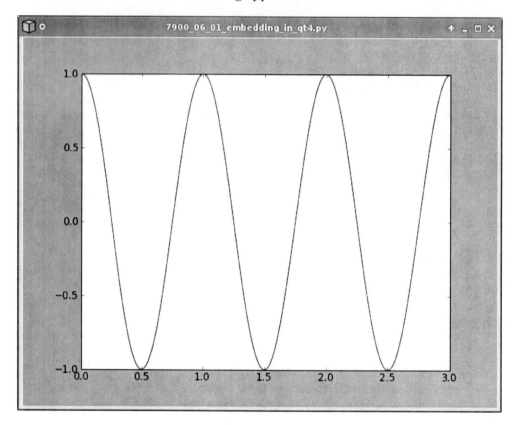

Including a navigation toolbar

Here we're going to add the navigation toolbar to the Matplotlib plot to explore some additional aspects of Qt.

```
import sys
```

This is used for command-line argument retrieval.

```
from PyQt4 import QtGui
```

We now import the Qt 4 GUI widget's submodule.

```
import numpy as np
```

This is the usual NumPy import to generate the plot data.

```
from matplotlib.figure import Figure
from matplotlib.backends.backend_qt4agg \
   import FigureCanvasQTAgg as FigureCanvas
from matplotlib.backends.backend_qt4agg \
   import NavigationToolbar2QTAgg as NavigationToolbar
```

Here we import the Matplotlib `Figure` object along with the `FigureCanvasQTAgg` and `NavigationToolbar2QTAgg`. Note that the last two are Qt 4 specific and also inherit from `QWidget`, so they can be used as Qt objects in a `QApplication`.

```
class Qt4MplCanvas(FigureCanvas):
```

We now define a new class and as it inherits from `FigureCanvas`, it is also a `QWidget` that can be embedded into a Qt application.

```
def __init__(self, parent):
    self.fig = Figure()
    self.axes = self.fig.add_subplot(111)
    t = np.arange(0.0, 3.0, 0.01)
    s = np.cos(2*np.pi*t)
    self.axes.plot(t, s)
```

This is the usual code to draw a Matplotlib example graph.

```
        FigureCanvas.__init__(self, self.fig)
```

We now initialize the `FigureCanvas` object, the Qt 4-specific figure canvas.

```
        self.setParent(parent)
```

We set the parent of this widget to the `parent` parameter of `__init__`.

```
FigureCanvas.setSizePolicy(self,
                           QtGui.QSizePolicy.Expanding,
                           QtGui.QSizePolicy.Expanding)
```

The `setSizePolicy()` `QWidget` method is used to set the widget size behavior. We set it to be freely expandable so that we can resize the window and have the `Figure` be resized accordingly.

```
FigureCanvas.updateGeometry(self)
```

We need to call this method because we have changed the size polices, so we now notify the layout system of this change.

```
class ApplicationWindow(QtGui.QMainWindow):
```

We create another class that will be our main application window.

The `QMainWindow` class provides a framework to create the main windows of application user interfaces; it's common to subclass it, when defining our own window.

As we've seen in the previous example, there are other ways to create a visible window (we did it with a `QWidget` without a parent), but using `QMainWindow` is the best way to build a full-featured GUI application.

```
def __init__(self):
    QtGui.QMainWindow.__init__(self)
```

We call the constructor of the superclass, since we inherit from it. It's necessary to initialize the base class (to be able to use its functionalities) while initializing our own class.

```
self.setWindowTitle("Matplotlib Figure in a Qt4 Window With
NavigationToolbar")
```

We set the window title, as we expect a real application to have a title.

```
self.main_widget = QtGui.QWidget(self)
```

We create a widget that will be the main widget displayed by our application.

```
vbl = QtGui.QVBoxLayout(self.main_widget)
```

Here is a vertical box: vertical and horizontal boxes are used to group widgets together (on a vertical or horizontal layout) and allow size transformations on all of them. They are also called *geometry* or *layout managers*, since they are able to automatically position and adjust the widgets they contain.

The idea behind layout managers is to pack widgets into an area where their positions are relative to the other widgets and to the window. Resize the window, and the layout managers will automatically adjust the size and position of widgets to accommodate this change.

```
qmc = Qt4MplCanvas(self.main_widget)
ntb = NavigationToolbar(qmc, self.main_widget)
```

Now we have the two Matplotlib objects we're interested in—the figure canvas and the toolbar. Note how one of the toolbar parameters is the figure canvas.

```
vbl.addWidget(qmc)
vbl.addWidget(ntb)
```

So now we can pack these two widgets into the vertical box that will align widgets from top to bottom.

```
self.main_widget.setFocus()
```

We set the focus on our main widget.

```
self.setCentralWidget(self.main_widget)
```

We now define it as the **central widget**. QApplication has the concept of central widget that we can think of as the main part of the application. It is not the toolbar, the menu, or anything else, rather it is the actual main functional area of the application.

```
qApp = QtGui.QApplication(sys.argv)
```

We create the QApplication instance.

```
aw = ApplicationWindow()
```

We instantiate our main window.

```
aw.show()
```
We show the main window.

```
sys.exit(qApp.exec_())
```

and at the end, start the Qt 4 main events loop.

The whole code is :

```
# for command-line arguments
import sys

# Python Qt4 bindings for GUI objects
from PyQt4 import QtGui
# Numpy functions for image creation
```

```python
import numpy as np

# Matplotlib Figure object
from matplotlib.figure import Figure
# import the Qt4Agg FigureCanvas object, that binds Figure to
# Qt4Agg backend. It also inherits from QWidget
from matplotlib.backends.backend_qt4agg \
    import FigureCanvasQTAgg as FigureCanvas
# import the NavigationToolbar Qt4Agg widget
from matplotlib.backends.backend_qt4agg \
    import NavigationToolbar2QTAgg as NavigationToolbar

class Qt4MplCanvas(FigureCanvas):
    """Class to represent the FigureCanvas widget"""
    def __init__(self, parent):
        # plot definition
        self.fig = Figure()
        self.axes = self.fig.add_subplot(111)

        t = np.arange(0.0, 3.0, 0.01)
        s = np.cos(2*np.pi*t)
        self.axes.plot(t, s)

        # initialization of the canvas
        FigureCanvas.__init__(self, self.fig)
        # set the parent widget
        self.setParent(parent)

        # we define the widget as expandable
        FigureCanvas.setSizePolicy(self,
                                    QtGui.QSizePolicy.Expanding,
                                    QtGui.QSizePolicy.Expanding)
        # notify the system of updated policy
        FigureCanvas.updateGeometry(self)

class ApplicationWindow(QtGui.QMainWindow):
    """Example main window"""
    def __init__(self):
        # initialization of Qt MainWindow widget
        QtGui.QMainWindow.__init__(self)
        # set window title
        self.setWindowTitle("Matplotlib Figure in a Qt4 Window With
NavigationToolbar")

        # instantiate a widget, it will be the main one
        self.main_widget = QtGui.QWidget(self)
        # create a vertical box layout widget
        vbl = QtGui.QVBoxLayout(self.main_widget)
        # instantiate our Matplotlib canvas widget
```

```
        qmc = Qt4MplCanvas(self.main_widget)
        # instantiate the navigation toolbar
        ntb = NavigationToolbar(qmc, self.main_widget)
        # pack these widget into the vertical box
        vbl.addWidget(qmc)
        vbl.addWidget(ntb)

        # set the focus on the main widget
        self.main_widget.setFocus()
        # set the central widget of MainWindow to main_widget
        self.setCentralWidget(self.main_widget)

# create the GUI application
qApp = QtGui.QApplication(sys.argv)
# instantiate the ApplicationWindow widget
aw = ApplicationWindow()
# show the widget
aw.show()
# start the Qt main loop execution, exiting from this script
# with the same return code of Qt application
sys.exit(qApp.exec_())
```

When we execute this application, it will show something similar to:

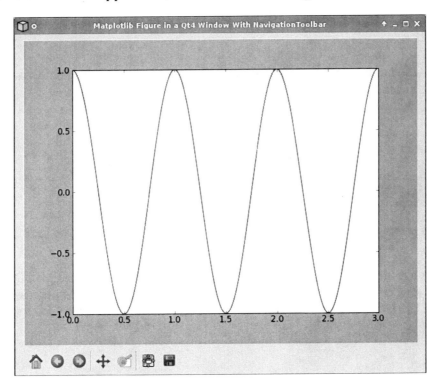

Real-time update of a Matplotlib graph

In this section, we will present a simple application—a CPU usage monitor, where we will update the Matplotlib graph in real-time (once every second over a period of 30 seconds).

As there are several indicators of CPU usage in a modern operating system, we decided to restrict our graph to the four main ones:

- **user**: The time consumed by processes executed by the users of the machine
- **nice**: The time consumed by processes executed by users but with a lower priority
- **system**: The time consumed by system tasks
- **idle**: The time consumed waiting for something to execute

The ignored indicators contribute for just a minimal part of the CPU usage, so their exclusion doesn't disturb the validity of the example.

Of those four indicators, what we will plot is the percentage of each of them against the total CPU usage.

Here we start:

```
import sys
from PyQt4 import QtGui
```

These are the modules for command-line parameters and for Python bindings of the `QtGui` submodule.

```
from matplotlib.figure import Figure
from matplotlib.backends.backend_qt4agg \
   import FigureCanvasQTAgg as FigureCanvas
```

The classic Matplotlib import for the required objects.

```
import psutil as p
```

Python is full of modules that do almost everything we can think of, so for our example, we leverage an existing module—`psutils`.

`psutil` is a multiplatform module (available for Windows, Linux, and Mac OS X) that exports a common interface to access system information such as processes, memory, CPU, and so on. We will use its functionalities to obtain the CPU usage.

```
MAXITERS = 30
```

This is the total number of iterations we want to perform. Since we perform an iteration every second, the total number of iterations equals 30 seconds of CPU usage monitoring.

```
class CPUMonitor(FigureCanvas):
```

As usual, we define a class for the Matplotlib graph elaboration.

```
def __init__(self):
    self.before = self.prepare_cpu_usage()
```

In the initialization method, we save the current CPU usage information. The algorithm we will use to update the graph needs a *previous* set of values.

```
self.fig = Figure()
self.ax = self.fig.add_subplot(111)
```

The basic Matplotlib `Figure` and `Axes` initialization.

```
FigureCanvas.__init__(self, self.fig)
```

Initialization for the canvas, referring to the `Figure` object defined earlier.

```
self.ax.set_xlim(0, 30)
self.ax.set_ylim(0, 100)
self.ax.set_autoscale_on(False)
```

We set the limits for the X-axis (to have a 30 seconds interval) and for the Y-axis (the range of percentage usage), and then disable the autoscale feature. This will allow us to have a fixed dimension `Axes`, where the plot can be redrawn without resizing the figure.

```
self.user, self.nice, self.sys, self.idle = [], [], [], []
self.l_user, = self.ax.plot([],self.user, label='User %')
self.l_nice, = self.ax.plot([],self.nice, label='Nice %')
self.l_sys,  = self.ax.plot([],self.sys,  label='Sys %')
self.l_idle, = self.ax.plot([],self.idle, label='Idle %')
```

This draws a placeholder line for the four datasets that we will use. This is important because we now have the references to the four line objects, and we can dynamically update their information without generating a new object at every iteration.

```
self.ax.legend()
```

Here, we add a legend.

```
self.fig.canvas.draw()
```

The preceding line of code forces a draw of the canvas.

```
self.cnt = 0
```

We initialize the iterations counter to 0.

```
self.timerEvent(None)
```

We make an explicit call to the method that we will use to update the graph dynamically: this is a little trick used to speed up the visualization of the plot.

```
self.timer = self.startTimer(1000)
```

With this command, we start a timer object and save the reference to `self.timer`. `QTimer` is a class that triggers an event every *n* milliseconds (the interval is specified on instantiation).

In this case, our timer will generate an event every second, and we will use this event to update our graph.

The main loop (started by `exec_()`) processes the timer events (along with all the others) and delivers them to this widget.

```
def prepare_cpu_usage(self):
```

This function will take care of preparing the CPU usage information we need.

```
t = p.cpu_times()
```

We use the `psutil cpu_times()` method to retrieve the current CPU usage.

```
if hasattr(t, 'nice'):
    return [t.user, t.nice, t.system, t.idle]
else:
    # special case for Windows, without 'nice' value
    return [t.user, 0, t.system, t.idle]
```

We check if the `nice` attribute is available. On a Unix-like system, that attribute is present, so we can return the whole set of data. On Windows, where there is no distinction between `user` and `nice` processes, the attribute is missing, so we set its value to `0` while still returning the other indicators. The net result is that we have a cross-platform code able to run on Windows and on Unix-like systems.

```
def get_cpu_usage(self):
```

We define another function to take the values from `prepare_cpu_usage()` and compute the information needed for plotting.

```
now = self.prepare_cpu_usage()
```

We take the current CPU usage values.

```
delta = [now[i]-self.before[i] for i in range(len(now))]
```

Then we compute the deltas from the previous measurement to the current one. *Delta* is the Greek letter for *d* (from difference), commonly used when dealing with differences.

Values returned from `psutil cpu_times()` are counters. They are monotonically increased from the moment the machine boots until it is turned off. What we're interested in is the amount of CPU taken by each of the four categories that we plot during the measurement interval. These commands do this evaluation.

```
total = sum(delta)
```

We compute the sum of the deltas.

```
self.before = now
```

We replace the `self.before` value with `now`, so at the next iteration, the current values will be used.

```
return [(100.0*dt)/total for dt in delta]
```

and we return the CPU usage percentage for our four categories. `dt/total` represents the fraction of the total time used by that category and multiplying it by `100.0` generates a percentage value.

```
def timerEvent(self, evt):
```

As said, events are an important part of Qt, and the main loop receives and dispatches them to the right widgets. A common way by which a widget processes events is by reimplementing *event handlers*.

In our example, `QTimer` object generates (at a regular rate of one event per second) a `QTimerEvent` that is sent to our widget (since it's the widget that started the timer).

To modify the widget behavior following the reception of an event, we need to define our own event handler, which in the case of a timer is called `timerEvent()`.

```
result = self.get_cpu_usage()
```

We get the current percentage values for CPU usage.

```
self.user.append(result[0])
self.nice.append(result[1])
self.sys.append( result[2])
self.idle.append(result[3])
```

We add them to the relevant datasets.

```
self.l_user.set_data(range(len(self.user)),  self.user)
self.l_nice.set_data(range(len(self.nice)),  self.nice)
self.l_sys.set_data( range(len(self.sys)),   self.sys)
self.l_idle.set_data(range(len(self.idle)), self.idle)
```

Now, we replot the lines with the updated information. We have added one item to each indicator's list, and now we are updating the line objects to reflect the new data. Updating the lines instead of creating a completely new plot (or removing the old lines and adding new ones) is faster and does not create any annoying visual effect on the window.

```
self.fig.canvas.draw()
```

We force a redraw of the canvas to actually show the changed lines.

```
if self.cnt == MAXITERS:
```

then we have to check if we've performed all the iterations or not.

```
self.killTimer(self.timer)
```

Once we have completed all the iterations, we stop the timer by calling `killTimer()` and passing the timer reference that we had created and saved when creating `startTimer()`.

```
else:
    self.cnt += 1
```

Alternatively, we simply increment the counter and wait for the next timer event to occur.

```
app = QtGui.QApplication(sys.argv)
```

we now start the main part of the application, and as the first thing, we create our wrapper `QApplication` instance.

```
widget = CPUMonitor()
```

Here, we create our `CPUMonitor` widget.

```
widget.setWindowTitle("30 Seconds of CPU Usage Updated in RealTime")
```

we set the window title.

```
widget.show()
```

We show the widget.

```
sys.exit(app.exec_())
```

and at the end, we start the main loop.

Here is the full example code:

```
# for command-line arguments
import sys

# Python Qt4 bindings for GUI objects
from PyQt4 import QtGui

# Matplotlib Figure object
from matplotlib.figure import Figure
# import the Qt4Agg FigureCanvas object, that binds Figure to
# Qt4Agg backend. It also inherits from QWidget
from matplotlib.backends.backend_qt4agg \
   import FigureCanvasQTAgg as FigureCanvas

# used to obtain CPU usage information
import psutil as p

# Total number of iterations
MAXITERS = 30

class CPUMonitor(FigureCanvas):
    """Matplotlib Figure widget to display CPU utilization"""
    def __init__(self):
        # save the current CPU info (used by updating algorithm)
        self.before = self.prepare_cpu_usage()

        # first image setup
        self.fig = Figure()
        self.ax = self.fig.add_subplot(111)

        # initialization of the canvas
        FigureCanvas.__init__(self, self.fig)

        # set specific limits for X and Y axes
        self.ax.set_xlim(0, 30)
        self.ax.set_ylim(0, 100)

        # and disable figure-wide autoscale
```

```
            self.ax.set_autoscale_on(False)

            # generates first "empty" plots
            self.user, self.nice, self.sys, self.idle =[], [], [], []

            self.l_user, = self.ax.plot([],self.user, label='User %')
            self.l_nice, = self.ax.plot([],self.nice, label='Nice %')
            self.l_sys,  = self.ax.plot([],self.sys,  label='Sys %')
            self.l_idle, = self.ax.plot([],self.idle, label='Idle %')

            # add legend to plot
            self.ax.legend()

            # force a redraw of the Figure
            self.fig.canvas.draw()

            # initialize the iteration counter
            self.cnt = 0

            # call the update method (to speed-up visualization)
            self.timerEvent(None)

            # start timer, trigger event every 1000 millisecs (=1sec)
            self.timer = self.startTimer(1000)

        def prepare_cpu_usage(self):
            """helper function to return CPU usage info"""

            # get the CPU times using psutil module
            t = p.cpu_times()

            # return only the values we're interested in
            if hasattr(t, 'nice'):
                return [t.user, t.nice, t.system, t.idle]
            else:
                # special case for Windows, without 'nice' value
                return [t.user, 0, t.system, t.idle]
        def get_cpu_usage(self):
            """Compute CPU usage comparing previous and current
    measurements"""

            # take the current CPU usage information
            now = self.prepare_cpu_usage()
            # compute delta between current and previous measurements
```

```
        delta = [now[i]-self.before[i] for i in range(len(now))]
        # compute the total (needed for percentages calculation)
        total = sum(delta)
        # save the current measurement to before object
        self.before = now
        # return the percentage of CPU usage for our 4 categories
        return [(100.0*dt)/total for dt in delta]

    def timerEvent(self, evt):
        """Custom timerEvent code, called at timer event receive"""
        # get the cpu percentage usage
        result = self.get_cpu_usage()

        # append new data to the datasets
        self.user.append(result[0])
        self.nice.append(result[1])
        self.sys.append( result[2])
        self.idle.append(result[3])

        # update lines data using the lists with new data
        self.l_user.set_data(range(len(self.user)), self.user)
        self.l_nice.set_data(range(len(self.nice)), self.nice)
        self.l_sys.set_data( range(len(self.sys)),  self.sys)
        self.l_idle.set_data(range(len(self.idle)), self.idle)

        # force a redraw of the Figure
        self.fig.canvas.draw()

        # if we've done all the iterations
        if self.cnt == MAXITERS:
            # stop the timer
            self.killTimer(self.timer)
        else:
            # else, we increment the counter
            self.cnt += 1

# create the GUI application
app = QtGui.QApplication(sys.argv)
# Create our Matplotlib widget
widget = CPUMonitor()
# set the window title
widget.setWindowTitle("30 Seconds of CPU Usage Updated in RealTime")
# show the widget
widget.show()
```

```
# start the Qt main loop execution, exiting from this script
# with the same return code of Qt application
sys.exit(app.exec_())
```

Here is a screenshot which was taken while running the preceding application:

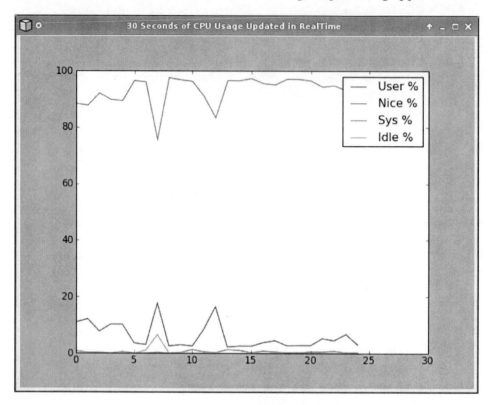

At the top of the window, we can see the green line for the CPU usage of `nice` processes, down below there is the blue line for user CPU usage, and very near the **0** we have system time (in red) and idle time (in cyan) lines, barely visible. In Chapter 7, we will present a similar technique to update a plot in real time, but with a much higher throughput.

Embedding Matplotlib in a GUI made with Qt Designer

For simple examples, designing the GUI in the Python code can be good enough, but for more complex applications, this solution does not scale.

There are some tools to help you design the GUI for Qt, and one of the most commonly used is **Qt Designer**.

Similar to Glade, we can design the user interface part of the application using on-screen form and drag-and-drop interface. Then we can connect the widgets with the backend code, where we develop the logic of the application.

The core of our example application will be plotting the frequencies of occurrences of letters in a text file: we will count the number of times each letter of the English alphabet appears in a given file and then plot this information in a bar graph.

First, we will show how to design our GUI with Qt Designer, in particular, how to create a custom Matplotlib widget managed by an external Python source file. Then, we will convert that GUI into a Python code that we can use for our main program.

This example is made up of several source files:

- `qtdesigner.ui`: UI file generated by Qt Designer
- `qtdesigner.py`: Python code generated from UI file
- `mplwidget.py`: Python code to control the custom Matplotlib widget
- `7900_06_04_qt_designer.py`: Main code used to execute the example

We start by looking at how we used the Qt Designer. This chapter is about Qt 4, so we have to use development tools for that version, for example, our Qt Designer is the one for Qt 4 (in particular, version 4.5.1).

Designing the GUI using Qt Designer

Once started, the Designer asks us what kind of form we want to design. For our purpose, we will create a *main window*. An empty window will show up, ready for designing the interface.

From that empty window, the final result will be:

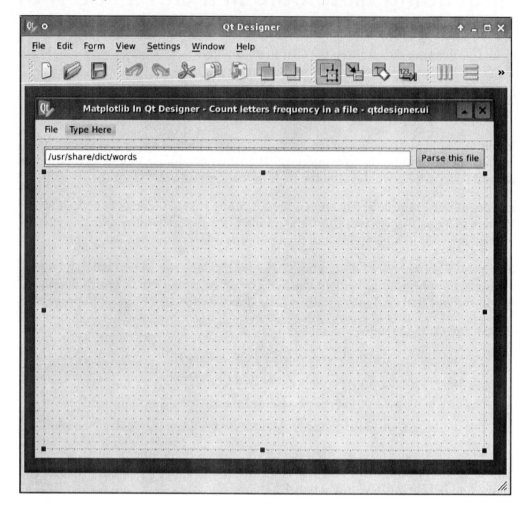

Let's see how to achieve this.

First, rename the main window to **MplMainWindow**. Double-click on the widget in the **Object Inspector** to change its name. We will rename all the widgets to start with mpl to recall Matplotlib. Then, we can also remove the status bar (as we do not use it) from the **Object Inspector**.

At this point, we can start adding the widgets that will make up our GUI.

The use of layout managers is important to obtain a nice-looking GUI. So we will add a **Horizontal Layout** widget, and then we add a **Line Edit** and a **PUSH BUTTON** widget to it.

As you can see, the **Horizontal Layout** is just *dropped* in the window right where we dragged it, without a specific layout. Now that we have a widget in the main window, we can decide its global layout. Right-click on the main window widget in the **Object Inspector**, and choose **Lay Out Vertically** from the **Lay Out** submenu.

We can see that our **Horizontal Layout** widget is now expanded to fill the whole window.

Now, place a widget right below the **Horizontal Layout**. This will be our custom widget, where we will plot Matplotlib `Figure`. Each widget is resized to take only half of the window space, but we want to give all the space we can to the custom widget.

We can achieve this by changing the size policy properties of the widget. Click on the widget, and in the **Property** editor, look for the **sizePolicy** section. Set both the, **Horizontal Policy** and **Vertical Policy** properties to **Expanding**, and the widget will be expanded to take much more space (as we expected).

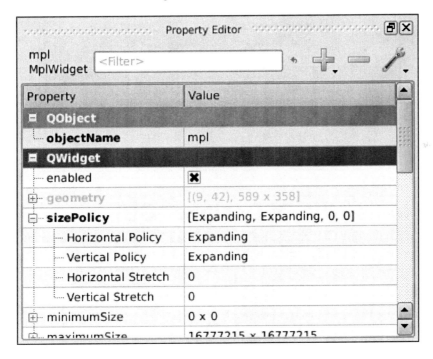

But how can we define the new widget as a custom widget? We have to *promote* it. This is the way to define a custom widget in Qt Designer:

Select the widget, right-click on it and select **Promote to...** and a window will pop up. This is where we will define our custom widget class name and the external library that manages it. We set **Promoted class name** to **MplWidget** to identify this as the widget for Matplotlib plotting, and **Header file** to **mplwidget**, that's the filename without the .py extension where we will write the Python code to govern its behavior. Add it to the promoted class, and finally promote the widget to it.

We have almost created the whole GUI, just another step left to go: add a menu with two items, one to select a file to parse and the other to close the application.

Let's see the widgets hierarchy showing the widgets names, their classes, and how they're related to each other:

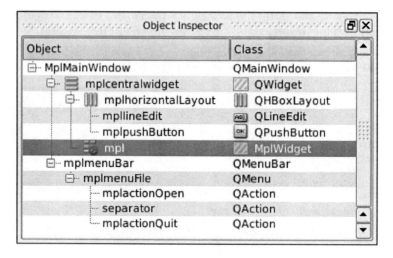

Code to use the Qt Designer GUI

Now that we have our GUI ready, let's save it to a file, we chose the filename qtdesigner.ui. The UI file format is XML, so we have to convert it to Python code, using pyuic4: pyuic4 generates Python code from the GUI designed with Qt 4 Designer.

The tool outputs the result to the terminal, so we have to redirect it into a file:

```
$ pyuic4 qtdesigner.ui > qtdesigner.py
```

If we look at the generated file, we can see that the code is structured as a single class that creates the GUI. On the last line we can see:

```
from mplwidget import MplWidget
```

```
Embed Matplotlib in Qt 4
```

This is the same name used in the **Header file** field when promoting the widget.

This import connects the custom widget with the external Python code that controls it; in our example, the file that contains that code is mplwidget.py.

So let's give it a look:

```
from PyQt4 import QtGui
from matplotlib.backends.backend_qt4agg \
   import FigureCanvasQTAgg as FigureCanvas
from matplotlib.figure import Figure
```

These are the usual imports for the Qt GUI widgets: the Matplotlib Qt4Agg backend canvas and the Figure object.

```
class MplCanvas(FigureCanvas):
    def __init__(self):
        self.fig = Figure()
        self.ax = self.fig.add_subplot(111)
        FigureCanvas.__init__(self, self.fig)
        FigureCanvas.setSizePolicy(self,
                              QtGui.QSizePolicy.Expanding,
                              QtGui.QSizePolicy.Expanding)
        FigureCanvas.updateGeometry(self)
```

This is the class that represents the Matplotlib Figure for the Qt backend; nothing new, we've already seen it in the previous examples.

```
class MplWidget(QtGui.QWidget):
```

This is an important class: the name must match with the one used for the custom widget defined in Qt Designer UI file, as this will manage widget drawing. The code is quite similar to what we already saw:

```
    def __init__(self, parent = None):
        QtGui.QWidget.__init__(self, parent)
```

Here, we initialize the widget.

```
        self.canvas = MplCanvas()
```

We instantiate the Matplotlib canvas object.

```
        self.vbl = QtGui.QVBoxLayout()
```

Here, we create a layout manager (in this case a vertical box).

```
        self.vbl.addWidget(self.canvas)
```

We add the Matplotlib canvas to the layout manager.

```
self.setLayout(self.vbl)
```

Here, we delegate the layout handling to the `vbl` object.

The main program, `7900_06_04_qt_designer.py`, will glue all the code together to create our application. It will:

- Import the UI
- Define the code to compose the application logic
- Instantiate the `QApplication` with the window layout defined by our GUI
- Start the main loop

At the beginning, we have the import part (as usual):

```
from __future__ import with_statement
```

This helps to open the file easily.

```
import numpy as np
```

NumPy is needed for its `array` support.

```
import sys
```

For command-line arguments, it is needed for `QApplication` instantiation.

```
from PyQt4 import QtCore
from PyQt4 import QtGui
```

Here, we also import `QtCore`, the Qt submodules for non-GUI, low-level functions.

```
from qtdesigner import Ui_MplMainWindow
```

We import the main window designed with Qt Designer; the name of the main window in Designer is `MplMainWindow` and so `pyuic4` creates a class called `Ui_MplMainWindow` that we can now import to have access to the main window object.

```
class DesignerMainWindow(QtGui.QMainWindow, Ui_MplMainWindow):
```

We now define a class to merge the UI we have designed (with the Qt Designer) with the code to develop the application.

```
def __init__(self, parent = None):
    super(DesignerMainWindow, self).__init__(parent)
```

We initialize the superclass.

```
self.setupUi(self)
```

`setupUi()` is a method of `Ui_MplMainWindow`, created by `pyuic4` at conversion time.It is used to create the UI. The parameter is the widget in which the user interface is created.

```
QtCore.QObject.connect(self.mplpushButton, QtCore.
SIGNAL("clicked()"), self.update_graph)
        QtCore.QObject.connect(self.mplactionOpen, QtCore.
SIGNAL('triggered()'), self.select_file)
        QtCore.QObject.connect(self.mplactionQuit, QtCore.
SIGNAL('triggered()'), QtGui.qApp, QtCore.SLOT("quit()"))
```

Here we need to introduce the concept of signals and slots.

Introduction to signals and slots

One of the fundamental (and most innovative) concepts in Qt is signals and slots.

They are a very elegant solution which was introduced by Qt to let widgets interact. **Signals** are emitted (sent) by an object that wants to notify the world that something interesting just happened (usually in response to a user interaction, such as a click), and by *connecting signals to slots*, the notification arrives to the slot of objects that are interested.

Slots are functions that respond to certain signals. When a signal is emitted, Qt executes all the slots that are connected to that signal.

We can also connect signals to other signals, creating a chain of notifications.

Signals and slots are primarily used for event handling, but they can also be used to let objects interact (keeping this fact *hidden* from them). Those objects know nothing about who emits the signals or where the slots are; it's all handled by Qt, so they are *loosely coupled*, resulting in more reusable components.

With the function `QtCore.QObject.connect()`, we connect a slot to a particular signal. The complementary function, `QtCore.QObject.disconnect()`, is used to remove the slot from the signal notification. If a signal isn't connected to a slot, nothing happens; the component that emits the signal does not know if the signal is being used or not.

The general line for `connect()` is:

```
QtCore.QObject.connect(objA, QtCore.SIGNAL("QtSig()"), objB, QtCore.
SLOT("QtSlot()"))
```

It's made of four parameters:

- The sender, `objA` — the object emitting the signal
- The signal, `QtSig` — the signal emitted
- The receiver, `objB` — the object that will receive the signal
- The slot, `QtSlot` — the slot that will react to the signal

In case `objB` is `self`, then we can omit the third argument:

```
QtCore.QObject.connect(objA, QtCore.SIGNAL("QtSig()"), QtCore.
SLOT("QtSlot()"))
```

`SIGNAL()` is used to refer a signal, while `SLOT()` is used to refer a slot. The strings passed to those functions are used to look up dictionaries of signals and slots into Qt engine, so we have to match the definition precisely.

PyQt allows any Python callable (functions mainly) to be used as a slot, not just Qt slots. This is done by simply referencing the callable. As Qt slots are implemented as class methods, they are also available as Python callables. Therefore, it is not usually necessary to use `QtCore.SLOT()` for Qt slots.

So, we will end up with a line like this one:

```
QtCore.QObject.connect(objA, QtCore.SIGNAL("QtSig()"),pyFunction)
```

In our example, we used both formats: `SLOT()` is used to connect the `quit()` slot of qApp to the `triggered()` signal of **Quit** menu item, while Python function references are used for button `clicked()` signal and **Open** menu item `triggered()` signal.

A note about the order of signals receiving: there is no fixed order for the arrival of signals at their destinations. If a signal is connected to more slots, then the slots are called in no particular order, every time the signal is emitted. Note that if two different signals are connected to two separated slots, then the slots are called in the order in which the signals are emitted.

Returning to the example

Getting back to where we stopped:

```
def select_file(self):
```

This is the function called when the menu item **Open** is selected.

```
file = QtGui.QFileDialog.getOpenFileName()
```

It creates a dialog to select a file, obtaining the selected file (if any).

```
if file:
    self.mpllineEdit.setText(file)
```

It saves the file to the **Line Edit** widget, but only if a file was selected in the dialog (think about what happens when we click on the **Cancel** button).

```
def parse_file(self, filename):
```

This function will take care of parsing the input file and extracting the information we will plot later.

```
letters = {}
```

We define the dictionary that will hold the letters information.

```
for i in range(97, 122 + 1):
    letters[chr(i)] = 0
```

we initialize that dictionary with all the lowercase English letters (identified in the ASCII table with numbers from 97 to 122) setting the value to 0.

```
with open(filename) as f:
    for line in f:
        for char in line:
            # counts only letters
            if ord(char.lower()) in range(97, 122 + 1):
                letters[char.lower()] += 1
```

For each line in the file and for each letter in that line, we check if it's a plain text letter, and in that case we increment the counter for it.

```
k = sorted(letters.keys())
v = [letters[ki] for ki in k]
return k, v
```

At the end, we return the sorted dictionary keys with the related values.

```
def update_graph(self):
```

This function is called when the **mplpushButton** button is clicked and handles the graph update.

```
l, v = self.parse_file(self.mpllineEdit.text())
```

First of all, we get the letters and their frequencies by passing the file set in the **Line Edit** widget to parse_file().

```
self.mpl.canvas.ax.clear()
```

Then we clear the `Axes` to ensure that the next plot will seem a completely new one, while we are reusing the same `Figure` and `Axes` instances.

```
self.mpl.canvas.ax.bar(np.arange(len(1))-0.25, v, width=0.5)
```

We plot a set of bars, one for each letter with the height set to the number of occurrences of that letter in the parsed file.

Note how we set up the bars: we shift their starting point by 0.25 to the left and the `width` is set to `0.5`; this will result in bars centered on the X ticks.

```
self.mpl.canvas.ax.set_xlim(xmin=-0.25, xmax=len(1)-0.75)
```

We have to adjust the X limits. As said earlier, we shifted bars start by 0.25, so the minimum X value is `-0.25`; the maximum X value is `len(1)-1` (the last tick position) but then we have to add 0.25 (half the bar width). With these limits, we have the bars perfectly fitting into the plot area.

```
self.mpl.canvas.ax.set_xticks(range(len(1)))
self.mpl.canvas.ax.set_xticklabels(1)
```

We set the X-axis ticks with their labels (the letters).

```
self.mpl.canvas.ax.get_yaxis().grid(True)
```

We draw a grid on the plot, but only for the Y-axis

```
self.mpl.canvas.draw()
```

Then we force a redraw of the canvas to show the changes we just did.

```
app = QtGui.QApplication(sys.argv)
```

As usual, we instantiate a `QApplication` to wrap our widget.

```
dmw = DesignerMainWindow()
```

we instantiate the main window.

```
dmw.show()
```

We show the main window.

```
sys.exit(app.exec_())
```

Then, we start the Qt main loop.

The complete source code for `mplwidget.py` is:

```python
# Python Qt4 bindings for GUI objects
from PyQt4 import QtGui

# import the Qt4Agg FigureCanvas object, that binds Figure to
# Qt4Agg backend. It also inherits from QWidget
from matplotlib.backends.backend_qt4agg \
  import FigureCanvasQTAgg as FigureCanvas

# Matplotlib Figure object
from matplotlib.figure import Figure

class MplCanvas(FigureCanvas):
    """Class to represent the FigureCanvas widget"""
    def __init__(self):
        # setup Matplotlib Figure and Axis
        self.fig = Figure()
        self.ax = self.fig.add_subplot(111)

        # initialization of the canvas
        FigureCanvas.__init__(self, self.fig)
        # we define the widget as expandable
        FigureCanvas.setSizePolicy(self,
                            QtGui.QSizePolicy.Expanding,
                            QtGui.QSizePolicy.Expanding)
        # notify the system of updated policy
        FigureCanvas.updateGeometry(self)


class MplWidget(QtGui.QWidget):
    """Widget defined in Qt Designer"""
    def __init__(self, parent = None):
        # initialization of Qt MainWindow widget
        QtGui.QWidget.__init__(self, parent)
        # set the canvas to the Matplotlib widget
        self.canvas = MplCanvas()
        # create a vertical box layout
        self.vbl = QtGui.QVBoxLayout()
        # add mpl widget to vertical box
        self.vbl.addWidget(self.canvas)
        # set the layout to th vertical box
        self.setLayout(self.vbl)
```

The whole source code for `7900_06_04_qt_designer.py` is:

```python
# used to parse files more easily
from __future__ import with_statement

# Numpy module
import numpy as np

# for command-line arguments
import sys

# Qt4 bindings for core Qt functionalities (non-GUI)
from PyQt4 import QtCore
# Python Qt4 bindings for GUI objects
from PyQt4 import QtGui

# import the MainWindow widget from the converted .ui files
from qtdesigner import Ui_MplMainWindow

class DesignerMainWindow(QtGui.QMainWindow, Ui_MplMainWindow):
    """Customization for Qt Designer created window"""
    def __init__(self, parent = None):
        # initialization of the superclass
        super(DesignerMainWindow, self).__init__(parent)
        # setup the GUI --> function generated by pyuic4
        self.setupUi(self)

        # connect the signals with the slots
        QtCore.QObject.connect(self.mplpushButton, QtCore.
SIGNAL("clicked()"), self.update_graph)
        QtCore.QObject.connect(self.mplactionOpen, QtCore.
SIGNAL('triggered()'), self.select_file)
        QtCore.QObject.connect(self.mplactionQuit, QtCore.
SIGNAL('triggered()'), QtGui.qApp, QtCore.SLOT("quit()"))

    def select_file(self):
        """opens a file select dialog"""
        # open the dialog and get the selected file
        file = QtGui.QFileDialog.getOpenFileName()
        # if a file is selected
        if file:
            # update the lineEdit text with the selected filename
            self.mpllineEdit.setText(file)

    def parse_file(self, filename):
```

```
        """Parse a text file to extract letters frequencies"""
        # dict initialization
        letters = {}

        # lower-case letter ordinal numbers
        for i in range(97, 122 + 1):
            letters[chr(i)] = 0

        # parse the input file
        with open(filename) as f:
            for line in f:
                for char in line:
                    # counts only letters
                    if ord(char.lower()) in range(97, 122 + 1):
                        letters[char.lower()] += 1

        # compute the ordered list of keys and relative values
        k = sorted(letters.keys())
        v = [letters[ki] for ki in k]

        return k, v

    def update_graph(self):
        """Updates the graph with new letters frequencies"""

        # get the letters frequencies
        l, v = self.parse_file(self.mpllineEdit.text())

        # clear the Axes
        self.mpl.canvas.ax.clear()

        # draw a bar chart for letters and their frequencies
        # set width to 0.5 and shift bars of 0.25, to be centered
        self.mpl.canvas.ax.bar(np.arange(len(l))-0.25, v, width=0.5)
        # reset the X limits
        self.mpl.canvas.ax.set_xlim(xmin=-0.25, xmax=len(l)-0.75)
        # set the X ticks & tickslabel as the letters
        self.mpl.canvas.ax.set_xticks(range(len(l)))
        self.mpl.canvas.ax.set_xticklabels(l)
        # enable grid only on the Y axis
        self.mpl.canvas.ax.get_yaxis().grid(True)
        # force an image redraw
        self.mpl.canvas.draw()
```

```
# create the GUI application
app = QtGui.QApplication(sys.argv)
# instantiate the main window
dmw = DesignerMainWindow()
# show it
dmw.show()
# start the Qt main loop execution, exiting from this script
# with the same return code of Qt application
sys.exit(app.exec_())
```

A screenshot of the application running, where we can see a bar for each letter with heights corresponding to the number of occurrences of that letter in the file is as follows:

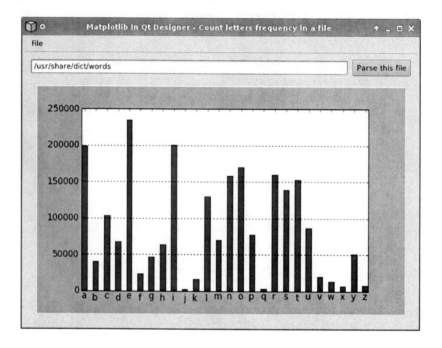

Summary

In this chapter, we learned how to use Qt and Matplotlib together. Now we know how to:

- Embed a `Figure` in a `QWidget`
- Use layout manager to pack a `Figure` and navigation toolbar in a `QWidget`
- Create a timer, react to events, and update a Matplotlib graph accordingly
- Use Qt Designer to draw a simple GUI and then refer it into our Python code

We are now ready to learn about another GUI library, wxWidgets.

7
Embedding Matplotlib in wxWidgets

This chapter will explain how we can use Matplotlib in the wxWidgets framework, particularly using the wxPython bindings.

The contents we will present in this chapter are:

- A brief introduction to wxWidgets and wxPython
- A simple example of embedding Matplotlib in wxWidgets
- Extending the previous example to include the Matplotlib navigation toolbar
- How to update a Matplotlib plot in real-time using the wxWidgets framework
- How to design a GUI with wxGlade and embed a Matplotlib `Figure` in it

Let's first start with an overview of the features of wxWidgets and wxPython.

Brief introduction to wxWidgets and wxPython

wxWidgets (formerly known as wxWindows, now available at `http://www.wxwidgets.org/`) is a widget toolkit used for creating GUIs.

One of its most important features is cross-platform portability: it currently supports Windows, Mac OS X, Linux (with X11, Motif, and GTK+ libraries), OS/2, and several other operating systems and platforms (including an embedded version which is currently under development).

wxWidgets would be best described as a *native mode toolkit* because it provides a thin API abstraction layer across platforms, and uses platform-native widgets under the hood, as opposed to emulating them. Using native controls gives wxWidgets applications a natural and familiar look and feel.

On the other hand, introducing an additional layer can result in a slight performance penalty, although this is unlikely to be noticed in the kind of applications we will commonly develop.

wxWidgets is not restricted to GUI development and it's more than just a graphics toolkit, providing a whole set of additional facilities, such as database libraries, inter-process communication layer, networking functionalities, and so on.

Though it's written in C++, there are several bindings for many commonly used programming languages. Among them is Python binding provided by wxPython.

wxPython (available at `http://www.wxpython.org/`) is a Python extension module that provides a set of bindings to the Python language from the wxWidgets library. This extension module allows Python programmers to create instances of wxWidgets classes and to invoke methods of those classes.

wxPython mirrors many of the wxWidgets GUI classes and functions, and the differences that exist are only because of the intrinsic differences between C++ and Python. Therefore, if we already know how to program with wxWidgets, using wxPython is quite straightforward.

Embedding a Matplotlib figure in a wxFrame

We will present examples by commenting each relevant source code block, and at the end, we will show the complete source code.

In the first example, we will describe how to embed a Matplotlib `Figure` in a `wxFrame`.

`wxFrame` is one of the most important widgets in wxWidgets. It's considered to be a *container* because it contains other widgets. `wxFrame` consists of a title bar, borders, and a center container area: the classic application window layout.

The example code starts with:

```
import wx
```

This is the main wxPython module. It contains all the submodules, objects, and functions for the wxWidgets library. Every application that uses wxPython imports this module.

```
from matplotlib.figure import Figure
import numpy as np
```

These are the usual imports of Matplotlib `Figure` and NumPy module.

```
from matplotlib.backends.backend_wxagg import \
    FigureCanvasWxAgg as FigureCanvas
```

Here is the import of the backend-specific `FigureCanvas` object: this class also inherits from `wxPanel`, so it's indeed a wxPython object that we can embed into a wxWidgets application.

```
class MplCanvasFrame(wx.Frame):
```

Every application must have a top-level `wxFrame`. What we are doing here is creating a customized `wxFrame`. In the classic object-oriented programming style, we inherit from a class and change its behavior to our own needs.

```
    def __init__(self):
```

In the initialization method, we will write the main code because in this small example, we don't need any additional methods.

```
        wx.Frame.__init__(self, None, wx.ID_ANY,
                    title='Matplotlib in Wx', size=(600, 400))
```

Here, we initialize the superclass. The parameters are:

- `parent`: In this case, set to `None` meaning we don't have a parent (it's a top-level window); it's common for a `wxFrame` to have no parent because it is the parent of *other* widgets.

- `id`: An identifier for the wxWidgets object, in this case set to `wx.ID_ANY`, which means to request an ID to the system (so we don't have to specify one). As `wx.ID_ANY` is equal to -1, sometimes we can also find this value specified in the initialization calls (although it's a bad practice).

- `title`: This will be the window title.

- `size`: We choose a size that is exactly the same as that of the `Figure`.

```
        self.figure = Figure(figsize=(6, 4), dpi=100)
        self.axes = self.figure.add_subplot(111)
        x = np.arange(0, 6, .01)
        y = np.sin(x**2)*np.exp(-x)
        self.axes.plot(x, y)
```

This is the Matplotlib code to create a sample plot.

```
self.canvas = FigureCanvas(self, wx.ID_ANY, self.figure)
```

Here we initialize the `FigureCanvas`: using the `WxAgg` backend, we pass the `parent` set to `self`, the current `wxFrame`, the `id` as a system-defined one, and then the `Figure` Matplotlib object to render.

```
app = wx.PySimpleApp()
```

Every wxWidgets application must be wrapped inside one `wxApp` instance which ensures that the GUI platform and wxWidgets are fully loaded and functional.

`PySimpleApp` is a simpler application class that we can use directly, particularly for small examples.

```
frame = MplCanvasFrame()
```

Now that we have created an application, we can also initialize the custom `wxFrame` object that will draw the Matplotlib plot.

```
frame.Show(True)
```

A call to `Show()` is needed to actually display the `wxFrame` on screen

```
app.MainLoop().
```

In the end, we start the main loop for events processing. After the `MainLoop()` is called, wxWidgets takes control and starts to check for events: whenever an event occurs, wxWidgets framework will dispatch it to the appropriate event handler.

The full code for this example is:

```
# wxPython module
import wx

# Matplotlib Figure object
from matplotlib.figure import Figure
# Numpy functions for image creation
import numpy as np
```

```
# import the WxAgg FigureCanvas object, that binds Figure to
# WxAgg backend. In this case, this is a wxPanel
from matplotlib.backends.backend_wxagg import \
  FigureCanvasWxAgg as FigureCanvas


class MplCanvasFrame(wx.Frame):
    """Class to represent a Matplotlib Figure as a wxFrame"""
    def __init__(self):
        # initialize the superclass, the wx.Frame
        wx.Frame.__init__(self, None, wx.ID_ANY,
                        title='Matplotlib in Wx', size=(600, 400))

        # usual Matplotlib functions
        self.figure = Figure()#figsize=(6, 4), dpi=100)
        self.axes = self.figure.add_subplot(111)
        x = np.arange(0, 6, .01)
        y = np.sin(x**2)*np.exp(-x)
        self.axes.plot(x, y)

        # initialize the FigureCanvas, mapping the figure to
        # the Wx backend
        self.canvas = FigureCanvas(self, wx.ID_ANY, self.figure)


# Create a wrapper wxWidgets application
app = wx.PySimpleApp()
# instantiate the Matplotlib wxFrame
frame = MplCanvasFrame()
# show it
frame.Show(True)
# start wxWidgets mainloop
app.MainLoop()
```

If we execute the previous example, the following screenshot will be displayed:

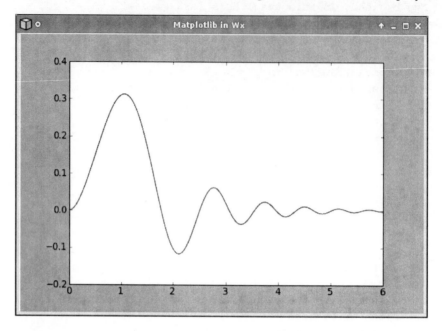

Including a navigation toolbar

Matplotlib's interactive plots present together with a graph, a very handy toolbar that has several buttons with common operations. We may be interested in using the same toolbar in our wxWidgets applications, so let's see how we can achieve this, extending the previous example:

```
import wx
```

First, we import the wx module needed to have access to wxPython library.

```
from matplotlib.figure import Figure
```

Here is the import for Matplotlib Figure object, the backend-independent plot representation.

```
import numpy as np
```

The import of NumPy module that is used to create a sample plot.

```
from matplotlib.backends.backend_wxagg import \
    FigureCanvasWxAgg as FigureCanvas
from matplotlib.backends.backend_wx import NavigationToolbar2Wx
```

These are the imports for the backend-specific `FigureCanvas` and a navigation toolbar.

```
class MplCanvasFrame(wx.Frame):
```

As we have seen before, we define our own `wxFrame` to render the `Figure` and toolbar. Let's repeat that the `wxFrame` is the classic application top-level window.

```
def __init__(self):
    wx.Frame.__init__(self, None, wx.ID_ANY, size=(600, 400),
            title='Matplotlib Figure with Navigation Toolbar')
```

We now initialize the superclass, calling its `__init__` method with `None` as `parent` (as it will be the top-level window, it has no parent object), then, we ask for a system-generated ID, we set the window dimensions, and lastly, we set the window title.

```
self.figure = Figure()
self.axes = self.figure.add_subplot(111)
x = np.arange(0, 6, .01)
y = np.sin(x**2)*np.exp(-x)
self.axes.plot(x, y)
```

This is the code to generate the Matplotlib plot.

```
self.canvas = FigureCanvas(self, wx.ID_ANY, self.figure)
```

This maps the `Figure` object to the backend-dependent canvas.

```
self.sizer = wx.BoxSizer(wx.VERTICAL)
```

Here we create a `BoxSizer` object. One of the biggest problems in GUI design is how to react to changes in canvas size, a problem commonly referred to as *layout management*.

The layout managers for wxWidgets are the **sizer widgets**: they are the containers for widgets (including other sizers) that will handle the visual arrangement of widgets' dimensions according to our configuration. BoxSizer takes one parameter, its orientation. In this case, we pass the constant. wx.VERTICAL to have widgets laid in a column, but there is also the constant. wx.HORIZONTAL to have a row of widgets.

```
self.sizer.Add(self.canvas, 1, wx.LEFT | wx.TOP | wx.EXPAND)
```

We are now able to add our FigureCanvas object to the sizer. The arguments of the Add() function are really important:

- The first parameter is a reference to the object to be added.
- Then, we have the second parameter: proportion—this is used to express how much of the additional free space should be assigned to this widget. Often, the widgets on a GUI don't take up all the space, so there is some extra space available. This space is redistributed to all the widgets based on the proportion value of each widget and all the widgets present in the GUI. Let's take an example: if we have three widgets respectively with proportion set to 0, 1, and 2, then the first (with proportion set to 0) will not change at all, while the third (with proportion set to 2) will change twice more than the second (with proportion set to 1). In the book example we set it to 1, so we declare that the widget should take one slot of the free space available when resizing.
- The third parameter is a combination of flags to further configure widget behavior in the sizer: it controls borders, alignment, separation between widgets, and expansions. Here we declare that the FigureCanvas should expand when the window is resized.

Note that adding a widget to a sizer does not make the sizer the parent widget: the canvas parent is still self (wxFrame).

```
self.toolbar = NavigationToolbar2Wx(self.canvas)
```

We now create an instance of the navigation toolbar, and we set the FigureCanvas object as the parent.

```
self.toolbar.Realize()
```

This call is not needed on Linux systems , however it is required on the Windows ones. This method must be called after all the buttons have been added to the toolbar (in case we have added custom ones), and it will reorder and place them in a platform-specific manner.

```
self.sizer.Add(self.toolbar, 0, wx.LEFT | wx.EXPAND)
```

We add the toolbar to the sizer; objects are packed in the sizer as they are added to it, so the navigation toolbar will be right below the `Figure` object. The `proportion` parameter is set to `0`, so that only the minimum sizes of the toolbar will be used. Nonetheless, we request the widget to expand, but this will happen only when resizing the width of the window. The height of the toolbar will always be the same.

```
self.toolbar.Show()
```

We explicitly show the toolbar, making a call to its `Show()` method.

```
self.SetSizer(self.sizer)
```

We now set this sizer as the layout manager for the main window. As we are inheriting from `wxPanel`, a call to `self` tells the top-level window to use this sizer.

```
self.Fit()
```

Then, we call the `Fit()` method on the `wxFrame` object. This method is used to calculate the initial size and position of each widget to fit nicely in the `wxFrame`.

```
class MplApp(wx.App):
```

Here we define a new class, inheriting from `wxApp` to create a customized application where we will embed the `Frame` object previously defined.

As said before, every wxWidgets application must be wrapped inside a `wxApp`: here, we can see how to inherit from it in order to customize its behavior to our needs.

```
def OnInit(self):
```

`OnInit` is the only method that we will write for this class, as it is called as part of system initialization when creating an application. The purpose of `OnInit` is to create a window and all the other objects necessary for the program to be operational.

```
frame = MplCanvasFrame()
```

We create an instance of our Matplotlib `wxFrame`.

```
self.SetTopWindow(frame)
```

We inform the wxWidgets system that our frame is one of the top-level windows. The application can only terminate when all the top-level windows have been closed.

```
frame.Show(True)
```

Then we force a show on the frame.

```
        return True
```

Finally, we return `True`: returning `True` signals to continue processing. If we had returned `False`, then the application would have exited immediately.

```
    mplapp = MplApp(False)
```

At this point, in the main part of the code, we create an instance of our application; the `redirect` parameter (the only one needed) is set to `False` to let errors go to the interpreter (instead of popping up a window).

```
    mplapp.MainLoop()
```

We can now start the main loop of events processing.

The full source code of the example is:

```
# wxPython module
import wx

# Matplotlib Figure object
from matplotlib.figure import Figure
# Numpy functions for image creation
import numpy as np

# import the WxAgg FigureCanvas object, that binds Figure to
# WxAgg backend. In this case, this is also a wxPanel
from matplotlib.backends.backend_wxagg import \
  FigureCanvasWxAgg as FigureCanvas
# import the NavigationToolbar WxAgg widget
from matplotlib.backends.backend_wx import NavigationToolbar2Wx


class MplCanvasFrame(wx.Frame):
    """Class to represent a Matplotlib Figure as a wxFrame"""
    def __init__(self):
        wx.Frame.__init__(self, None, wx.ID_ANY, size=(600, 400),
                title='Matplotlib Figure with Navigation Toolbar')
        # usual Matplotlib functions
        self.figure = Figure()
        self.axes = self.figure.add_subplot(111)
        x = np.arange(0, 6, .01)
        y = np.sin(x**2)*np.exp(-x)
        self.axes.plot(x, y)
```

```python
        # initialize the FigureCanvas, mapping the figure to
        # the WxAgg backend
        self.canvas = FigureCanvas(self, wx.ID_ANY, self.figure)

        # create an BoxSizer, to define the layout of our window
        self.sizer = wx.BoxSizer(wx.VERTICAL)
        # add the figure canvas
        self.sizer.Add(self.canvas, 1, wx.LEFT | wx.TOP | wx.EXPAND)

        # instantiate the Navigation Toolbar
        self.toolbar = NavigationToolbar2Wx(self.canvas)
        # needed to support Windows systems
        self.toolbar.Realize()
        # add it to the sizer
        self.sizer.Add(self.toolbar, 0, wx.LEFT | wx.EXPAND)
        # explicitly show the toolbar
        self.toolbar.Show()

        # sets the window to have the given layout sizer
        self.SetSizer(self.sizer)
        # adapt sub-widget sizes to fit the window size,
        # following sizer specification
        self.Fit()

class MplApp(wx.App):
    """Define customized wxApp for MplCanvasFrame"""
    def OnInit(self):
        # instantiate our custom wxFrame
        frame = MplCanvasFrame()
        # set it at the top-level window
        self.SetTopWindow(frame)
        # show it
        frame.Show(True)
        # return True to continue processing
        return True

# we instantiate our wxApp class
mplapp = MplApp(False)
# and start the main loop
mplapp.MainLoop()
```

If we execute the preceding application, then the following window will appear

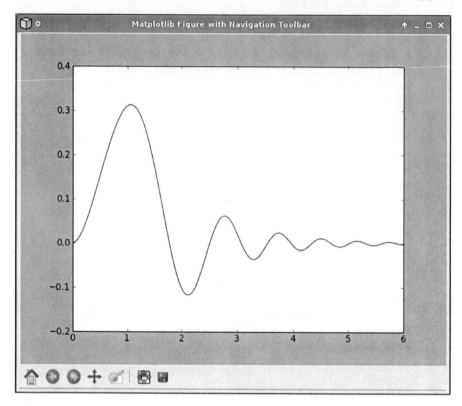

Real-time plots update

In several situations, data is generated in real time, and we want to plot it as it comes. Being able to process data and generate dynamic plots that are continuously updated is very interesting.

We are going to present an example where we take a sample of a quantity, and we show its progression in a real-time plot.

The information we will collect is CPU utilization; in a modern operating system, there are several processes always running on a machine, each using a part of the CPU time. On a Unix system, we can identify the major part of the time as being used by:

- System processes (sys)
- User processes (user)

- User processes with lower priority, for example, for background processing (`nice`)
- Time not used (`idle`)

Between parenthesis, we reported the name that we will use in our code to represent that slice of CPU usage.

We will use an additional module, `psutil` (available at `http://code.google.com/p/psutil/`), to gather information about CPU usage. The module is cross-platform (it's available for Linux, Windows, and Mac OS X), and it abstracts from the operating system to present a common layer to access run-time information. It allows us to query process information along with several other system indicators.

We will also use a particular way to update the plot in real time (borrowed from computer graphics) that grants a very high throughput (but requires a bit of additional work).

We now start to show the code, and we discuss some aspects in details during description:

```
import wx
```

this module is needed to access wxWidgets library objects, widgets, and functions.

```
from matplotlib.figure import Figure
import matplotlib.font_manager as font_manager
```

We import the usual Matplotlib `Figure` but this time we also need the font manager.

```
from matplotlib.backends.backend_wxagg import \
  FigureCanvasWxAgg as FigureCanvas
```

Then, we import the backend-specific `FigureCanvas`.

```
import psutil as p
```

Here, we import `psutil`: in this example, we are interested in CPU usage, and `psutil` allows us to run the code on Linux, Mac OS X, and Windows without modifications.

```
TIMER_ID = wx.NewId()
```

Now we define an ID (that is guaranteed to be unique during application lifecycle) to identify the timer in the application.

A **timer** is an object that triggers an event at every given time interval. We will use those events to update the plot.

```
POINTS = 300
```

The number of data points we will use in our plot.

```
class PlotFigure(wx.Frame):
```

This will be the main wxFrame of the application where we will embed the animated Matplotlib Figure.

```
    def __init__(self):
        wx.Frame.__init__(self, None, wx.ID_ANY, title="CPU Usage
Monitor", size=(600, 400))
```

As usual, while initializing this object, we also initialize the superclass where we specify the window's title and size.

```
        self.fig = Figure((6, 4), 100)
        self.canvas = FigureCanvas(self, wx.ID_ANY, self.fig)
        self.ax = self.fig.add_subplot(111)
```

Here we prepare the Matplotlib Figure object, creating a new one and binding it to the backend-specific FigureCanvas; at the end, we create the Axes instance by adding a subplot to the Figure.

```
        self.ax.set_ylim([0, 100])
        self.ax.set_xlim([0, POINTS])
        self.ax.set_autoscale_on(False)
```

We want our plot to have constant dimensions to avoid the unpleasant effect of axes resizing at each update.

To do so, we set the X and Y limits, by using the xlim() and ylim() functions (we prefer two separate function calls instead of a call to axis() for clarity) and then disable the autoscale feature.

The Axes limits are set to be percentage values on the Y-axis (so between 0 and 100) and the number of data points we want to keep on the X-axis (300).

```
        self.ax.set_xticks([])
```

We remove the ticks and labels from the X-axis as the update effect can be unpleasant.

```
        self.ax.set_yticks(range(0, 101, 10))
```

As the percentage value varies from 0 to 100, we decided to partition the Y-axis every 10 units. We use `101` as the higher value in `range()` as a trick to make the value "100" appear in the list.

```
self.ax.grid(True)
```

We draw the grid: this will be made up of only horizontal lines, originating from the Y ticks, as we removed the ticks from the X-axis.

```
self.user = [None] * POINTS
self.nice = [None] * POINTS
self.sys  = [None] * POINTS
self.idle = [None] * POINTS
```

Here, we create four lists of `POINTS` (300) items to contain the data we will be plotting. We use `None` to initialize them because `None` represents *lack of data* and is not plotted (at the contrary of 0, which represents a valid position in the axes and hence is plotted).

```
self.l_user,=self.ax.plot(range(POINTS),self.user,label='User %')
self.l_nice,=self.ax.plot(range(POINTS),self.nice,label='Nice %')
self.l_sys, =self.ax.plot(range(POINTS),self.sys, label='Sys %')
self.l_idle,=self.ax.plot(range(POINTS),self.idle,label='Idle %')
```

We now plot four empty lines; they are just markers and will be updated as the data comes in.

```
self.ax.legend(loc='upper center',
               ncol=4,
               prop=font_manager.FontProperties(size=10))
```

We would also like to draw a legend on the plot. The parameters of the `legend()` function are:

- `loc`: The location of the legend, in this case at the upper center of the `figure`.
- `ncol`: The number of columns in the legend; it's usually 1, so the legend is rendered as a vertical list. But in this case, we prefer a horizontal list, so we set the number of columns equal to the number of lines.
- `prop`: The properties for the legend text; here we have reduced the text font to `10` points.

```
self.canvas.draw()
```

We force a draw on the canvas: this is needed to let the grid and the legend be rendered on the `Figure`; without this call, we would not be able to see them.

```
self.bg = self.canvas.copy_from_bbox(self.ax.bbox)
```

This is the first part of the particular method we will use to animate the plot. We save the plot background that is currently made up of empty Axes (no visible lines), the grid, and the legend.

Technically, what we are doing here is saving a rectangular region into a pixel buffer, in this case, the Axes bounding box (bbox).

```
self.before = self.prepare_cpu_usage()
```

We take the first set of values of CPU usage because the update algorithm needs two sets to work — (the current and the *previous* one).

```
wx.EVT_TIMER(self, TIMER_ID, self.onTimer)
```

As said, we use a timer to trigger an event at the specified interval: now we are defining that in response to those timer events. The callback function to call is self.onTimer. Note how we have used the TIMER_ID identifier to match the timer object.

```
def prepare_cpu_usage(self):
```

This function is used to get the CPU information and return them in a format we expect.

```
t = p.cpu_times()
```

We use psutil module's cpu_times() function to obtain the CPU usage information.

```
if hasattr(t, 'nice'):
    return [t.user, t.nice, t.system, t.idle]
else:
    return [t.user, 0, t.system, t.idle]
```

As t.nice is not available on Windows systems, we check if that attribute is present. If it is, we return the complete dataset, otherwise we return 0 in replacement of the missing attribute. This grants for portable code that works on both Unix-like and Windows systems.

```
def get_cpu_usage(self):
```

This is the function that will generate the information we will plot: the CPU usage percentage.

```
now = self.prepare_cpu_usage()
```

Here we take a snapshot of the current CPU usage.

```
delta = [now[i]-self.before[i] for i in range(len(now))]
```

Now we compute the deltas between the current and previous relative values. We need to do this because operating systems keep CPU usage as additive counters while we are interested in the difference between the previous and the current measurements.

```
total = sum(delta)
```

We compute the total CPU usage by summing up the `delta` items.

```
self.before = now
```

We replace the `before` variable with the current CPU information stored in now.

```
return [(100.0*dt)/total for dt in delta]
```

At the end, we return the usage percentage for each category, dividing each `delta` item by the `total` CPU usage and multiplying it by `100.0`.

```
def onTimer(self, evt):
```

This is the callback function called upon receiving timer events, and it will update our plot.

```
tmp = self.get_cpu_usage()
```

We get the CPU usage percentage as the first thing.

```
self.canvas.restore_region(self.bg)
```

Then we restore the background (the `Axes` bounding box) saved during the execution of the __init__ method.

```
self.user = self.user[1:]  + [tmp[0]]
self.nice = self.nice[1:]  + [tmp[1]]
self.sys  = self.sys[1:]   + [tmp[2]]
self.idle = self.idle[1:]  + [tmp[3]]
```

Then we update the data lists. We remove the first item from the lists and append the new values. This will keep the data points' count constant, generating a *flow* in the line's plot from right to left.

```
self.l_user.set_ydata(self.user)
self.l_nice.set_ydata(self.nice)
self.l_sys.set_ydata( self.sys)
self.l_idle.set_ydata(self.idle)
```

We now update the lines `ydata` with the updated lists.

```
self.ax.draw_artist(self.l_user)
self.ax.draw_artist(self.l_nice)
self.ax.draw_artist(self.l_sys)
self.ax.draw_artist(self.l_idle)
```

and we force a draw only on the `Lines` objects over the clean background.

```
self.canvas.blit(self.ax.bbox)
```

Here comes the magic: the `blit()` function.

A simple approach to the animation problem would lead to a solution where we redraw the complete `Figure` each time (by using `draw()` method, for example), even if just one element was updated.

The idea behind `blit()` is drawing the background and animating objects over it.

Once we have restored the clean background with `self.canvas.restore_region(self.bg)`, we can draw the animated lines on top of it with `self.ax.draw_artist(<line ref>)`, and afterwards, the `blit()` function copies this result to the window.

Even though Matplotlib is not designed specifically for animated plots, with this technique, we can obtain a very high rate of **FPS (frames per second)**.

```
if __name__ == '__main__':
    app = wx.PySimpleApp()
```

When we execute the example, we instantiate the wxWidgets wrapper application.

```
frame = PlotFigure()
```

then we instantiate the `wxFrame` object defined earlier.

```
t = wx.Timer(frame, TIMER_ID)
```

We create a timer by binding it to the frame instance and assigning the `TIMER_ID`: this will allow us to identify the timer throughout the application.

```
t.Start(50)
```

We start the timer, specifying that it should trigger an event every 50 milliseconds: the `blit()` technique allows a very fast update cycle.

```
frame.Show()
```

Then we show the frame.

```
app.MainLoop()
```

Now, we start the application main loop for events processing.

Here is the full example code:

```python
# wxPython module
import wx

# Matplotlib Figure object
from matplotlib.figure import Figure
# Matplotlib font manager
import matplotlib.font_manager as font_manager

# import the WxAgg FigureCanvas object, that binds Figure to
# WxAgg backend. In this case, this is also a wxPanel
from matplotlib.backends.backend_wxagg import \
  FigureCanvasWxAgg as FigureCanvas

# used to obtain CPU usage information
import psutil as p

# wxWidgets object ID for the timer
TIMER_ID = wx.NewId()

# number of data points
POINTS = 300

class PlotFigure(wx.Frame):
    """Matplotlib wxFrame with animation effect"""

    def __init__(self):
        # initialize the super class
        wx.Frame.__init__(self, None, wx.ID_ANY, title="CPU Usage
Monitor", size=(600, 400))

        # Matplotlib Figure
        self.fig = Figure((6, 4), 100)
        # bind the Figure to the backend specific canvas
        self.canvas = FigureCanvas(self, wx.ID_ANY, self.fig)
        # add a subplot
        self.ax = self.fig.add_subplot(111)
```

```
# limit the X and Y axes dimensions
# we prefer 2 separate functions for clarity
self.ax.set_ylim([0, 100])
self.ax.set_xlim([0, POINTS])
# but we want a "frozen" window (defined by y/xlim functions)
self.ax.set_autoscale_on(False)

# we do not want ticks on X axis
self.ax.set_xticks([])
# we want a tick every 10 point on Y (101 is to have 100 too)
self.ax.set_yticks(range(0, 101, 10))
# disable autoscale, since we don't want the Axes to adapt
# draw a grid (it will be only for Y)
self.ax.grid(True)

# generates first "empty" plots
self.user = [None] * POINTS
self.nice = [None] * POINTS
self.sys  = [None] * POINTS
self.idle = [None] * POINTS

self.l_user,=self.ax.plot(range(POINTS),self.user,label='User
%')
self.l_nice,=self.ax.plot(range(POINTS),self.nice,label='Nice
%')
self.l_sys, =self.ax.plot(range(POINTS),self.sys, label='Sys
%')
self.l_idle,=self.ax.plot(range(POINTS),self.idle,label='Idle
%')

# add the legend
self.ax.legend(loc='upper center',
                ncol=4,
                prop=font_manager.FontProperties(size=10))

# force a draw on the canvas()
# trick to show the grid and the legend
self.canvas.draw()

# save the clean background - everything but the line
# is drawn and saved in the pixel buffer background
self.bg = self.canvas.copy_from_bbox(self.ax.bbox)

# take a snapshot of CPU usage, needed for the update
algorithm
```

```
        self.before = self.prepare_cpu_usage()

        # bind events coming from timer with id = TIMER_ID
        # to the onTimer callback function
        wx.EVT_TIMER(self, TIMER_ID, self.onTimer)


    def prepare_cpu_usage(self):
        """helper function to return CPU usage info"""

        # get the CPU times using psutil module
        t = p.cpu_times()

        # return only the values we're interested in
        if hasattr(t, 'nice'):
            return [t.user, t.nice, t.system, t.idle]
        else:
            # special case for Windows, without 'nice' value
            return [t.user, 0, t.system, t.idle]

    def get_cpu_usage(self):
        """Compute CPU usage comparing previous and current
measurements"""

        # take the current CPU usage information
        now = self.prepare_cpu_usage()
        # compute deltas between current and previous measurements
        delta = [now[i]-self.before[i] for i in range(len(now))]
        # compute the total (needed for percentages calculation)
        total = sum(delta)
        # save the current measurement to before object
        self.before = now
        # return the percentage of CPU usage for our 4 categories
        return [(100.0*dt)/total for dt in delta]


    def onTimer(self, evt):
        """callback function for timer events"""

        # get the CPU usage information
        tmp = self.get_cpu_usage()

        # restore the clean background, saved at the beginning
        self.canvas.restore_region(self.bg)
```

```
            # update the data
            self.user = self.user[1:] + [tmp[0]]
            self.nice = self.nice[1:] + [tmp[1]]
            self.sys  = self.sys[1:]  + [tmp[2]]
            self.idle = self.idle[1:] + [tmp[3]]

            # update the plot
            self.l_user.set_ydata(self.user)
            self.l_nice.set_ydata(self.nice)
            self.l_sys.set_ydata( self.sys)
            self.l_idle.set_ydata(self.idle)

            # just draw the "animated" objects
            self.ax.draw_artist(self.l_user)
            self.ax.draw_artist(self.l_nice)
            self.ax.draw_artist(self.l_sys)
            self.ax.draw_artist(self.l_idle)

            # "blit" the background with the animated lines
            self.canvas.blit(self.ax.bbox)


if __name__ == '__main__':
    # create the wrapping application
    app = wx.PySimpleApp()
    # instantiate the Matplotlib wxFrame object
    frame = PlotFigure()

    # Initialize the timer - wxPython requires this to be connected to
    # the receiving event handler
    t = wx.Timer(frame, TIMER_ID)
    t.Start(50)

    # show the frame
    frame.Show()
    # start application event loop processing
    app.MainLoop()
```

When we run this application, a similar window will come up:

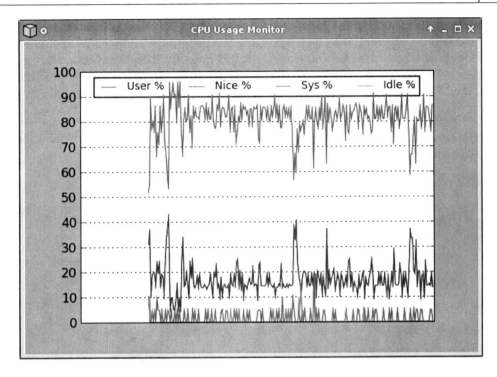

In this screenshot, we can see the nice time (green line) on the top of the image, the user time (blue line) between 10% and 20% lines, the system time (red line) is always almost low, and idle time (cyan line) only present at some spots.

Embedding Matplotlib in a GUI made with wxGlade

For very simple applications with limited GUIs, we can design the interface from inside the application source code. Once the GUI becomes more complex, this solution is not acceptable, and we need a tool to support us in the GUI design.

One of the most well-known tools for this activity in wxWidgets is **wxGlade**. wxGlade is an interface design program written in Python using wxPython, and this allows it to run on all the platforms where these two are available.

The philosophy is similar to Glade, the famous GTK+ GUI designer, and the look and feel is very similar as well. wxGlade is a program that helps us to create wxWidgets or wxPython user interfaces, but it is not a fully-featured code editor: it's just a *designer*, and the code it generates does nothing more than displaying the created widgets.

For this example, we are going to design a GUI with wxGlade to let us select a file, parse its content, and draw a Matplotlib plot of the number of occurrences of each letter in the file.

The GUI we are about to design will look like this:

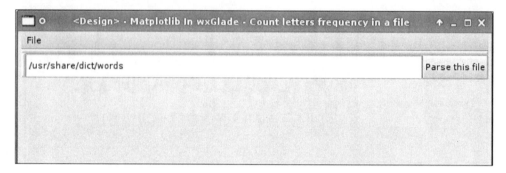

Let's see how we can come to this result.

When opening wxGlade, it presents an empty application. We start adding a **frame** to it by clicking on the corresponding button in the widgets panel: an empty window will pop up and the **Properties** window changes to show the attributes of the widgets just created. We rename both the frame and the class to **MplFrame**. To recall, this is a Matplotlib example. We also change the **frame** title (which will be the application title) by changing the **Title** property.

As we can see, adding a **frame** to the application automatically also adds a sizer. Sizers are really important for GUI layout, and presenting a default sizer is a smart idea particularly because every widget in wxGlade must be inside a sizer.

First, we rename this default sizer to **mplsizer1**, then we right-click on it on the **Tree** object's window and then on **Add slot**: we now see our window divided into two empty parts, one above the other. We will use these slots like this:

- A text area and a button in the upper slot
- The Matplotlib Figure in the lower slot

Let's start with the upper one: we add another sizer to it by selecting **Add a BoxSizer** from the widgets panel and then click on the slot. A configuration window is now shown: just select two slots and click on **OK**, and a new sizer is added. Lastly, we rename it to **mplsizer2**.

Now we can select **TextCtrl** from the widgets panel, and add it to the left slot of **mplsizer2**, then select a **Button**, and add it to the right slot of **mplsizer2**.

While we are here, we rename the **TextCtrl** to **mpltextctrl** and set the default text by modifying the **Value** field in the **Widget** tab of the **Properties** window. Additionally, we rename the button to **mplbutton**, change the **Label** value, and define a **handler** for it; we select the **Events** tab in the **Properties** sheet and set a value for the **EVT_BUTTON** event:

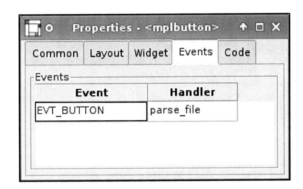

This defines the function that the wxWidgets framework will call when the button is clicked: in this case, the function will take care of parsing the file and drawing the chart.

The layout is far from optimal: what we want is the **TextCtrl** to be expanded to occupy the entire window length, while the extra space below the text control and the button to be assigned to the lower slot. Of course, we can do that:

1. We select the **mplsizer2** in the **Tree** view, and in its **Properties** window, we set **Proportion 0**: this value handles how the available extra space is distributed (spread) over widgets. When it is set to **0**, the sizer shrinks to accommodate the widgets it contains.

2. We click on **mpltextctrl**, then go to the **Properties** window, and select the **Layout** tab: set **Proportion** to **1** and add the **wxEXPAND** property in the **Alignment** section. We can see that the **mpltextctrl** expands to fill all the extra space in **mplsizer2**.

The net result of this is an empty, unused area as the second slot of **mplsizer1**: this is the area that we are going to use for the Matplotlib `Figure`.

We select a **panel** from the widgets window and add it to the empty area, which will be completely filled by it.

We now declare it as a custom **panel**. We select the **panel**, and go into the **Common** tab of the **Properties** window; we now set **Name** as **mplpanel**, in **Class** we replace **wxPanel** with **MplPanel** (the name of our custom class), and then enable **Base class** and set it to **wxPanel**.

In this way, we declared a custom **panel mplpanel** managed by the custom class **MplPanel**, which will control the Matplotlib `Figure`.

Let's see the whole tree of objects, just to have a global view of the widgets relationships:

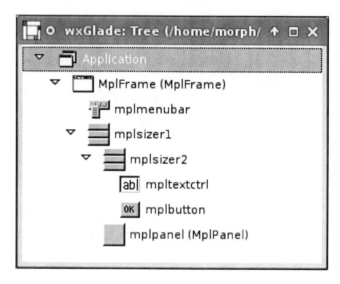

As we can see, there is a menubar also: to add one, we select the **MplFrame**, select the **Widget** tab of the **Properties** window, we check the **Has MenuBar** property, and a menubar widget is added to the **Tree** widget window.

We now click on it to rename it to **mplmenubar** and then in the **Properties** window, we click on **Edit menus...** to create our menu items. The result is:

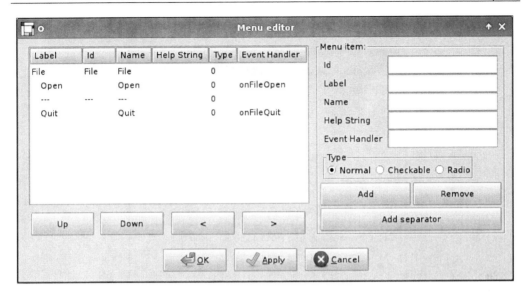

As we can see, we have also defined the event handlers and the callback functions that will react when a menu item is selected.

The GUI design has been completed.

At this point, we want wxGlade to generate the Python code to implement the GUI itself.

To do this, we select the **Application** object from the widgets **Tree** (it's at the root), and the **Application** tab appears on **Properties** window. This panel also presents an option for **Code Generation**:

The **Application** tab on the **Properties** windows looks like this:

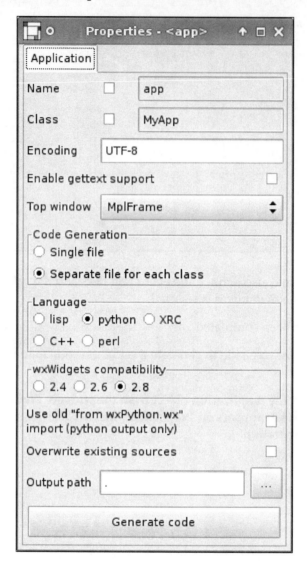

We select **Separate file for each class** so that each class is written in a different file, instead of having just one big file. This is very important for big projects. After this, we select **python** as the **Language** and **2.8** for the **wxWidgets compatibility** version and then we configure the **Output path**. To generate the code, we can click on the **Generate code** button.

But there is more than the GUI in an application: we have to add all the logic to it, to define how the application reacts to a users inputs, the interactions, and so on.

The code generated by wxGlade for this example is separated in three files:

- `app.py`: The code to execute the application
- `MplFrame.py`: The frame where we designed the GUI
- `MplPanel.py`: The custom panel that contains the Matplotlib `Figure`

wxGlade uses the well-known technique of *guarded region*. The autogenerated code of wxGlade is wrapped inside comments blocks that are actually instructions for wxGlade; for example:

```
# begin wxGlade: ...
... wxGlade generated code ...
# end wxGlade
```

Code between these comments is overwritten completely everytime we ask wxGlade to regenerate the code. Outside these regions, the code is preserved. This is where we can add our logic while still letting wxGlade modify its own parts.

Let's look at the source code files, and in details, the code that we added (the code that was not generated by wxGlade).

`app.py` is really simple:

```
import wx
from MplFrame import MplFrame
if __name__ == "__main__":
    app = wx.PySimpleApp(0)
    wx.InitAllImageHandlers()
    MplFrame = MplFrame(None, -1, "")
    app.SetTopWindow(MplFrame)
    MplFrame.Show()
    app.MainLoop()
```

It contains the code to initialize and show the `MplFrame`. `app.py` is the file to execute to run the application.

`MplFrame.py` contains the code to create the main window, and it's almost completely generated except for the bodies of callback functions (the function's headers are generated by wxGlade):

```
def onFileQuit(self, event): # wxGlade: MplFrame.<event_handler>
    self.Close(True)
def onFileOpen(self, event): # wxGlade: MplFrame.<event_handler>
    filename = wx.FileSelector()
    if filename:
        self.mpltextctrl.SetValue(filename)
```

These are the functions called once we select an item in the menu: to close the application and to open a file selector to choose a file to parse.

```
def parse_file(self, event): # wxGlade: MplFrame.<event_handler>
    self.mplpanel.update_graph(self.mpltextctrl.GetValue())
```

This is called when the button is clicked.

But it's in `MplPanel.py` where there is the biggest part of custom code:

```
from __future__ import with_statement
```

At the head of the file, we add the import for the `with` statement that will be used to open the file for parsing.

```
from matplotlib.figure import Figure
import numpy as np
from matplotlib.backends.backend_wxagg import \
    FigureCanvasWxAgg as FigureCanvas
```

Still in the heading part, we import the `Figure` class, the NumPy module, and the `FigureCanvas` specific for the `WxAgg` backend.

```
class MplPanel(wx.Panel):
    def __init__(self, *args, **kwds):
        # begin wxGlade: MplPanel.__init__
        wx.Panel.__init__(self, *args, **kwds)
        self.__set_properties()
        self.__do_layout()
        # end wxGlade
        self.figure = Figure(figsize=(6, 4), dpi=100)
        self.axes = self.figure.add_subplot(111)
        self.canvas = FigureCanvas(self, wx.ID_ANY, self.figure)
```

This is the `__init__` method of our custom class: we can see the guarded region for wxGlade, and then we can add our code to set up an empty `Axes` where we will draw the plot later.

```
def parse_file(self, filename):
```

We add a function to parse the file: its task is to count the occurrences of each letter in the given file.

```
letters = {}
for i in range(97, 122 + 1):
    letters[chr(i)] = 0
```

So we first initialize the `letters` dictionary with a value of `0` for each letter; `97` is the ordinal number for the lowercase letter *a*, while `122` is the ordinal number for the the lowercase letter *z*.

```
with open(filename) as f:
    for line in f:
        for char in line:
            if ord(char.lower()) in range(97, 122 + 1):
                letters[char.lower()] += 1
```

The actual parse code for each character in each line of the file checks if it's a letter, and if it is, increments its counter.

```
return sorted(letters.keys()), [letters[k] for k in
    sorted(letters.keys())]
```

The last instruction is the `return` statement: we return two lists, one containing the ordered letters (the keys of the dictionary) and the second containing the corresponding letter's frequencies (the values of the dictionary, indexed by ordered letters).

```
def update_graph(self, filename):
```

We need another function, one that will take care of updating the `Axes` instance with the occurrences of the frequencies of letters of the current file.

```
l, v = self.parse_file(filename)
```

At the beginning, we take the resultset from the `parse_file()` function.

```
self.axes.clear()
```

Then we clear the `Axes` instance: this will reset all `Axes` information (such as X and Y limits), will remove any objects from it, and so on.

```
self.axes.bar(np.arange(len(l))-0.25, v, width=0.5)
```

So now we can draw the bar plot for the letters frequencies. We set the bars width to be `0.5` units; to have bars centered around the X ticks we shift the bars starting point (as specified by the first list in `bar()`) by `0.25` to the left: the center of the bar will now match the tick position with half the bar on the left and half on the right.

```
self.axes.set_xlim(xmin=-0.25, xmax=len(l)-0.75)
```

We fine tune the X limits: the first bar would have started at position 0, but as we have shifted all bars beginning by `0.25` to the left, the first bar now starts at `-0.25`. At the opposite, the last bar ends at the last tick position (`len(l) - 1`) plus an additional half-bar width of `0.25`. That's how the limit values are obtained.

```
self.axes.set_xticks(range(len(l)))
self.axes.set_xticklabels(l)
```

We set the `xticks` to be right below each bar, labeling them with the letters.

```
self.axes.get_yaxis().grid(True)
```

We enable a grid, but only for the Y-axis. Note that a grid is drawn per axis, and so calling `grid()` on the `Axes` instance is like calling `grid()` on each of the axis separately.

```
self.figure.canvas.draw()
```

At the end, we force a draw on the `Figure` canvas.

If we execute the `app.py` file and parse the default file, then we will see a window like this:

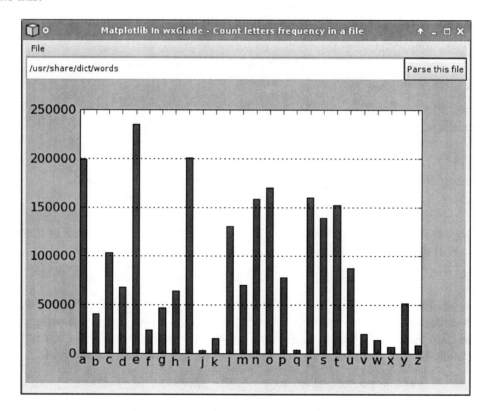

Summary

With what we have seen here, we are now able to develop wxWidgets applications and then embed Matplotlib in them.

In particular, we have seen how to:

- Embed a Matplotlib `Figure` in a `wxFrame`
- Use a sizer to embed both `Figure` and navigation toolbar in a `wxFrame`
- Update a plot in real time using wxWidgets timer and Matplotlibs `blit()`
- Use wxGlade to design a GUI, generate the source code to implement it, and embed Matplotlib into it

We are now ready to move further and see how to integrate Matplotlib into the Web.

8

Matplotlib for the Web

The World Wide Web is pervasive in all of our activities. Today, we are seeing a gradual shift from the desktop to the Web: applications that were earlier installed on personal desktop computers are now used through the browser and so on.

Programming for the Web has become an even hotter topic since the rise of the so-called Web 2.0. So if we want to be a part of this, then we need powerful tools at hand, and a web graphing solution is one of them.

In this chapter, we will explore how to expose Matplotlib on the Web using:

- CGI (through Apache `mod_cgi`)
- mod_python
- Django
- Pylons

The first two are low-level methods for programming the Web, while the latter are two of the most popular web frameworks for Python.

The world of programming is always evolving, so it's important to have a common ground from where we can start productively. Here are the versions of the tools that we will use during this chapter. We suggest you to use the same versions to try the examples to avoid problems with missing or changed functionalities in older or newer versions:

- **Apache**: version 2.2.11, available at `http://www.apache.org/`
- **mod_python**: version 3.3.1, available at `http://www.modpython.org/`
- **Django**: version 1.0.2, available at `http://www.djangoproject.com/`
- **Pylons**: version 0.9.7, available at `http://pylonshq.com/`

Each section will start with a brief introduction to the technology, moving on to explaining, with the help of some examples, how to use Matplotlib into it.

Please note that this is not a book about those tools, so we expect the user to have them installed and working, and in case of problems, refer to the tool documentation and/or the operating system support.

Matplotlib and CGI

CGI, being quite simple, is the perfect start for Matplotlib on the Web.

What is CGI

CGI is the acronym for **Common Gateway Interface**, and it's one of the oldest (and hence well-supported by almost every web server) ways to write web applications.

CGI defines a way for a web server to interact with external content-generating programs, which are often referred to as *CGI programs* or *CGI scripts*. It is the simplest, and the most common way to put dynamic content on a web site.

At a very low level, we can see a CGI script as just a script executed by a web server, receiving the inputs (if any) from the request and then returning the result to the user browser.

The CGI programs code must be interpreted by a web server. As there are far too many web servers available, each with its own configuration, we decided to show how to configure the most widely used one: Apache.

Configuring Apache for CGI execution

In this section, we are about to see how to configure Apache to permit CGI execution.

Apache default configuration usually has a `cgi-bin` directory to contain CGI scripts, a special directory that is separated from the rest of the contents (mainly for security reasons).

It is possible to add as many directories for CGI execution as we need, and so we decided to create a new directory to contain the CGI scripts for Matplotlib examples.

So we edit the general Apache configuration file, `httpd.conf`, and change the `VirtualHosts` (if any) we are using. In any case, the additional configuration we need is:

```
ScriptAlias /matplotlib/cgi-bin/ /path/to/cgi-bin/
<Directory "/path/to/cgi-bin/">
```

```
            Options +ExecCGI
            Order allow,deny
            Allow from all
      </Directory>
```

where /path/to/ indicates a the full path to the location of the cgi-bin directory, whatever we may choose it to be.

 A change to Apache's configuration requires a service restart to be applied.

Let's describe these directives.

Apache has a default location for web contents, the DocumentRoot. Apache is said to expose a web space: the hierarchy of pages provided by the web server, retrieved from the DocumentRoot. Anything outside the DocumentRoot is not (by default) accessible by Apache web sites.

The Alias directive maps an additional *web space* to an external directory (the tree of files and directory) from the *filesystem space* (what is stored on the hard drives). This way we can serve contents outside the DocumentRoot.

For CGI scripts, there is a more specific directive, ScriptAlias that works the same way as that of Alias but additionally, it will force all the content located at that target to be treated as CGI scripts.

In our configuration, we map the /matplotlib/cgi-bin/ web space to the /path/to/cgi-bin/ directory that will contain our scripts.

As the directory specified in ScriptAlias is outside the DocumentRoot, we have to define what options to use for it; Apache provides the Directory directive to do it.

Here we have to specify that the files in it are CGI scripts and that they need to be processed by the mod_cgi script handler by enabling the option ExecCGI.

We also need to explicitly permit access to the target directory using:

```
            Order allow,deny
            Allow from all
```

Now, all the files in the directory will be treated as CGI scripts.

Please note these simple tips to prevent common mistakes:

- A CGI script must be a working script, with a correct **shebang** (the first line of the script, starting with **#!** and then specifying the full path to the interpreter to use) and without syntax errors.

- The scripts must be readable and executable by any users. Apache is usually run by an unprivileged user, so it must be able to read the script and execute it (and the same applies to any file that the script uses).

Simple CGI example

Writing a CGI script in Python is simple—it's just a script that receives user input and then generates an output that the web server will redirect to the client browser.

Python's standard library supplies modules to handle common CGI-related tasks:

- `cgi`: To handle user inputs in CGI scripts
- `cgitb`: To display a nice traceback in case an error occurs

It's now time for an example; let's take the following code:

```
#!/usr/bin/python
print "Content-Type: text/html"      # headers; HTML is following
print                                 # blank line, end of headers
print """<html>
<head><title>Simple CGI script</title></head>
<body><h2>Hello, world!</h2></body>
</html>"""
```

Save it to a file named `7900_08_01.py` in our `cgi-bin` directory (the one defined earlier), and then point the browser to `http://localhost/matplotlib/cgi-bin/7900_08_01.py`. **Hello, world!** will be displayed:

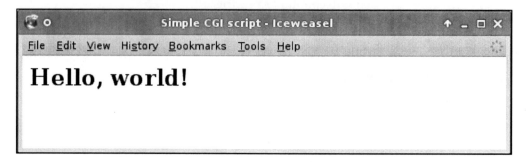

Even though this example is very simple, it demonstrates an important aspect of CGI scripts.

The output of any CGI script must consist of two sections, separated by one (or more) blank line: first comes the headers, telling the client (the browser) what kind of data will follow. The second section contains the data itself (such as HTML code, an image, and so on).

In the previous script, the `Content-Type` HTTP header (which must be always present) specifies that the data is to be parsed as HTML, we then have the separation line, and finally some simple HTML text.

However, there is a downside with CGI: as the processes are started by the web server itself, every request starts a new Python interpreter to execute the script, and it takes some time to start up. This poses a big limitation for situations where a fast response is required or where high-load applications are running.

Matplotlib in a CGI script

We are now ready to see how to use Matplotlib in a CGI script. It's not really different from writing a Python script, but there are some tips to do it nicely. Here is the code:

```
import sys
```

At the beginning of the script, we import the `sys` module because we need it to access the standard output.

```
import matplotlib
matplotlib.use('Agg')
import matplotlib.pyplot as plt
```

Many web servers don't have a graphical environment enabled, so we have to select a Matplotlib backend that doesn't rely on a GUI library to render the figure. As we are going to generate PNG images, we will use the `Agg` backend that uses the `antigrain` rendering engine to create nice PNGs.

 Remember that to change the Matplotlib backend, `matplotlib.use()` must be called before any Matplotlib plotting module is imported.

```
plt.plot([1, 2, 3, 2, 3, 4])
```

Here we generate the graph, as always.

```
print "Content-Type: image/png\n"
```

Then we can start to output the result to the client: we must specify the `Content-Type`, and select the MIME string to represent a PNG image. This means that what will follow is a PNG image. The `'\n'` notation in `print` grants us an additional new line to inform the browser that the headers section is over and the data comes next.

```
plt.savefig(sys.stdout, format='png')
```

Here is the trick: we save the plot directly to the standard output. This will make the web server send the image data to the client (the browser) that will handle it correctly because we specified the correct `Content-Type`.

If we now call the URL `http://localhost/matplotlib/cgi-bin/7900_08_02.py`, we will see this:

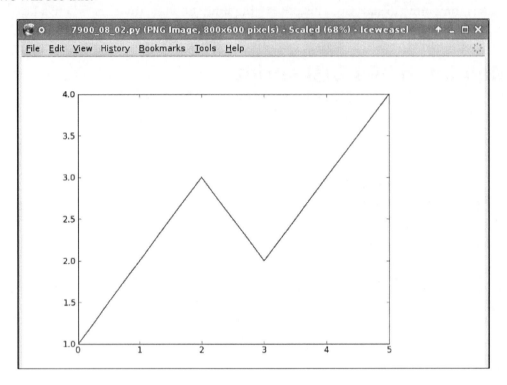

Passing parameters to a CGI script

CGI scripts can also receive user data, for example, using the `GET` method for passing parameters. Let's see how we can process them and generate a dynamic graph with Matplotlib.

```
import sys
```

We import the `sys` module to output the graph in a standard output.

```
import cgitb
cgitb.enable()
```

Debugging CGI scripts has traditionally been difficult, mainly because it is hard to study the output (standard output and error) from scripts which fail to run properly and because the information is sent only to the Apache logs that are not always accessible by developers.

cgitb can help us with this: it activates a special exception handler that will display detailed information in the web browser (in case any errors occur), instead of only writing the traceback into the Apache log files.

Without cgitb, in case of an error the interpreter just crashes and a non-descriptive **Internal Server Error** message is displayed on the browser, and the Python traceback is printed only in the Apache error.log.

It's important that cgitb is imported before cgi, so that the exception handler is replaced before cgi is loaded.

> A security note: remember to disable cgitb for production CGI scripts, as it can expose internal or confidential information, and also because all exceptions should be caught and handled.

Continuing with the scripts we have:

```
import cgi
```

The standard library's cgi module that allows to access GET parameters.

```
import matplotlib
matplotlib.use('Agg')
import matplotlib.pyplot as plt
```

We select the non-GUI Agg backend and then import pyplot.

```
form = cgi.FieldStorage()
```

the FieldStorage instance contains parameters passed in GET or POST, and it provides a handy way to access them.

```
form_data = form.getfirst('data', '1,3,2,2,4')
```

getfirst() returns only one value associated to the requested field name (note that browser can reorder parameters, so it's the first in the order it is received), even if more are specified.

This is a security tip: we should never expect users to provide valid inputs (either due to mistakes or malevolent attempts), so while using `getfirst()`, the script won't crash if more parameters with the same name are passed.

The additional argument is the default value, which is used in case the requested field is missing.

In this case, we try to access the `data` parameter that should contain a **comma-separated values (CSV)** list of integers to plot, but if it's missing, we fall back to the default value.

```
data = [int(x) for x in form_data.split(',')]
```

Here we parse the list, splitting on the `','` character to generate a list of integers to be plotted.

```
plt.plot(data)
```

We generate the plot starting from the `data` list.

```
print "Content-Type: image/png\n"
plt.savefig(sys.stdout, format='png')
```

Finally, we plot the resulting image to the standard output, so it is directly sent to the client program.

Calling the URL `http://localhost/matplotlib/cgi-bin/7900_08_03.py?data=2,3,2,1,2,3,2` generates the following screenshot:

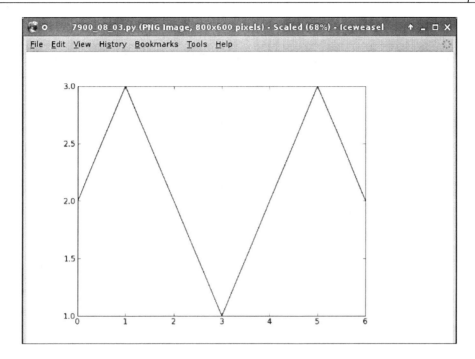

This script represents a real image, so we can also embed it in web pages, using:

```
<img src="/matplotlib/cgi-bin/7900_08_03.py" />
```

as done for any other image file.

Matplotlib and mod_python

Let's first introduce what mod_python is and then show some examples.

What is mod_python

mod_python is an Apache module that embeds the Python interpreter within the web server.

With CGI, a separate process is spawn and its output is then returned to the client's application; every request to a CGI script creates a new process, and this results in unnecessary CPU and I/O activity that poses serious problems to application scalability.

mod_python solves this problem by embedding the Python interpreter directly into the Apache processes, thus speeding up the applications response time. Not having to start a Python interpreter at every request eliminates the typical startup penalty of CGI.

The result is that you can make web applications that are many times faster than the CGI approach and have full access to advanced features (such as database connection retention between hits) and to Apache internals.

Also, simple Python scripts and programs benefit from this approach. They don't have to pay the price of starting the Python interpreter at each request, thus providing a fast response mechanism well suited for exposing function libraries on the Web.

But we have to notice that there are also some drawbacks:

- Every Apache child process needs to load the whole Python interpreter, even if it doesn't use it. This will result in a higher memory usage and a slow startup of the child process (however a child remains active for several requests).

- mod_python uses a specific version of Python (in particular, linking against a given version of `libpython`), so it's not possible to upgrade Python without upgrading mod_python too.

- The Python interpreter is loaded and remains active, and as Python uses caching when executing files, if a script is changed, the whole Apache server must be restarted to see the change. A restart is also needed to free memory if the memory usage increased due to a higher number of requests or if there was a memory leak in the application.

Apache configuration for mod_python

As it's an Apache module, we have to configure the `httpd` server before we can start using mod_python.

After the installation of mod_python, we have to let Apache load it by specifying the following line in the `httpd.conf` file:

```
LoadModule python_module modules/mod_python.so
```

Then, we can edit our `VirtualHost` (for example, `/etc/apache2/sites-available/default` – default vhost on Debian) to add:

```
ScriptAlias /matplotlib/mod_python/ /path/to/mod_python/
<Directory "/path/to/mod_python/ ">
    Order allow,deny
    Allow from all
```

```
        AddHandler mod_python .py .psp
        PythonHandler mod_python.publisher | .py
        PythonHandler mod_python.psp | .psp
        PythonDebug On
    </Directory>
```

Alternatively, we can do this configuration in the .htaccess file in the same directory. In this last case, Apache restart is not needed.

The first two options are needed to allow users to access the directory, if it's outside the DocumentRoot of Apache server. Then, there are the mod_python-specific options.

Even if we use the ScriptAlias directive to specify that the directory will contain only the script, we might need to have more handlers for them. By using this line.

```
        AddHandler mod_python .py .psp
```

We tell Apache that every request for .py and .psp filename extensions in this directory (or its subdirectories) needs to be served by the mod_python handler.

PythonHandler specifies which is the main response handler (where the contents of the response are typically generated); we use a particular syntax:

```
        PythonHandler mod_python.publisher | .py
        PythonHandler mod_python.psp | .psp
```

Since we have multiple resource types that need to be processed by distinct handler functions, we have to qualify what extensions should be served by what handler.

Our configuration is such that:

- The publisher handler will take care of the Python script (with .py extension) execution
- The psp handler will process text documents with Python code embedded in them (.psp extensions)

The last option:

```
        PythonDebug On
```

instructs mod_python to output any Python errors to the browser instead of only in the Apache error log (but that does not imply not to check log files); this is very useful for debugging purposes during development phases.

Due to security concerns (as it can expose internal information), it's highly recommended to disable the `PythonDebug` option for production usage, but keeping it active while developing.

After changing the Apache configuration file, we have to restart the web server (not needed when using `.htaccess`).

Matplotlib in a mod_python example

In this example, we will see how to generate a simple image using Matplotlib and mod_python.

```
import matplotlib
matplotlib.use('Agg')
import matplotlib.pyplot as plt
import numpy as np
```

This is the usual import to set a non-GUI backend and for modules needed to generate the plot.

```
from cStringIO import StringIO
```

We will use this module to simulate file writing to Matplotlib functions while we are actually writing into a `StringIO` object (no disk access is needed).

```
def index(req):
```

This is the function that gets called when an access request is made to a resource under mod_python control.

There is always one argument—the **request object**. The `req` object is automatically created and provides all the information about that particular request, such as the IP address of a client, the headers, URI, and so on. Note that the communication back to the client is also done through the request object: there is no **response object**.

```
plt.cla()
```

We clear the `Axes`. As the Python interpreter is loaded and then never closed until Apache shutdown, if we don't clean the `Axes`, successive plots will be drawn over the previous ones.

```
x = np.arange(0, 6, .01)
plt.plot(x, np.sin(x)**3 + 0.5*np.cos(x))
```

We prepare our plot.

```
s = StringIO()
```

We instantiate the `StringIO` object.

```
plt.savefig(s)
```

Then save the figure on it.

```
req.content_type = "image/png"
```

We set the `Content-Type` HTTP header. We have to be sure to write the `Content-Type` before any `write()` call. This is because once the first `write()` is called, the HTTP headers (and thus including `Content-Type`) are sent to the client, and all subsequent headers are simply lost.

```
req.write(s.getvalue())
```

Next, we write the content of `s` (that's actually the Matplotlib plot) to the `req` object.

If we save this script in a file named `7900_08_04.py` and visit this URL `http://localhost/matplotlib/mod_python/7900_08_04.py`, then we will see a web page similar to the following screenshot:

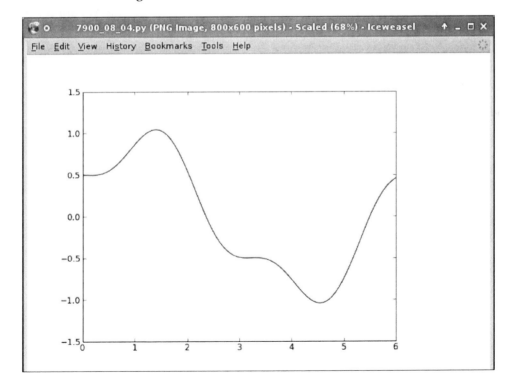

Matplotlib and mod_python's Python Server Pages

mod_python provides presentation support—a templating system called **Python Server Pages (PSP)**. PSP is a framework that allows us to embed Python code within HTML, similar to what PHP, JSP or ASP does.

Anything in between the `<%` and `%>` delimiters is interpreted as Python code, and whatever is in between `<%=` and `%>` is replaced with the result of the expression contained.

Our example starts with an open tag for PSP, `<%` at the top of the file, and then we have.

```
import matplotlib
matplotlib.use('Agg')
```

We select a non-GUI backend.

```
from matplotlib.backends.backend_agg import \
    FigureCanvasAgg as FigureCanvas
```

we import the `Figure` and `FigureCanvasAgg` (that maps a `Figure` into a backend-dependent representation, `Agg` in this case): we will use the API approach in this example.

```
from cStringIO import StringIO
```

We import the `StringIO` module to simulate a file write.

```
if (form.has_key('data')) and form.getfirst('data') != '':
```

It's real Python code, so we can check for a variable existence and so on; here we check if the `data` GET parameter is present (and not empty). The first time a `form` variable is accessed in a PSP file, an instance of `FieldStorage` is automatically created, containing the necessary functions to handle the submitted data.

```
data = [int(x) for x in form.getfirst('data').split(',')]
```

We expect the `data` to be a CSV of integer values, so we now parse that parameter to generate a list of integers.

Note that `getfirst()` will return the first parameter submitted by the form with the given name (this will avoid any unexpected problems, should some malicious users pass the same parameter more than once).

```
fig = Figure()
canvas = FigureCanvas(fig)
ax = fig.add_subplot(111)
```

```
        ax.plot(data)
```

We generate the plot.

```
        s = StringIO()
        canvas.print_figure(s)
```

Print it to the `StringIO` object.

```
        req.content_type = "image/png"
```

Now, we set the `Content-Type`.

```
        req.write(s.getvalue())
```

Write the image to the req object, sending it to the client.

```
    else:
```

If we don't have the `data` parameter (or it's empty), then we present an HTML page with a textbox where we can enter values to the plot.

```
    %>
    <html><head>
    <title>A simple script to generate a plot</title>
    <head>
    <body>
    <form method="POST" action="/matplotlib/mod_python/7900_08_05.psp">
    <p>
    <hr>
    <br />
    <input type="text" name="data" size=30 />
    <br />
    <input type="submit" value="Generate the Plot" />
    <br />
    <hr>
    </form>
    </body></html>
```

Note how the `form action` recalls the script itself by passing the value set in the `data` input box.

Now, by calling the URL at `http://localhost/matplotlib/mod_python/7900_08_05.psp`, we can enter some values:

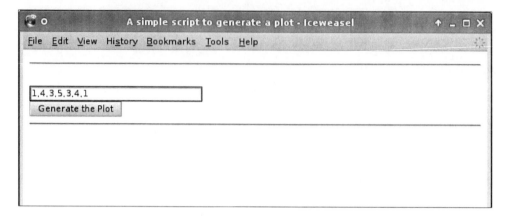

and see them plotted as:

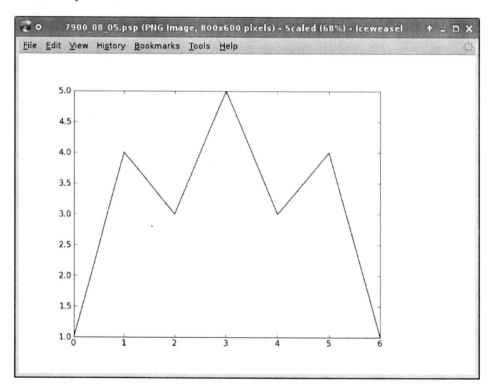

Web Frameworks and MVC

The previous approaches are perfectly fine for independent scripts or for very simple web applications.

But, as soon as the application starts to grow, they suddenly show their limits:

- Common parts of the code (for example, database connection) must be shared between the scripts
- Developers should concentrate on coding the application core, without dwelling on the technicalities of the web infrastructure (such as setting `Content-Type`)
- Deploying the application in a different environment often requires a lot of changes (parameters, setup, and so on)

A **web framework** provides the programming infrastructure for creating web applications so that the developers can focus on writing clean maintainable code without reinventing the wheel and creating sites that are faster and more robust.

Modern frameworks give us everything we need to start working: a template engine, a way to save and access data in a database, and many more features.

Usually, a web framework is a collection of packages or modules that allow developers to write web applications whose main advantage is to spare developers from handling low-level details such as protocols, sockets, or process/thread management.

Recently one web application pattern arose as the winning one: MVC.

MVC, the acronym for **Model-View-Controller**, is a way of organizing the project, not a programming technique. It is quite interesting to note that MVC was conceived significantly before the explosion of WWW, in particular the design traces back to 1979, as a part of Smalltalk programming language.

In the MVC pattern, we have a clear separation between these three aspects:

- **Model**: The interface used to access data resources (usually a database) where data is stored and retrieved
- **View**: How the data is presented to the users, the user interface
- **Controller**: The application core logic that manipulates the data from the model to present it to the users (using a view) and controls the users' interactions with it

Organizing the code by following the MVC pattern will result in a web application that is easily extensible, flexible, and scalable.

Matplotlib and Django

Django is a very well-known Python web framework. Let's first introduce it and then present the example.

What is Django

Django grew from a practical need: create a framework for building intensive web applications for journalism or news web sites.

As Django was born in the news environment, it offers several features which are particularly well suited for content web sites. Although Django is particularly good for developing those sorts of sites, that doesn't preclude it from being an effective tool for building any kind of dynamic web site.

Moreover, it's a common misinterpretation that Django is a Content Management System (CMS); well, it is not. It's a web framework, a programming tool, as well as something that we can use to *create* a CMS.

Django changes the MVC pattern slightly; in its interpretation:

- The view describes the data that gets presented to the users (not necessarily *how* the data will be presented, but *which* data to present). This is basically a Python callback function for a particular URL.
- The controller is (probably) Django itself: the machinery that delivers requests to the appropriate view.

It might be quite confusing because a controller in MVC is a view in Django, and a view in MVC is a template in Django. For these reasons, Django is often referred to as an **MTV** framework: **Model-Template-View**.

Some of the fundamental aspects of Django are:

- **Simplicity**: It has been designed to make common web development tasks fast and easy, reducing the pain of repetitive tasks.
- **Loose coupling**: Even if it's a full stack of convenience components, the various layers of the framework should not know about each other.
- **Less code**: A Django app should use as little code as possible.
- **Quick development**: Makes the tedious task of web development fast, so that developers can concentrate on the real core of the application.

- **Elegant URL scheme**: URLs should be as flexible as possible and completely decoupled from the underlying Python code: in fact, Django uses a very interesting feature for this, a regular expression-based URLs dispatching mechanism.

Matplotlib in a Django application

The first step in creating a Django application is to create a Django *project*. Before that, we create a directory (that will contain our project) and move into it. It's not a good idea to store the Django project files and directories under the web server document root because we risk the possibility that people may be able to view the code over the Web. So, using a directory outside the document root is highly encouraged.

Then we can issue this command:

```
$ django-admin startproject mpldjango
```

This commands creates a directory called `mpldjango` (we must use a name that would not conflict with other Python components, because it will be imported) that will contain our project.

If we look at the `mpldjango` directory contents, we can see this hierarchy:

```
mpldjango/
|-- __init__.py
|-- manage.py
|-- settings.py
`-- urls.py
```

Let's have a look at the following table for a brief description of these files:

Filename	Description
`__init__.py`	Empty file, used only to tell Python that this directory can be imported by other Python packages.
`manage.py`	A command-line utility to interact with this Django project.
`settings.py`	Settings or configuration for this Django project.
`urls.py`	The URLs or the functions mapping of this Django project; consider it like the "Table of contents" of the site, the file that specifies which view is called for a given URL pattern.

Now that we have our environment (project) set up, we are ready to start doing some work, and this work is done by an *application* (also called *app*).

Let's first look at the differences between an application and a project:

- An application is a web application that does something (which can be useful to a project)
- A project is a collection of settings and applications for a given web site
- A project can contain multiple applications
- An application can be in multiple projects

So the applications are the building blocks of a Django project.

To create an app from within the `mpldjango` project directory, we execute this commands:

```
$ python manage.py startapp mpl
```

that creates a new directory named `mpl` with this content:

```
mpl/
|-- __init__.py
|-- models.py
`-- views.py
```

where:

Filename	Description
__init__.py	Has the same function as that of the project's __init__.py
models.py	Contains the database layout classes
views.py	Contains the views for the application, the core logic for the pages

A view is a *type* of web pages in our Django app that serves a specific function.

The contents of the page are produced by a `view` function, so we are about to write a function in the `views.py` file to generate and return a Matplotlib plot.

```python
import django
# import Figure and FigureCanvas, we will use API
from matplotlib.backends.backend_agg import \
   FigureCanvasAgg as FigureCanvas
from matplotlib.figure import Figure
# used to generate the graph
import numpy as np
def mplimage(request):
    # do the plotting
    fig = Figure()
    canvas = FigureCanvas(fig)
    ax = fig.add_subplot(111)
```

```
x = np.arange(-2,1.5,.01)
y = np.sin(np.exp(2*x))
ax.plot(x, y)
# prepare the response, setting Content-Type
response=django.http.HttpResponse(content_type='image/png')
# print the image on the response
canvas.print_png(response)
# and return it
return response
```

The only difference from other examples is the import of the django module and the preparation of the response object.

Now that we have the view ready, we need to *expose* it in Django.

Django provides a clean and elegant URL schema where the requests are mapped to the Python code using a map between URLs and callback functions. Moreover, the map is done using regular expressions, granting an extreme flexibility.

The map is stored in the file indicated by ROOT_URLCONF item in settings.py that usually points to <app>/urls.py.

So in our example, the file mpldjango/urls.py contains the URLs dispatching configuration, so we're going to add a line to the urlpatterns tuple there:

```
urlpatterns = patterns('',
    (r'mplimage.png', 'mpl.views.mplimage'),
)
```

The previous code snippet maps the URL (the first field) to the location of the callback function to call to serve that request (the second field).

In this case, it's really simple (not even using a regular expression), but generally speaking, when a user requests a page, Django runs through each pattern (in the order they are written in the file) and stops at the first one that matches the requested URL. At this point, Django imports and calls the given view.

Regular expressions are compiled at load time, so this mechanism is extremely fast.

But we are curious to see what we've just developed, so let's start the Django development web server with:

```
$ python manage.py runserver
Validating models...
0 errors found
Django version 1.0.2 final, using settings 'mpldjango.settings'
Development server is running at http://127.0.0.1:8000/
Quit the server with CONTROL-C.
```

This is a lightweight web server shipped with Django to develop things rapidly. An important note: do **not** ever use it for production environment, as it's intended to be used only while developing.

So now, by pointing the browser to http://127.0.0.1:8000/mplimage.png, we see the next screenshot:

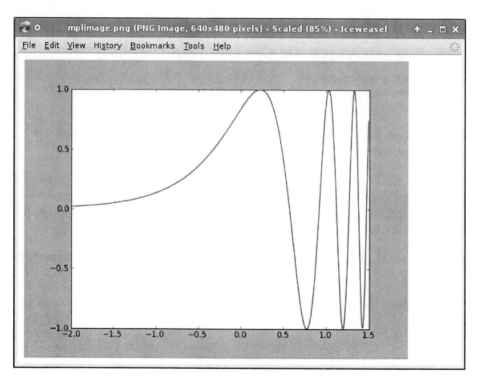

Matplotlib and Pylons

First, we will introduce Pylons, and then we will see how to use Matplotlib with it.

What is Pylons

Pylons provides a structured but extremely flexible Python web framework.

It works a bit differently from other frameworks. Instead of presenting a rigid structure or recreating all the pieces that a web application framework should provide, it chooses a loosely coupled approach.

Pylons is a collection of very carefully selected components that are well known and widespread, and almost any of them can be exchanged (that's what we meant by *loosely coupled*). Pylons is just a thin *glue* layer used to merge all these components, abstract them, and present a consistent and flexible environment.

This allows developers to model Pylons to their needs, and to use the tools they know best. It also allows to choose the best components for the specific job at hand.

Just to give an example of the available components, here is a (short) list of supported projects along with their function in Pylons:

- **Data model**: SQLAlchemy, SQLObject, CouchDB, and so on
- **Templating**: Mako, Genshi, Jinja2, and so on
- **Helpers**: WebHelpers, FormAlchemy, and so on
- **URL dispatching**: Routes, and so on

Pylons is built on top of **Paste**, which is mainly a web server and an extensive set of tools to help developers and system administrators develop and deploy web applications.

Pylons uses the MVC pattern—requests are dispatched to the controller that interact with the model to retrieve the relevant information which is then presented to the user using a view.

And Pylons is also much more than just a framework, for example it has:

- **Interactive web debugger**: In case of an exception, a traceback is displayed on the browser, and we can interact with it.
- **Built-in web server**: When using Paste, Pylons doesn't need to use any external web server (such as Apache), and that makes the upgrade and the deploy processes easier.

Matplotlib in a Pylons application

We start by creating a new Pylons project, using Paste's `paster` command:

```
$ paster create --template=pylons mplpylons
Selected and implied templates:
  Pylons#pylons  Pylons application template
Variables:
  egg:      mplpylons
  package:  mplpylons
  project:  mplpylons
Enter template_engine (mako/genshi/jinja2/etc: Template language)
['mako']: mako
Enter sqlalchemy (True/False: Include SQLAlchemy 0.5 configuration)
[False]: False

...
```

The previous command creates a project called `mplpylons` using the `pylons` template (that specifies directories and file structure for the project), the default one.

Then several output lines are printed. We are prompted to choose the templating engine and whether to include SQLAlchemy support. We will not use them, so any response is fine.

This generates a complex directory tree that we have reduced to the following because these are the items we will be using:

```
mplpylons/
|-- <several other files and directories>
|-- mplpylons
|    |-- <several other files and directories>
|    `--   controllers
`-- development.ini
```

where:

- `development.ini`: This is the application project configuration file. It contains settings to run the Pylons application in a development environment. For example, when developing a Pylons application, it is very useful to be able to see a debug report every time an error occurs. For a production environment, there will be a different file.

- `mplpylons` subdirectory: This is the main application directory, and the name is the same as we gave in the `paster create` command line (lowercase) — it is the place where our code is stored.

- `mplpylons/controllers`: This is where the application controllers are written; as said, controllers are the core of the application, handling requests, interacting with models and views.

At this point, we already have a working web application. Even though it is empty, we can start it with:

```
$ cd mplpylons
$ paster serve --reload development.ini
Starting subprocess with file monitor
Starting server in PID 20006.
serving on http://127.0.0.1:5000
```

This command will start a web server that listens to localhost on port `5000` (it's all written in `development.ini` file) with our application running, so we can visit `http://127.0.0.1:5000/` and see the Pylons welcome page.

It's recommended to use the Paste HTTP web server; we can think of Paste for Pylons as being like Apache for PHP. It listens for HTTP requests and dispatches them to the running applications, returning the result through HTTP to the client's browser.

Note the `--reload` option: it ensures that the server is automatically reloaded, if changes are made to Python files or to `development.ini`; this way changes are immediately reflected on the live site. This is very useful during development. To stop the server, press `Ctrl+c` or the platform's equivalent.

What we need to do now is create a new controller to generate an image using Matplotlib.

In the MVC pattern, the controller receives a request, interprets its inputs, and interacts with the model to prepare data for representation, which is then rendered using a view (for example, using a templating language).

In our situation, we don't have a model to query, or a view—our controller will directly generate an image and will send it to the client.

There are two options for serving images to the user:

1. Writing a temporary file and serve that
2. Directly output the image data to the browser

We will use the second option, as it's the most efficient.

To create the controller, we use the `paster` command:

```
$ paster controller mpl
```

```
Creating .../mplpylons/controllers/mpl.py
```

```
Creating .../mplpylons/tests/functional/test_mpl.py
```

As we can see, it adds two files—the actual controller and a test file, which is used to run some of the functional tests.

The controller file is just a skeleton, so we need to add a method to it. In the Pylons terminology, a method in a controller is called an **action**.

The code is nothing new. We just have some little additions for the Pylons framework:

```
import logging
from pylons import request, response, session, tmpl_context as c
from pylons.controllers.util import abort, redirect_to
from mplpylons.lib.base import BaseController, render
log = logging.getLogger(__name__)
```

This is a big part, autogenerated by `paster` for importing Pylons' modules.

```
import matplotlib
matplotlib.use('Agg')
from matplotlib.backends.backend_agg import \
    FigureCanvasAgg as FigureCanvas
from matplotlib.figure import Figure
import numpy as np
```

Here we add the imports for Matplotlib plot generation.

```
from cStringIO import StringIO
```

This is used to simulate file writing.

```
class MplController(BaseController):
    def index(self):
```

Then, we have the definition of the controller class and the response method. Note how the controller class is the concatenation of the controller's name with `Controller` (in camel case).

In the body of the `index()` function, we'll be writing the Matplotlib code:

```
fig = Figure()
canvas = FigureCanvas(fig)
ax = fig.add_subplot(111)
x = np.arange(-2,2,.01)
y = x*np.sin(x**3)
ax.plot(x, y)
s = StringIO()
```

```
canvas.print_figure(s)
response.headers['Content-Type'] = 'image/png'
return s.getvalue()
```

In every action, we have access to the `request` object (created automatically at each request) that contains all the information about HTTP request, parameters, and so on.

To return data to the client, we use the `response` object, where we set the `Content-Type` HTTP header and the payload, retuning the image bytes (anytime we return something from a controller action, Pylons automatically writes it to the `response` objects).

The `--reload` option makes the Paste server reload after the new controller changes:

```
.../mplpylons/controllers/mpl.py changed; reloading...
------------------- Restarting --------------------
Starting server in PID 21188.
serving on http://127.0.0.1:5000
```

Now we can point our browser to `http://127.0.0.1:5000/mpl/index` and see that the controller generates the Matplotlib `Figure`.

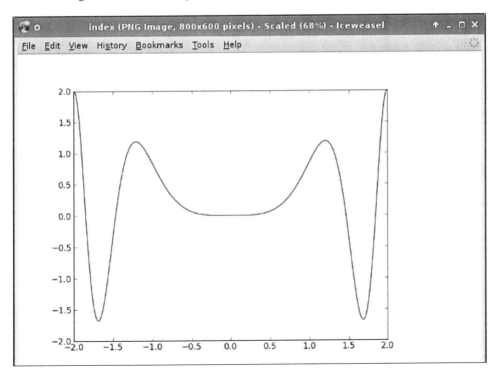

Note how the URLs are mapped to the controller and then to the function to call. Pylons uses Routes package that allows for very sophisticated URL mapping.

The default URL map is `http://<server>:<port>/<controller>/<action>`. So with this URL, we are invoking the `index()` action (method) of the `MplController` class that generates our graph.

Summary

Being able to create plots with Matplotlib in web applications is really interesting. In this chapter, we've seen how Matplotlib can interact with older but consolidated techniques such as:

- CGI
- mod_python

Along with that, this chapter also covered Matplotlib interaction with recent, but very popular Python application web frameworks such as:

- Django
- Pylons

Matplotlib in the Real World

9

In this chapter you will see several examples of Matplotlib usage in real-world situations, showing some of the common cases where we can use Matplotlib to draw a plot of some values.

There is a common workflow for this kind of job:

1. Identify the best data source for the information we want to plot
2. Extract the data of interest and elaborate it for plotting
3. Plot the data

Usually, the hardest part is to extract and prepare the data for plotting. Due to this, we are going to show several examples of the first two steps.

The examples are:

- Plotting data from a database
- Plotting data from a web page
- Plotting the data extracted by parsing an Apache log file
- Plotting the data read from a comma-separated values (CSV) file
- Plotting extrapolated data using curve fitting
- Third-party tools using Matplotlib (NetworkX and mpmath)
- Plotting geographical data using Basemap

Let's begin

Plotting data from a database

Databases often tend to collect much more information than we can simply extract and watch in a tabular format (let's call it the "Excel sheet" report style).

Databases not only use efficient techniques to store and retrieve data, but they are also very good at *aggregating* it.

One suggestion we can give is to let the database do the work. For example, if we need to sum up a column, let's make the database sum the data, and not sum it up in the code. In this way, the whole process is much more efficient because:

- There is a smaller memory footprint for the Python code, since only the aggregate value is returned, not the whole result set to generate it
- The database has to read all the rows in any case. However, if it's smart enough, then it can sum values up as they are read
- The database can efficiently perform such an operation on more than one column at a time

The data source we're going to query is from an open source project: the Debian distribution. Debian has an interesting project called **UDD**, **Ultimate Debian Database**, which is a relational database where a lot of information (either historical or actual) about the distribution is collected and can be analyzed.

On the project website `http://udd.debian.org/`, we can find a full dump of the database (quite big, honestly) that can be downloaded and imported into a local *PostgreSQL* instance (refer to `http://wiki.debian.org/ UltimateDebianDatabase/CreateLocalReplica` for import instructions).

Now that we have a local replica of UDD, we can start querying it:

```
# module to access PostgreSQL databases
import psycopg2
# matplotlib pyplot module
import matplotlib.pyplot as plt
```

Since UDD is stored in a *PostgreSQL* database, we need `psycopg2` to access it. `psycopg2` is a third-party module available at `http://initd.org/projects/ psycopg`.

```
# connect to UDD database
conn = psycopg2.connect(database="udd")
# prepare a cursor
cur = conn.cursor()
```

We will now connect to the database server to access the udd database instance, and then open a cursor on the connection just created.

```
# this is the query we'll be making
query = """
select to_char(date AT TIME ZONE 'UTC', 'HH24'), count(*)
  from upload_history
 where to_char(date, 'YYYY') = '2008'
 group by 1
 order by 1"""
```

We have prepared the select statement to be executed on UDD. What we wish to do here is extract the number of packages uploaded to the Debian archive (per hour) in the whole year of 2008.

A couple of notes:

- date AT TIME ZONE 'UTC': As date field is of the type timestamp with time zone, it also contains time zone information, while we want something independent from the local time. This is the way to get a date in UTC time zone.

- group by 1: This is what we have encouraged earlier, that is, let the database do the work. We let the query return the already aggregated data, instead of coding it into the program.

```
# execute the query
cur.execute(query)
# retrieve the whole result set
data = cur.fetchall()
```

We execute the query and fetch the whole result set from it.

```
# close cursor and connection
cur.close()
conn.close()
```

Remember to always close the resources that we've acquired in order to avoid memory or resource leakage and reduce the load on the server (removing connections that aren't needed anymore).

```
# unpack data in hours (first column) and
# uploads (second column)
hours, uploads = zip(*data)
```

The query result is a list of tuples, (in this case, hour and number of uploads), but we need two separate lists—one for the hours and another with the corresponding number of uploads. `zip()` solves this with `*data`, we *unpack* the list, returning the sublists as separate arguments to `zip()`, which in return, aggregates the elements in the same position in the parameters into separated lists. Consider the following example:

```
In [1]: zip(['a1', 'a2'], ['b1', 'b2'])
Out[1]: [('a1', 'b1'), ('a2', 'b2')]
```

To complete the code:

```
# graph code
plt.plot(hours, uploads)
# the the x limits to the 'hours' limit
plt.xlim(0, 23)
# set the X ticks every 2 hours
plt.xticks(range(0, 23, 2))
# draw a grid
plt.grid()
# set title, X/Y labels
plt.title("Debian packages uploads per hour in 2008")
plt.xlabel("Hour (in UTC)")
plt.ylabel("No. of uploads")
```

The previous code snippet is the standard plotting code, which results in the following screenshot:

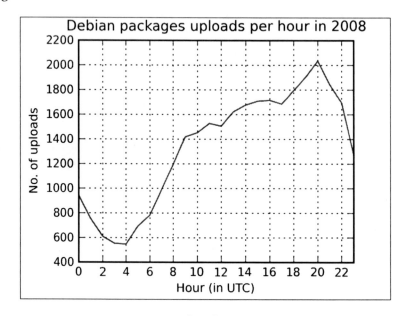

From this graph we can see that in 2008, the main part of Debian packages uploads came from European contributors. In fact, uploads were made mainly in the evening hours (European time), after the working days are over (as we can expect from a voluntary project).

Plotting data from the Web

Often, the information we need is not distributed in an easy-to-use format such as XML or a database export but for example only on web sites.

More and more often we find interesting data on a web page, and in that case we have to parse it to extract that information: this is called **web scraping**.

In this example, we will parse a Wikipedia article to extracts some data to plot. The article is at http://it.wikipedia.org/wiki/Demografia_d'Italia and contains lots of information about Italian demography (it's in Italian because the English version lacks a lot of data); in particular, we are interested in the population evolution over the years.

Probably the best known Python module for web scraping is **BeautifulSoup** (http://www.crummy.com/software/BeautifulSoup/). It's a really nice library that gets the job done quickly, but there are situations (in particular with JavaScript embedded in the web page, such as for Wikipedia) that prevent it from working.

As an alternative, we find lxml quite productive (http://codespeak.net/lxml/). It's a library mainly used to work with XML (as the name suggests), but it can also be used with HTML (given their quite similar structures), and it is powerful and easy–to-use.

Let's dig into the code now:

```
# to get the web pages
import urllib2
# lxml submodule for html parsing
from lxml.html import parse
# regular expression module
import re
# Matplotlib module
import matplotlib.pyplot as plt
```

Along with the Matplotlib module, we need the following modules:

- `urllib2`: This is the module (from the standard library) that is used to access resources through URL (we will download the webpage with this).

- `lxml`: This is the parsing library.

- `re`: Regular expressions are needed to parse the returned data to extract the information we need. `re` is a module from the standard library, so we don't need to install a third-party module to use it.

```
# general urllib2 config
user_agent = 'Mozilla/5.0 (compatible; MSIE 5.5; Windows NT)'
headers = { 'User-Agent' : user_agent }
url = "http://it.wikipedia.org/wiki/Demografia_d'Italia"
```

Here, we prepare some configuration for `urllib2`, in particular, the `user_agent` header is used to access Wikipedia and the URL of the page.

```
# prepare the request and open the url
req = urllib2.Request(url, headers=headers)
response = urllib2.urlopen(req)
```

Then we make a request for the URL and get the HTML back.

```
# we parse the webpage, getroot() return the document root
doc = parse(response).getroot()
```

We parse the HTML using the `parse()` function of `lxml.html` and then we get the root element. XML can be seen as a tree, with a root element (the node at the top of the tree from where every other node descends), and a hierarchical structure of elements.

```
# find the data table, using css elements
table = doc.cssselect('table.wikitable')[0]
```

We leverage the structure of HTML accessing the first element of type `table` of class `wikitable` because that's the table we're interested in.

```
# prepare data structures, will contain actual data
years = []
people = []
```

Preparing the lists that will contain the parsed data.

```
# iterate over the rows of the table, except first and last ones
for row in table.cssselect('tr')[1:-1]:
```

We can start parsing the table. Since there is a header and a footer in the table, we skip the first and the last line from the lines (selected by the `tr` tag) to loop over.

```
# get the row cell (we will use only the first two)
data = row.cssselect('td')
```

We get the element with the `td` tag that stands for *table data*: those are the cells in an HTML table.

```
# the first cell is the year
tmp_years = data[0].text_content()
# cleanup for cases like 'YYYY[N]' (date + footnote link)
tmp_years = re.sub('\[.\]', '', tmp_years)
```

We take the first cell that contains the year, but we need to remove the additional characters (used by Wikipedia to link to footnotes).

```
# the second cell is the population count
tmp_people = data[1].text_content()
# cleanup from '.', used as separator
tmp_people = tmp_people.replace('.', '')
```

We also take the second cell that contains the population for a given year. It's quite common in Italy to separate thousands in number with a `'.'` character: we have to remove them to have an appropriate value.

```
# append current data to data lists, converting to integers
years.append(int(tmp_years))
people.append(int(tmp_people))
```

We append the parsed values to the data lists, explicitly converting them to integer values.

```
# plot data
plt.plot(years,people)
# ticks every 10 years
plt.xticks(range(min(years), max(years), 10))
plt.grid()
# add a note for 2001 Census
plt.annotate("2001 Census", xy=(2001, people[years.index(2001)]),
            xytext=(1986, 54.5*10**6),
            arrowprops=dict(arrowstyle='fancy'))
```

Running the example results in the following screenshot that clearly shows why the annotation is needed:

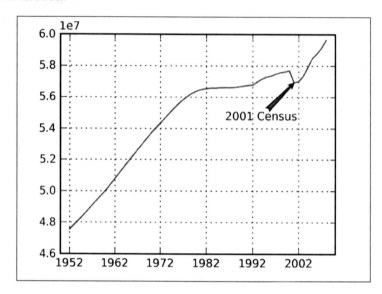

In 2001, we had a national census in Italy, and that's the reason for the drop in that year: the values released from the National Institute for Statistics (and reported in the Wikipedia article) are just an estimation of the population. However, with a census, we have a precise count of the people living in Italy.

Plotting data by parsing an Apache log file

Plotting data from a log file can be seen as the *art* of extracting information from it.

Every service has a log format different from the others. There are some exceptions of similar or same format (for example, for services that come from the same development teams) but then they may be customized and we're back at the beginning.

The main differences in log files are:

- **Fields orders**: Some have time information at the beginning, others in the middle of the line, and so on
- **Fields types**: We can find several different data types such as integers, strings, and so on
- **Fields meanings**: For example, log levels can have very different meanings

From all the data contained in the log file, we need to extract the information we are interested in from the surrounding data that we don't need (and hence we skip).

In our example, we're going to analyze the log file of one of the most common services: Apache. In particular, we will parse the `access.log` file to extract the total number of hits and amount of data transferred per day.

Apache is highly configurable, and so is the log format. Our Apache configuration, contained in the `httpd.conf` file, has this log format:

```
"%h %l %u %t \"%r\" %>s %b \"%{Referer}i\" \"%{User-Agent}i\""
```

This is in `LogFormat` specification where:

Log directive	Description
%h	The host making the request
%l	Identity of the client (which is usually not available)
%u	User making the request (usually not available)
%t	The time the request was received
%r	The request
%>s	The status code
%b	The size (in bytes) of the response sent to the client (excluding the headers)
%{Referer}i	The page from where the requests originated (for example, the HTML page where a PNG image is requested)
%{User-Agent}i	The user agent used to make the request

This resulting log looks like this:

```
127.0.0.1 - - [08/Aug/2009:00:26:05 +0200] \
    "GET /doc/apache2-doc/manual/images/down.gif HTTP/1.1" 200 56 \
    "http://localhost/doc/apache2-doc/manual/en/logs.html" \
    "Mozilla/5.0 (X11; U; Linux x86_64; en-US; rv:1.9.0.11) \
    Gecko/2009061317 Iceweasel/3.0.11 (Debian-3.0.11-1)"
```

where we introduced the line breaks for clarity.

Let's look at the code to parse this log:

```
# to read Apache log file
from __future__ import with_statement
```

We open the file using the `with` statement.

```
# Numpy and matplotlib modules
import numpy as np
import matplotlib.pyplot as plt
# needed for formatting Y axis
from matplotlib.ticker import FuncFormatter
```

This is the standard import for Numpy and Matplotlib `pyplot` module, along with the `FuncFormatter` that is needed to properly format the Y-axis.

```
# to parse the log file
import re
```

We need to parse the log file and the best way to do this is by using regular expressions.

```
def megabytes(x, pos):
    """Formatter for Y axis, values are in megabytes"""
    return '%1.f' % (x/(1024*1024))
```

This function will be used for formatting the Y-axis: it is called for each tick, passing the value of the label and its position. We gather values in bytes, and this function will display values in megabytes.

```
# prepare the regular expression to match
# the day and the size of the request
apa_line = re.compile(r'.*\[([^:]+):.* ([0-9]+) .+ .+')
```

Here we prepare the regular expression to extract the day and the transferred data for the request. It consists of the following parts:

Pattern	Description
`.*`	Matches a string of any length made of any character
`\[`	The literal `[` is needed to mark the positions where the interesting data begins
`([^:]+)`	A non-zero string of characters (none of them equals to `': '`) will match the day, the parentheses signal to save the value for further reference
`:.*`	A literal colon `:` followed by a string of any length made of any character
`([0-9]+)`	A space followed by a number
`.+ .+`	A space followed by two non-empty strings (separated by a space)

In this way, we extract the day of the request along with the response size from every line.

```
# prepare dictionaries to contain the data
day_hits = {}
day_txn = {}
```

These dictionaries will store the parsed data.

```
# we open the file
with open('<location of the Apache>/access.log') as f:
    # and for every line in it
    for line in f:
```

we open the file (we have to select the proper location of `access.log` as it differs between operating systems and/or installation), and for every line in it

```
    # we pass the line to regular expression
    m = apa_line.match(line)
    # and we get the 2 values matched back
    day, call_size = m.groups()
```

We parse the line and take the resulting values.

```
    # if the current day is already present
    if day in day_hits:
        # we add the call and the size of the request
        day_hits[day] += 1
        day_txn[day] += int(call_size)
```

else if the current day is already present in the dictionaries, then add the hit and the size to the respective dictionaries.

```
    else:
        # else we initialize the dictionaries
        day_hits[day] = 1
        day_txn[day] = int(call_size)
```

If the current day is not present, then we need to initialize the dictionaries for a new day.

```
# prepare a list of the keys (days)
keys = sorted(day_hits.keys())
```

We prepare a sorted list of dictionary keys, since we need to access it several times.

```
# prepare a figure and an Axes in it
fig = plt.figure()
ax1 = fig.add_subplot(111)
```

We prepare a `Figure` and an `Axes` in it.

```
# bar width
width = .4
```

We define the bars width.

```
# for each key (day) and it's position
for i, k in enumerate(keys):
```

Then we enumerate the item in `keys` so that we have a progressive number associated with each key.

```
    # we plot a bar
    ax1.bar(i - width/2, day_hits[k], width=width, color='y')
```

Now we can plot a bar at position i (but shifted by `width/2` to center the tick) with its height proportional to the number of hits, and width set to `width`. We set the bar color to yellow.

```
# for each label for the X ticks
for label in ax1.get_xticklabels():
    # we hide it
    label.set_visible(False)
```

We hide the labels on the X-axis to avoid its superimposition with the other `Axes` labels (for transfer size).

```
# add a label to the Y axis (for the first plot)
ax1.set_ylabel('Total hits')
```

We set a label for the Y-axis.

```
# create another Axes instance, twin of the previous one
ax2 = ax1.twinx()
```

We now create a second `Axes`, sharing the X-axis with the previous one.

```
# plot the total requests size
ax2.plot([day_txn[k] for k in keys], 'k', linewidth=2)
```

We plot a line for the transferred size, using the black color and with a bigger width.

```
# set the Y axis to start from 0
ax2.set_ylim(ymin=0)
```

We let the Y-axis start from 0 so that it can be congruent with the other Y-axis.

```
# set the X ticks for each element of keys (days)
ax2.set_xticks(range(len(keys)))
# set the label for them to keys, rotating and align to the right
ax2.set_xticklabels(keys, rotation=25, ha='right')
```

We set the ticks for the X-axis (that will be shared between this and the bar plot) and the labels, rotating them by 25 degrees and aligning them to the right to better fit the plot.

```
# set the formatter for Y ticks labels
ax2.yaxis.set_major_formatter(FuncFormatter(megabytes))
# add a label to Y axis (for the second plot)
ax2.set_ylabel('Total transferred data (in Mb)')
```

Then we set the formatter for the Y-axis so that the labels are shown in megabytes (instead of bytes).

```
# add a title to the whole plot
plt.title('Apache hits and transferred data by day')
```

Finally, we set the plot title.

On executing the preceding code snippet, the following screenshot is displayed:

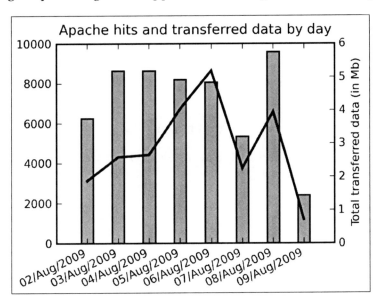

The preceding screenshot tells us that it is not a very busy server, but it still shows what's going on.

Plotting data from a CSV file

A common format to export and distribute datasets is the **Comma-Separated Values (CSV)** format. For example, spreadsheet applications allow us to export a CSV from a working sheet, and some databases also allow for CSV data export. Additionally, it's a common format to distribute datasets on the Web.

In this example, we'll be plotting the evolution of the world's population divided by continents, between 1950 and 2050 (of course they are predictions), using a new type of graph: **bars stacked**.

Using the data available at http://www.xist.org/earth/pop_continent.aspx (that fetches data from the official UN data at http://esa.un.org/unpp/index.asp), we have prepared the following CSV file:

```
Continent,1950,1975,2000,2010,2025,2050
Africa,227270,418765,819462,1033043,1400184,1998466
Asia,1402887,2379374,3698296,4166741,4772523,5231485
Europe,547460,676207,726568,732759,729264,691048
Latin America,167307,323323,521228,588649,669533,729184
Northern America,171615,242360,318654,351659,397522,448464
Oceania,12807,21286,31160,35838,42507,51338
```

In the first line, we can find the header with a description of what the data in the columns represent. The other lines contain the continent's name and its population (in thousands) for the given years.

There are several ways to parse a CSV file, for example:

- NumPy's `loadtxt()` (what we are going to use here)
- Matplotlib's `mlab.csv2rec()`
- The `csv` module (in the standard library)

but we decided to go with `loadtxt()` because it's very powerful (and it's what Matplotlib is standardizing on).

Let's look at how we can plot it then:

```
# for file opening made easier
from __future__ import with_statement
```

We need this because we will use the `with` statement to read the file.

```
# numpy
import numpy as np
```

NumPy is used to load the CSV and for its useful array data type.

```
# matplotlib plotting module
import matplotlib.pyplot as plt
# matplotlib colormap module
import matplotlib.cm as cm
# needed for formatting Y axis
from matplotlib.ticker import FuncFormatter
# Matplotlib font manager
import matplotlib.font_manager as font_manager
```

In addition to the classic `pyplot` module, we need other Matplotlib submodules:

- `cm` (color map): Considering the way we're going to prepare the plot, we need to specify the color map of the graphical elements
- `FuncFormatter`: We will use this to change the way the Y-axis labels are displayed
- `font_manager`: We want to have a legend with a smaller font, and `font_manager` allows us to do that

```
def billions(x, pos):
    """Formatter for Y axis, values are in billions"""
    return '%1.fbn' % (x*1e-6)
```

This is the function that we will use to format the Y-axis labels. Our data is in thousands. Therefore, by dividing it by one million, we obtain values in the order of billions. The function is called at every label to draw, passing the label value and the position.

```
# bar width
width = .8
```

As said earlier, we will plot bars, and here we define their width.

The following is the parsing code. We know that it's a bit hard to follow (the data preparation code is usually the hardest one) but we will show how powerful it is.

```
# open CSV file
with open('population.csv') as f:
```

The function we're going to use, NumPy `loadtxt()`, is able to receive either a filename or a file descriptor, as in this case. We have to open the file here because we have to strip the header line from the rest of the file and set up the data parsing structures.

```
# read the first line, splitting the years
years = map(int, f.readline().split(',')[1:])
```

Here we read the first line, the header, and extract the years. We do that by calling the `split()` function and then mapping the `int()` function to the resulting list, from the second element onwards (as the first one is a string).

```
# we prepare the dtype for exacting data; it's made of:
# <1 string field> <len(years) integers fields>
dtype = [('continents', 'S16')] + [('', np.int32)]*len(years)
```

NumPy is flexible enough to allow us to define new data types. Here, we are creating one ad hoc for our data lines: a string (of maximum 16 characters) and as many integers as the length of `years` list. Also note how the first element has a name, `continents`, while the last integers have none: we will need this in a bit.

```
# we load the file, setting the delimiter and the dtype above
y = np.loadtxt(f, delimiter=',', dtype=dtype)
```

With the new data type, we can actually call `loadtxt()`. Here is the description of the parameters:

- `f`: This is the file descriptor. Please note that it now contains all the lines except the first one (we've read above) which contains the headers, so no data is lost.

- `delimiter`: By default, `loadtxt()` expects the delimiter to be spaces, but since we are parsing a CSV file, the separator is comma.

- `dtype`: This is the data type that is used to apply to the text we read. By default, `loadtxt()` tries to match against float values

```
# "map" the resulting structure to be easily accessible:
# the first column (made of string) is called 'continents'
# the remaining values are added to 'data' sub-matrix
# where the real data are
y = y.view(np.dtype([('continents', 'S16'),
                     ('data', np.int32, len(years))]))
```

Here we're using a trick: we *view* the resulting data structure as made up of two parts, `continents` and `data`. It's similar to the `dtype` that we defined earlier, but with an important difference. Now, the integer's values are mapped to a field name, `data`. This results in the column `continents` with all the continents names, and the matrix `data` that contains the year's values for each row of the file.

```
data = y['data']
continents = y['continents']
```

We can separate the `data` and the `continents` part into two variables for easier usage in the code.

```
# prepare the bottom array
bottom = np.zeros(len(years))
```

We prepare an array of zeros of the same length as `years`. As said earlier, we plot stacked bars, so each dataset is plot over the previous ones, thus we need to know where the bars below finish. The `bottom` array keeps track of this, containing the height of bars already plotted.

```
# for each line in data
for i in range(len(data)):
```

Now that we have our information in `data`, we can loop over it.

```
# create the bars for each element, on top of the previous bars
bt = plt.bar(range(len(data[i])), data[i], width=width,
             color=cm.hsv(32*i), label=continents[i],
             bottom=bottom)
```

and create the stacked bars. Some important notes:

- We select the the i-th row of `data`, and plot a bar according to its element's size (`data[i]`) with the chosen `width`.

- As the bars are generated in different loops, their colors would be all the same. To avoid this, we use a color map (in this case `hsv`), selecting a different color at each iteration, so the sub-bars will have different colors.

- We label each bar set with the relative continent's name (useful for the legend)

- As we have said, they are stacked bars. In fact, every iteration adds a piece of the global bars. To do so, we need to know where to start drawing the bar from (the lower limit) and `bottom` does this. It contains the value where to start drowing the current bar.

```
# update the bottom array
bottom += data[i]
```

We update the `bottom` array. By adding the current data line, we know what the bottom line will be to plot the next bars on top of it.

```
# label the X ticks with years
plt.xticks(np.arange(len(years))+width/2,
           [int(year) for year in years])
```

We then add the tick's labels, the `years` elements, right in the middle of the bar.

```
# some information on the plot
plt.xlabel('Years')
plt.ylabel('Population (in billions)')
plt.title('World Population: 1950 - 2050 (predictions)')
```

Add some information to the graph.

```
# draw a legend, with a smaller font
plt.legend(loc='upper left',
           prop=font_manager.FontProperties(size=7))
```

We now draw a legend in the upper-left position with a small font (to better fit the empty space).

```
# apply the custom function as Y axis formatter
plt.gca().yaxis.set_major_formatter(FuncFormatter(billions))
```

Finally, we change the Y-axis label formatter, to use the custom formatting function that we defined earlier.

The result is the next screenshot where we can see the composition of the world population divided by continents:

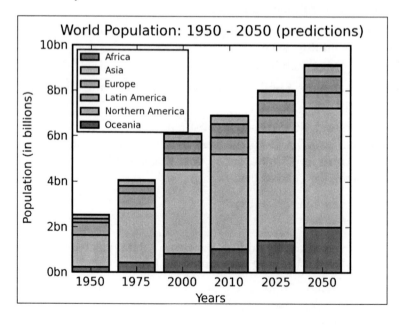

In the preceding screenshot, the whole bar represents the total world population, and the sections in each bar tell us about how much a continent contributes to it. Also observe how the custom color map works: from bottom to top, we have represented Africa in red, Asia in orange, Europe in light green, Latin America in green, Northern America in light blue, and Oceania in blue (barely visible as the top of the bars).

Plotting extrapolated data using curve fitting

While plotting the CSV values, we have seen that there were some columns representing predictions of the world population in the coming years. We'd like to show how to obtain such predictions using the mathematical process of *extrapolation* with the help of *curve fitting*.

Curve fitting is the process of constructing a curve (a mathematical function) that better fits to a series of data points.

This process is related to other two concepts:

- `interpolation`: A method of constructing new data points **within** the range of a known set of points
- `extrapolation`: A method of constructing new data points **outside** a known set of points

The results of `extrapolation` are subject to a greater degree of uncertainty and are influenced a lot by the fitting function that is used.

So it works this way:

1. First, a known set of measures is passed to the curve fitting procedure that computes a function to approximate these values
2. With this function, we can compute additional values that are not present in the original dataset

Let's first approach curve fitting with a simple example:

```
# Numpy and Matplotlib
import numpy as np
import matplotlib.pyplot as plt
```

These are the classic imports.

```
# the known points set
data = [[2,2],[5,0],[9,5],[11,4],[12,7],[13,11],[17,12]]
```

This is the data we will use for curve fitting. They are the points on a plane (so each has a X and a Y component)

```
# we extract the X and Y components from previous points
x, y = zip(*data)
```

We aggregate the X and Y components in two distinct lists.

```
# plot the data points with a black cross
plt.plot(x, y, 'kx')
```

Then plot the original dataset as a black cross on the Matplotlib image.

```
# we want a bit more data and more fine grained for
# the fitting functions
x2 = np.arange(min(x)-1, max(x)+1, .01)
```

We prepare a new array for the X values because we wish to have a wider set of values (one unit on the right and one on to the left of the original list) and a fine grain to plot the fitting function nicely.

```
# lines styles for the polynomials
styles = [':', '-.', '--']
```

To differentiate better between the polynomial lines, we now define their `styles` list.

```
# getting style and count one at time
for d, style in enumerate(styles):
```

Then we loop over that list by also considering the item count.

```
    # degree of the polynomial
    deg = d + 1
```

We define the actual polynomial degree.

```
    # calculate the coefficients of the fitting polynomial
    c = np.polyfit(x, y, deg)
```

Then compute the coefficients of the fitting polynomial whose general format is:

```
c[0]*x**deg + c[1]*x**(deg - 1) + ... + c[deg]
```

```
    # we evaluate the fitting function against x2
    y2 = np.polyval(c, x2)
```

Here, we generate the new values by evaluating the fitting polynomial against the x2 array.

```
    # and then we plot it
    plt.plot(x2, y2, label="deg=%d" % deg, linestyle=style)
```

Then we plot the resulting function, adding a label that indicates the degree of the polynomial and using a different style for each line.

```
# show the legend
plt.legend(loc='upper left')
```

We then show the legend, and the final result is shown in the next screenshot:

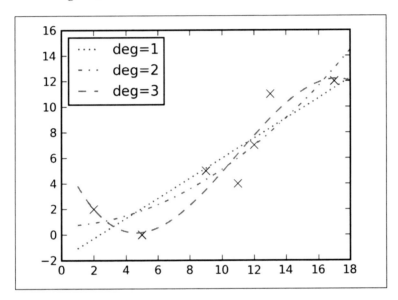

Here, the polynomial with degree=1 is drawn as a dotted blue line, the one with degree=2 is a dash-dot green line, and the one with degree=3 is a dashed red line.

We can see that the higher the degree, the better is the fit of the function against the data.

Let's now revert to our main intention, trying to provide an extrapolation for population data. First a note: we take the values for 2010 as real data and not predictions (well, we are quite near to that year) else we have very few values to create a realistic extrapolation.

Let's see the code:

```
# for file opening made easier
from __future__ import with_statement
# numpy
import numpy as np
# matplotlib plotting module
import matplotlib.pyplot as plt
# matplotlib colormap module
```

```
import matplotlib.cm as cm
# Matplotlib font manager
import matplotlib.font_manager as font_manager
# bar width
width = .8
# open CSV file
with open('population.csv') as f:
    # read the first line, splitting the years
    years = map(int, f.readline().split(',')[1:])

    # we prepare the dtype for exacting data; it's made of:
    # <1 string field> <6 integers fields>
    dtype = [('continents', 'S16')] + [('', np.int32)]*len(years)
    # we load the file, setting the delimiter and the dtype above
    y = np.loadtxt(f, delimiter=',', dtype=dtype)

    # "map" the resulting structure to be easily accessible:
    # the first column (made of string) is called 'continents'
    # the remaining values are added to 'data' sub-matrix
    # where the real data are
    y = y.view(np.dtype([('continents', 'S16'),
                         ('data', np.int32, len(years))]))
# extract fields
data = y['data']
continents = y['continents']
```

This is the same code that is used for the CSV example (reported here for completeness).

```
x = years[:-2]
x2 = years[-2:]
```

We are dividing the years into two groups: before and after 2010. This translates to split the last two elements of the `years` list.

What we are going to do here is prepare the plot in two phases:

1. First, we plot the data we consider certain values

2. After this, we plot the data from the UN predictions next to our extrapolations

```
# prepare the bottom array
b1 = np.zeros(len(years)-2)
```

We prepare the array (made of zeros) for the `bottom` argument of `bar()`.

```
# for each line in data
for i in range(len(data)):
    # select all the data except the last 2 values
```

```
        d = data[i][:-2]
```

For each `data` line, we extract the information we need, so we remove the last two values.

```
        # create bars for each element, on top of the previous bars
        bt = plt.bar(range(len(d)), d, width=width,
                     color=cm.hsv(32*(i)), label=continents[i],
                     bottom=b1)
        # update the bottom array
        b1 += d
```

Then we plot the bar, and update the `bottom` array.

```
    # prepare the bottom array
    b2_1, b2_2 = np.zeros(2), np.zeros(2)
```

We need two arrays because we will display two bars for the same year — one from the CSV and the other from our fitting function.

```
    # for each line in data
    for i in range(len(data)):

        # extract the last 2 values
        d = data[i][-2:]
```

Again, for each line in the `data` matrix, we extract the last two values that are needed to plot the bar for CSV.

```
        # select the data to compute the fitting function
        y = data[i][:-2]
```

Along with the other values needed to compute the fitting polynomial.

```
        # use a polynomial of degree 3
        c = np.polyfit(x, y, 3)
```

Here, we set up a polynomial of degree 3; there is no need for higher degrees.

```
        # create a function out of those coefficients
        p = np.poly1d(c)
```

This method constructs a polynomial starting from the coefficients that we pass as parameter.

```
        # compute p on x2 values (we need integers, so the map)
        y2 = map(int, p(x2))
```

We use the polynomial that was defined earlier to compute its values for $x2$. We also map the resulting values to integer, as the `bar()` function expects them for height.

```
# create bars for each element, on top of the previous bars
bt = plt.bar(len(b1)+np.arange(len(d)), d, width=width/2,
             color=cm.hsv(32*(i)), bottom=b2_1)
```

We draw a bar for the data from the CSV. Note how the `width` is half of that of the other bars. This is because in the same `width` we will draw the two sets of bars for a better visual comparison.

```
# create the bars for the extrapolated values
bt = plt.bar(len(b1)+np.arange(len(d))+width/2, y2,
             width=width/2, color=cm.bone(32*(i+2)),
             bottom=b2_2)
```

Here, we plot the bars for the extrapolated values, using a dark color map so that we have an even better separation for the two datasets.

```
# update the bottom array
b2_1 += d
b2_2 += y2
```

We update both the `bottom` arrays.

```
# label the X ticks with years
plt.xticks(np.arange(len(years))+width/2,
           [int(year) for year in years])
```

We add the years as ticks for the X-axis.

```
# draw a legend, with a smaller font
plt.legend(loc='upper left',
           prop=font_manager.FontProperties(size=7))
```

To avoid a very big legend, we used only the labels for the data from the CSV, skipping the interpolated values. We believe it's pretty clear what they're referring to. Here is the screenshot that is displayed on executing this example:

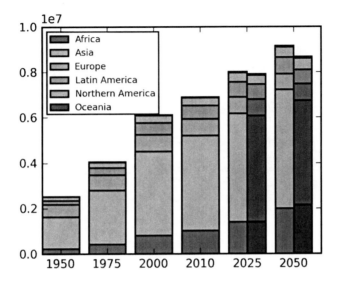

The conclusion we can draw from this is that the United Nations uses a different function to prepare the predictions, especially because they have a continuous set of information, and they can also take into account other environmental circumstances while preparing such predictions.

Tools using Matplotlib

Given that it's has an easy and powerful API, Matplotlib is also used inside other programs and tools when plotting is needed. We are about to present a couple of these tools:

- NetworkX
- Mpmath

NetworkX

NetworkX (http://networkx.lanl.gov/) is a Python module that contains tools for creating and manipulating (complex) *networks*, also known as graphs.

A **graph** is defined as a set of nodes and edges where each edge is associated with two nodes. NetworkX also adds the possibility to associate properties to each node and edge.

NetworkX is not primarily a graph drawing package but, in collaboration with Matplotlib (and also with Graphviz), it's able to show the graph we're working on.

In the example we're going to propose, we will show how to create a random graph and draw it in a circular shape.

```
# matplotlib
import matplotlib.pyplot as plt
# networkx nodule
import networkx as nx
```

In addition to `pyplot`, we also import the `networkx` module.

```
# prepare a random graph with n nodes and m edges
n = 16
m = 60
G = nx.gnm_random_graph(n, m)
```

Here, we set up a graph with 16 nodes and 60 edges, chosen randomly from all the graphs with such characteristics. The graph returned is *undirected*: edges just connect two nodes, without a direction information (from node A to node B or vice versa).

```
# prepare a circular layout of nodes
pos = nx.circular_layout(G)
```

Then we are using a node positioning algorithm, particularly to prepare a circular layout for the nodes of our graphs; the returned variable `pos` is a 2D array of nodes' positions forming a circular shape.

```
# define the color to select from the color map
# as n numbers evenly spaced between color map limits
node_color = map(int, np.linspace(0, 255, n))
```

We want to give a nice coloring to our nodes, so we will use a particular color map, but before that we have to identify what colors of the color map would be assigned to each node. We do this by selecting 16 numbers evenly spaced in the 256 available colors in the color map. We now have a progression of numbers that will result in a nice fading effect in the nodes' colors.

```
# draw the nodes, specifying the color map and the list of color
nx.draw_networkx_nodes(G, pos,
                       node_color=node_color, cmap=plt.cm.hsv)
```

We start drawing the graph from the nodes. We pass the graph object, the position `pos` to draw nodes in a circular layout, the color map, and the list of colors to be assigned to the nodes.

```
# add the labels inside the nodes
nx.draw_networkx_labels(G, pos)
```

We then request to draw the labels for the nodes. They are numbers identifying the nodes plotted inside them.

```
# draw the edges, using alpha parameter to make them lighter
nx.draw_networkx_edges(G, pos, alpha=0.4)
```

Finally, we draw the edges between nodes. We also specify the `alpha` parameter so that they are a little lighter and don't just appear as a complicated web of lines.

```
# turn off axis elements
plt.axis('off')
```

We then remove the Matplotlib axis lines and labels. The result is as shown in the next screenshot where the nodes' colors are distributed across the whole color spectrum:

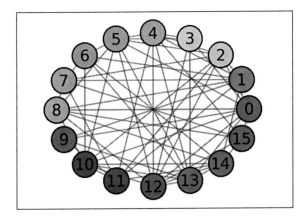

We advise you to look at the examples available on the NetworkX web site. If you like this kind of stuff, then you'll enjoy it for sure.

Mpmath

mpmath (`http://code.google.com/p/mpmath/`) is a mathematical library, written in pure Python for multiprecision floating-point arithmetic, which means that every calculation done using mpmath can have an arbitrarily high number of precision digits. This is extremely important for fields such as numerical simulation and analysis.

It also contains a high number of mathematical functions, constants, and a library of tools commonly needed in mathematical applications with an astonishing performance.

In conjunction with Matplotlib, mpmath provides a convenient plotting interface to display a function graphically.

It is extremely easy to plot with mpmath and Matplotlib:

```
In [1]: import mpmath as mp
In [2]: mp.plot(mp.sin, [-6, 6])
```

In this example, the mpmath `plot()` method takes the function to plot and the interval where to draw it.

Running this code, the following window pops up:

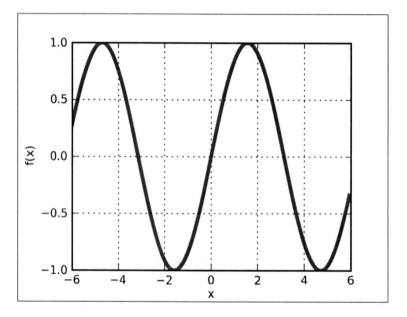

We can also plot multiple functions at a time and define our own functions too:

```
In [1]: import mpmath as mp
In [2]: mp.plot([mp.sqrt, lambda x: -0.1*x**3 + x-0.5], [-3, 3])
```

On executing the preceding code snippet, we get the following screenshot where we have plotted the square root (in blue, upper part) and the function we defined (in red, lower part):

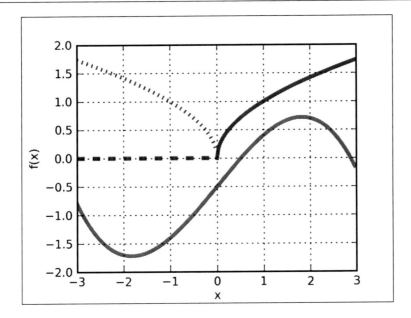

To plot more functions, simply provide a list of them to `plot()`. To define a new function, we use a `lambda` expression.

Note how the square root plot is done in full lines for positive values of X, while it's dotted in the negative part. This is because for X negatives, the result is a complex number: mpmath represents the real part with dashes and the imaginary part with dots.

Plotting geographical data

We can also use Matplotlib to draw on geographical map projections using the Basemap external toolkit. **Basemap** provides an efficient way to draw Matplotlib plots over real world maps.

Basemap is a Matplotlib toolkit, a collection of application-specific functions that extends Matplotlib functionalities, and its complete documentation is available at `http://matplotlib.sourceforge.net/basemap/doc/html/index.html`.

Toolkits are not present in the default Matplotlib installation (in fact, they also have a different namespace, `mpl_toolkits`), so we have to install Basemap separately. We can download it from `http://sourceforge.net/projects/matplotlib/`, under the **matplotlib-toolkits** menu of the **download** section, and then install it following the instructions in the documentation link mentioned previously.

Basemap is useful for scientists such as oceanographers and meteorologists, but other users may also find it interesting. For example, we could parse the Apache log and draw a point on a map using GeoIP localization for each connection.

We use the 0.99.3 version of Basemap for our examples.

First example

Let's start playing with the library. It contains a lot of things that are very specific, so we're going to just give an introduction to the basic functions of Basemap.

```
# pyplot module import
import matplotlib.pyplot as plt
# basemap import
from mpl_toolkits.basemap import Basemap
# Numpy import
import numpy as np
```

These are the usual imports along with the basemap module.

```
# Lambert Conformal map of USA lower 48 states
m = Basemap(llcrnrlon=-119, llcrnrlat=22, urcrnrlon=-64,
            urcrnrlat=49, projection='lcc', lat_1=33, lat_2=45,
            lon_0=-95, resolution='h', area_thresh=10000)
```

Here, we initialize a Basemap object, and we can see it has several parameters depending upon the projection chosen.

Let's see what a **projection** is: In order to represent the curved surface of the Earth on a two-dimensional map, a *map projection* is needed.

This conversion cannot be done without distortion. Therefore, there are many map projections available in Basemap, each with its own advantages and disadvantages. Specifically, a projection can be:

- equal-area (the area of features is preserved)
- conformal (the shape of features is preserved)

No projection can be both (equal-area and conformal) at the same time.

In this example, we have used a Lambert Conformal map. This projection requires additional parameters to work with. In this case, they are lat_1, lat_2, and lon_0.

Along with the projection, we have to provide the information about the portion of the Earth surface that the map projection will describe. This is done with the help of the following arguments:

Argument	Description
llcrnrlon	Longitude of lower-left corner of the desired map domain
llcrnrlat	Latitude of lower-left corner of the desired map domain
urcrnrlon	Longitude of upper-right corner of the desired map domain
urcrnrlat	Latitude of upper-right corner of the desired map domain

The last two arguments are:

Argument	Description
resolution	Specifies what is the resolution of the features added to the map (such as coast lines, borders, and so on), here we have chosen high resolution (h), but crude, low, and intermediate are also available.
area_thresh	Specifies what is the minimum size for a feature to be plotted. In this case, only features bigger than 10,000 square kilometer

```
# draw the coastlines of continental area
m.drawcoastlines()
# draw country boundaries
m.drawcountries(linewidth=2)
# draw states boundaries (America only)
m.drawstates()
```

We start adding features to the map. In this case, we have just added:

- The coast lines

- The country borders (with a bigger line style)

- The state borders inside the country (they are only available for America)

```
# fill the background (the oceans)
m.drawmapboundary(fill_color='aqua')
# fill the continental area
# we color the lakes like the oceans
m.fillcontinents(color='coral',lake_color='aqua')
```

We give some colors to our map. We color the ocean with aqua color and the interior of the continents are coral (but lakes have the same color of the ocean).

```
# draw parallels and meridians
m.drawparallels(np.arange(25,65,20),labels=[1,0,0,0])
m.drawmeridians(np.arange(-120,-40,20),labels=[0,0,0,1])
```

We draw a 20 degrees graticule of parallels and meridians for the map. Note how the `labels` argument controls the positions where the graticules are labeled. `labels` is an array having four elements:

```
[left, right, top, bottom]
```

These elements define the label of the parallels and the meridian when they intersect the borders of the plot. In this case, parallels are labeled when they intersect the left border and meridians are labeled at the bottom.

After adding a title to it, the result is as shown:

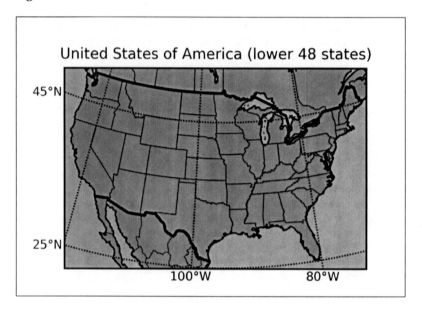

Using satellite background

Basemap can also use a terrain image as a map background.

```
m = Basemap(llcrnrlon=-119, llcrnrlat=22, urcrnrlon=-64,
            urcrnrlat=49, projection='lcc', lat_1=33, lat_2=45,
            lon_0=-95, resolution='h', area_thresh=10000)
```

We are using the same map as before.

```
# display blue marble image (from NASA) as map background
m.bluemarble()
```

We add the satellite images taken from the NASA images library.

```
# draw the coastlines of continental area
```

```
m.drawcoastlines()
# draw country boundaries
m.drawcountries(linewidth=2)
# draw states boundaries (America only)
m.drawstates()
```

Then, we draw the Basemap features over it, as done before, and this results in a very pretty image, as shown in the following screenshot:

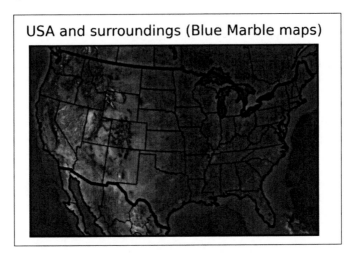

USA and surroundings (Blue Marble maps)

Plot data over a map

We got to know Matplotlib as a tool that can plot datasets easily. It would be really nice if we can mix this with Basemap projections. Well, of course it's possible, and this is how it is done.

We need some geographical data to plot over a map, so we take a group of cities, and we'll plot them on a map. The cities along with their coordinates (taken from Wikipedia) are:

City	Latitude	Longitude
London	51° 30' 28" N	0° 7' 41" W
New York	40° 43' 0" N	74° 0' 0" W
Madrid	40° 24' 0" N	3° 41' 0" W
Cairo	30° 3' 28.8" N	31° 13' 44.4" E
Moscow	55° 45' 6" N	37° 37' 4" E
Delhi	28° 36' 36" N	77° 13' 48" E
Dakar	14° 41' 34" N	17° 26' 48" W

From the previous table, we can prepare these three lists:

```
# Cities names and coordinates
cities = ['London', 'New York', 'Madrid', 'Cairo', 'Moscow',
          'Delhi', 'Dakar']
lat    = [51.507778, 40.716667, 40.4, 30.058, 55.751667,
          28.61, 14.692778]
lon    = [-0.128056, -74, -3.683333, 31.229, 37.617778,
          77.23, -17.446667]
```

where we have recorded the names and coordinates of different cities.

```
# orthogonal projection of the Earth
m = Basemap(projection='ortho', lat_0=45, lon_0=10)
```

We now prepare a map using an orthogonal projection that displays the Earth in the way a satellite would see it. The additional arguments, `lat_0` and `lon_0`, represent the points at the center of the projection (what the satellite looks down at).

```
# draw the borders of the map
m.drawmapboundary()
# draw the coasts borders and fill the continents
m.drawcoastlines()
m.fillcontinents()
```

We then draw the map's border (the edge of the map projection region) and the coastal lines, and then fill the continents.

```
# map city coordinates to map coordinates
x, y = m(lon, lat)
```

Here we convert the latitude and longitudes of the different cities into map domain coordinates—in particular, note that the resulting lists are values in meters on the map.

Calling a Basemap instance with arrays of longitudes and latitudes returns those locations in the native map projection coordinates.

```
# draw a red dot at cities coordinates
plt.plot(x, y, 'ro')
```

Now that we have the cities' locations in the map coordinates, we can plot a red dot at their positions.

```
# for each city,
for city, xc, yc in zip(cities, x, y):
# draw the city name in a yellow (shaded) box
    plt.text(xc+250000, yc-150000, city,
             bbox=dict(facecolor='yellow', alpha=0.5))
```

We also want to display the name of the city next to the point in the map. In order to do this, we use the `text()` function to write the name of the city (inside a nice yellow box, a bit translucent because of the `alpha` channel) next to the points position. Note the big numbers that are used to adapt the text's position. They need a little bit of hand tweaking and remember that they are in meters.

The following image is created as a result of executing the preceding code:

Plotting shapefiles with Basemap

Through the `DATA.gov` portal, the US government is releasing a huge quantity of high quality datasets that are free to use and analyze. Some of the datasets contain geographical information in a particular format: Shapefile.

A **Shapefile**, which commonly refers to a collection of files, is a popular geospatial data format for **Geographical Information Systems (GIS)**.

Shapefiles store geometrical primitives such as points, lines, and polygons (the shapes) to represent a geographical feature in a dataset. Each item can also have attributes and information associated to it, which are used to describe what it represents.

We will use the dataset available at the URL http://www.data.gov/details/16. It represents the locations of the copper smelters in the world (it also contains several other attributes and characteristics about the smelters, but we are not going to use them here).

```
# the map, a Miller Cylindrical projection
m = Basemap(projection='mill',
            llcrnrlon=-180. ,llcrnrlat=-60,
            urcrnrlon=180. ,urcrnrlat=80.)
```

We use a map from a **Miller cylindrical projection**. We limit the latitude (while keeping the world-wide longitude) because the excluded areas don't have smelters, and so we have more space for the zones where they are present.

```
# read the shapefile archive
s = m.readshapefile('<location of shapefile>/copper', 'copper')
```

Reading a shapefile is as simple as calling the readshapefile() function and passing the shapefile location. The additional argument (in this case, copper) is the name of the map attribute that will be created to hold the shapefiles' vertices and features. m.copper will contain the smelters locations in map domain coordinates, while s contains only general information about the Shapefile.

```
# prepare map coordinate lists for copper smelters locations
x, y = zip(*m.copper)
```

We prepare a list of coordinates (in the map domain) for the copper smelters locations; zip() receives the m.copper array unpacked (each sublist is passed as a separate parameter to zip()).

```
# draw coast lines and fill the continents
m.drawcoastlines()
m.fillcontinents()
```

We draw the coast lines and fill the continents

```
# draw a blue dot at smelters location
plt.plot(x, y, 'b.')
```

We can then draw a blue dot at the smelters' locations.

When we run the example, we can see a map with dots (in blue) that represent the places where the smelters are located:

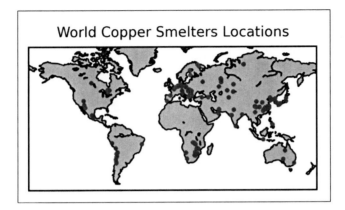

Summary

In this chapter, we have seen several examples of real world Matplotlib usage, including:

- How to plot data read from a database
- How to plot data extracted from a parsed Wikipedia article
- How to plot data from parsing an Apache log file
- How to plot data from a CSV file
- How to plot extrapolated data using a curve fitting polynomial
- How to plot using third-party tools such as NetworkX and mpmath
- How to plot geographical data using Basemap

We hope these practical examples have increased your interest in exploring Matplotlib, if you haven't already explored it!

Index

Thank you for buying
Matplotlib for Python Developers

Packt Open Source Project Royalties

When we sell a book written on an Open Source project, we pay a royalty directly to that project. Therefore by purchasing Matplotlib for Python Developers, Packt will have given some of the money received to the Matplotlib project.

In the long term, we see ourselves and you—customers and readers of our books—as part of the Open Source ecosystem, providing sustainable revenue for the projects we publish on. Our aim at Packt is to establish publishing royalties as an essential part of the service and support a business model that sustains Open Source.

If you're working with an Open Source project that you would like us to publish on, and subsequently pay royalties to, please get in touch with us.

Writing for Packt

We welcome all inquiries from people who are interested in authoring. Book proposals should be sent to author@packtpub.com. If your book idea is still at an early stage and you would like to discuss it first before writing a formal book proposal, contact us; one of our commissioning editors will get in touch with you.

We're not just looking for published authors; if you have strong technical skills but no writing experience, our experienced editors can help you develop a writing career, or simply get some additional reward for your expertise.

About Packt Publishing

Packt, pronounced 'packed', published its first book "Mastering phpMyAdmin for Effective MySQL Management" in April 2004 and subsequently continued to specialize in publishing highly focused books on specific technologies and solutions.

Our books and publications share the experiences of your fellow IT professionals in adapting and customizing today's systems, applications, and frameworks. Our solution-based books give you the knowledge and power to customize the software and technologies you're using to get the job done. Packt books are more specific and less general than the IT books you have seen in the past. Our unique business model allows us to bring you more focused information, giving you more of what you need to know, and less of what you don't.

Packt is a modern, yet unique publishing company, which focuses on producing quality, cutting-edge books for communities of developers, administrators, and newbies alike. For more information, please visit our website: www.PacktPub.com.

Expert Python Programming

ISBN: 978-1-847194-94-7   Paperback: 372 pages

Best practices for designing, coding, and distributing your Python software

1. Learn Python development best practices from an expert, with detailed coverage of naming and coding conventions

2. Apply object-oriented principles, design patterns, and advanced syntax tricks

3. Manage your code with distributed version control

CherryPy Essentials: Rapid Python Web Application Development

ISBN: 978-1-904811-84-8   Paperback: 272 pages

Design, develop, test, and deploy your Python web applications easily

1. Walks through building a complete Python web application using CherryPy 3

2. The CherryPy HTTP:Python interface

3. Use CherryPy with other Python libraries

4. Design, security, testing, and deployment

Please check **www.PacktPub.com** for information on our titles

Grok 1.0 Web Development

ISBN: 978-1-847197-48-1   Paperback: 250 pages

Create flexible, agile web applications using the power of Grok—a Python web framework

1. Develop efficient and powerful web applications and web sites from start to finish using Grok, which is based on Zope 3

2. Integrate your applications or web sites with relational databases easily

3. Extend your applications using the power of the Zope Toolkit

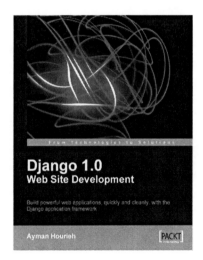

Django 1.0 Website Development

ISBN: 978-1-847196-78-1   Paperback: 272 pages

Build powerful web applications, quickly and cleanly, with the Django application framework

1. Teaches everything you need to create a complete Web 2.0-style web application with Django 1.0

2. Learn rapid development and clean, pragmatic design

3. No knowledge of Django required

4. Packed with examples and screenshots for better understanding

Please check **www.PacktPub.com** for information on our titles

Lightning Source UK Ltd.
Milton Keynes UK
UKOW020925191012

200778UK00004B/64/P